LONDON RECORD SOCIETY
PUBLICATIONS

VOLUME LI

To the memory of the Voicites 1910–13

THE ANGELS' VOICE

A MAGAZINE FOR YOUNG MEN IN BRIXTON, LONDON, 1910–1913

EDITED BY

ALAN ARGENT

LONDON RECORD SOCIETY
THE BOYDELL PRESS
2016

First published 2016

A London Record Society publication
Published by The Boydell Press
an imprint of Boydell & Brewer Ltd
PO Box 9, Woodbridge, Suffolk IP12 3DF, UK
and of Boydell & Brewer Inc.
668 Mt Hope Avenue, Rochester, NY 14620–2731, USA
website: www.boydellandbrewer.com

ISBN 978-0-900952-57-9

A CIP catalogue record for this book is available
from the British Library

The publisher has no responsibility for the continued existence or accuracy of URLs for
external or third-party internet websites referred to in this book, and does not guarantee that
any content on such websites is, or will remain, accurate or appropriate

This publication is printed on acid-free paper

Printed and bound in Great Britain by
TJ International Ltd, Padstow, Cornwall

MIX
Paper from
responsible sources
FSC® C013056

CONTENTS

ILLUSTRATIONS vi

FOREWORD vii

ACKNOWLEDGEMENTS ix

ABBREVIATIONS x

INTRODUCTION I

Number 1, November 1910 33
Number 2, December 1910 49
Number 3, January 1911 63
Number 5, March 1911 85
Number 6, April 1911 105
Number 7, November 1911 127
Number 8, July 1912 159
Number 9, December 1912 185
Number 10, July 1913 209
Number 11, August 1913 229
Number 12, September 1913 239
Number 13, October 1913 253
Number 15, December 1913 271

APPENDIX: LIST OF NAMES 299

BIBLIOGRAPHY 317

INDEX 321

ILLUSTRATIONS

I   Lambeth sketch plan   2
2   Trinity Chapel 2015 (photograph by Jane Giscombe)   16
3   Brixton pre–1914 (*Philips ABC Pocket Atlas Guide to London*)   21
4   The editor, James G. Godden – *AV* I (Nov. 1910), 26   45
5   'Art and Literature' – *AV* 3 (Jan. 1911), 4   65
6   'Temptation' – *AV* 3 (Jan. 1911), 9   67
7   Roller skating – *AV* 6 (Apr. 1911), 16   113
8   Ideas for Vol. II' – *AV* 6 (Apr. 1911), 24   116
9   Trinity Ladies Hockey Club – *AV* 7 (Nov. 1911), 41   145
10   There are moments when one wants to be alone' – *AV* 7 (Nov. 1911), 42   146
11   Dan C. Messent – *AV* 7 (Nov. 1911), 43   147
12   James G. Godden – *AV* 7 (Nov. 1911), 43   148
13   'The landlady' – *AV* 7 (Nov. 1911), 61   157
14   'The editor preparing the summer number' – *AV* 8 (July 1912), 1   159
15   'Before … ' – *AV* 10 (July 1913), 33   223
16   ' … and After' – *AV* 10 (July 1913), 35   225
17   War memorial, Trinity Congregational Church   300

FOREWORD

In 1909, the Liberal politician C. F. G. Masterman published a bitter attack on 'The Suburbans' as part of a manifesto on *The Condition of England*. 'They form a homogeneous civilisation, -- detached, self-centred, unostentatious':

> Suburban life has often little conception of social services, no tradition of disinterested public duty, but a limited outlook beyond a personal ambition. Here the individualism of the national character exercises its full influence: unchecked by the horizontal links of the industrial peoples, organising themselves into unions, or by the vertical links of the older aristocracy with a conception of family service which once passed from parent to child.

Now, too, the suburb 'is losing its old religions', and with them any object 'for contemplation beyond the orderly suburban road and the well-trimmed suburban garden'.[1]

Of all the seven million or so Londoners in the opening years of the twentieth century, these 'suburbans' remain most obscure and anonymous. We know a great deal about the life and condition of the London poor, and the lives of the London rich and the London intelligentsia have been documented in countless biographies and memoirs. But despite the efforts of the suburbs' own literary laureate in H. G. Wells, and the work of a sympathetic historian in Geoffrey Crossick, the stereotypes of Masterman and numerous others still come most easily to mind when we think about the twentieth-century London suburbs and their residents.

It seems unlikely that Charles Masterman ever met the young men of Trinity Congregational Church in Brixton. Had he done so he might have tempered his easy generalisations with the thought that really not everywhere in the suburbs was the same, and that the suburbs could boast a complexity as rich, say, as St James's at one end of the London spectrum or Whitechapel at the other. Everything about these young men of Trinity Church contradicts Masterman's strictures. For *The Angels' Voice* testifies by its very existence that a conception of social service and disinterested public duty was to be found as readily in the suburbs as anywhere else in the metropolis – indeed,

---

[1]   C. F. G. Masterman, *The Condition of England*, 1910, ch. III.

perhaps more so. Here, too, in great detail is evidence of an outlook unconfined by the limits of personal ambition, with horizontal links in every direction (most tangibly on the playing fields of south London), with vertical links to an older generation a source of wry comment, and with religious practice still offering a vista for contemplation far beyond the suburban privet hedge.

For the modern reader, perhaps, it will be the sheer exuberance and joy of living that shines through these numbers of *The Angels' Voice*. We meet these young men on the football field, cycling round Surrey's country lanes and rambling over its fields, sharing the excitement of trips across the Channel and letting friends know of the adventures offered by the chance to work or even live abroad. For this was a time when the world had never been less bounded by 'the orderly suburban road and the well-trimmed suburban garden'. And these young men were ready to take full advantage of it.

They did not know it, of course, but theirs was a world just about to be turned savagely upside down. This book is published just days before the hundredth anniversary of the Battle of the Somme, when so many young men lost their lives. Among men killed then or in the other actions of the Great War, or who died of their wounds or disease during army service, were some two dozen from Trinity's Young Men's Bible Class. *The Angels' Voice*, and much of the world it recounted, died with them. The London Record Society hopes that this volume, testimony to the lives these young men led before 1914, will add eloquently to their memorial.

Jerry White
Birkbeck, University of London
March 2016

ACKNOWLEDGEMENTS

I am grateful to the members of Trinity Congregational Church, Brixton, for granting me permission to publish the texts contained in this volume. In addition, I should like to thank those ministers, especially T. F. Camsey and John Stott, and the deacons, in particular R. F. Nichols, who kept alive and unwittingly maintained in later generations the traditions of fun, freedom and faith which inform the magazines here transcribed. As a youth, I was especially impressed by Kathleen Pratt, Trinity's long-serving church secretary, whose example, intelligence and memory often recalled her own upbringing in Brixton and her absorption of the values of the Messent family.

I am, of course, indebted to several friends for encouragement and for the generous giving of their time and advice. Among these are Trinity's present deacons, Lesley Dean and Peter Young, whose researches into the background of many of the Voicites have proved indispensable. Jerry White has been instrumental in guiding this work and its editor from the beginning. He deserves thanks for this and other kindnesses. Lastly I am grateful for the love and support of my wife, Jane, whose interest throughout in this project, especially the illustrations, has sustained me.

ABBREVIATIONS

AV	*The Angels' Voice.* Page numbers given are those in square brackets in the transcription.
Booth	Charles Booth, *Life and Labour of the People in London* (1902), 3rd series.
Cox	Jeffrey Cox, *The English Churches in a Secular Society. Lambeth, 1870–1930* (Oxford, 1982).
CUEW	Congregational Union of England and Wales.
CWGC	Commonwealth War Graves Commission. Records accessed through <http://www.cwgc.org/find-war-dead.aspx> multiple dates.
CYB	*Congregational Year Book.*
ILP	Independent Labour Party
LCC	London County Council
LMA	London Metropolitan Archives. Documents accessed through <http://search.ancestry.co.uk/search/db.aspx?dbid=1623> multiple dates.
LMS	London Missionary Society
McLeod	Hugh McLeod, *Class and Religion in the late Victorian City* (1974).
n.d.	no date
ODNB	*Oxford Dictionary of National Biography.*
POLCSD	*Post Office London County Suburbs Directory.* Accessed through University of Leicester <http://specialcollections.le.ac.uk/cdm/> multiple dates.
POLD	*Post Office London Directory.* Accessed through University of Leicester <http://specialcollections.le.ac.uk/cdm/> multiple dates.
PPR *Calendar*	Principal Probate Registry, *Calendar of the Grants of Probate and Letters of Administration made in the Probate Registries of the High Court of Justice in England.* Accessed through <http://search.ancestry.co.uk/search/db.aspx?dbid=1904> multiple dates.
TCC	Trinity Congregational Church, Brixton.
TCC Deacons	Trinity Congregational Church, Brixton, Deacons' Meeting minutes 1906–20, 1920–26. MSS at Trinity Congregational Church, Brixton.

TCC Marriage	Trinity Congregational Church, Brixton, Marriage registers 1899–1918, 1918–50. MSS at Trinity Congregational Church, Brixton.
TCC Meeting	Trinity Congregational Church, Brixton, Church Meeting minutes 1906–20. MS at Trinity Congregational Church, Brixton.
TLHC	Trinity Ladies Hockey Club/Long Haired Chums.
TNA	The National Archives, Kew. Documents accessed through <https://search.livesofthefirstworldwar.org/search/world-records/armed-forces-and-conflict> and <http://search.ancestry.co.uk/search/> multiple dates.
TYMBC	Trinity Young Men's Bible Class (sometimes YMBC: Young Men's Bible Class)

Notes

The page numbers given for *The Angels' Voice* are those in square brackets in the transcription. The place of publication is London unless stated otherwise.

INTRODUCTION

The Angels' Voice was a magazine produced by the Young Men's Bible Class of Trinity Congregational Church, Brixton. Fifteen issues appeared between 1910 and 1913. It touched the lives of some 30 to 40 young men, many of whom were to serve and some of whom were to die in the First World War. Rather than confining its articles to strictly religious topics, *The Angels' Voice* recorded their rambles, day trips, sporting activities, holidays abroad, smoking cigarettes and growing moustaches, as well as their first innocent attractions to members of the opposite sex. Through their illustrations, attempts at poetry and comments on politics, women's rights and cycling, the reader gains insights into a society about to be overwhelmed by war.

That this was the end of an age was unknown to those whose lives are recorded in the magazine. Rather *The Angels' Voice* reveals youths emerging into manhood; teasing each other; aping, and sometimes defying, their elders, whose own characters would have been shaped in the nineteenth century. Yet this was post-Victorian London, a new century when social and political change was anticipated, influenced by militant trades unionists and suffragists. Against this backcloth *The Angels' Voice* offers a vision of the regular round of south London shop-workers, clerks and other aspirant members of the lower middle classes.

The venture was conceived by James Godden, the Bible Class secretary, who presented his first offering to over 20 subscribers who paid 3*d.* each.[1] Few copies were produced at any one time. References were made to copies sent overseas, and in July 1912 five copies were in circulation. Also in July 1912 the editor noted an 'illustrated number and a carbon copy', implying that other versions were not illustrated.[2] The magazines now extant carry the original illustrations. Sluggish movement between the almost 40 subscribers which the magazine gained led to complaints that individuals kept it longer than they should have. Aware of this, the editor and sub-editor prepared a calendar (covering about a month) so that a single reader or a household of readers knew when to expect it and when and to whom they must pass

---

[1]   *AV* 3 (Jan. 1911), 25; *AV* 5 (Mar. 1911), 3. Judging by the cash account, in *AV* 6 (Apr. 1911), 20, the 3*d.* covered several issues, perhaps being half-yearly.

[2]   *AV* 8 (July 1912), 2, 56; *AV* 10 (July 1913), 19.

I

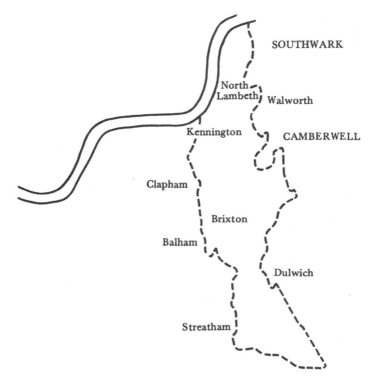

Lambeth in 1910

it on. Given the large families then prevalent, some non-members of the Young Men's Bible Class, perhaps sisters, may have read it. Indeed the young women of the church were the butt of mild jokes in the publication.

Copies of *The Angels' Voice* have been retained in the vestry of Trinity Congregational Church, Brixton, which some of these men continued to attend until the 1950s and '60s. The surviving copies probably belonged to the Bible Class leader, Dan C. Messent, perhaps donated at his death. Over the years church members and ministers have admired them, without necessarily realising their worth. Trinity has almost a complete set, although two missing issues have proved impossible to recover.

The magazine was consistently 9 inches by 7½ inches in size (normally in 'portrait' format; uniquely no. 9 is in 'landscape'), the pages being secured by a ribbon passed through punched holes. The number of pages varied from approximately 30 to 50. The issues held at Trinity are carbon copies of an original typescript, now lost. Allowing that the content was typed by hand, some errors crept in. The transcription in this work retains some but not all of the original typographical errors. A few errors have been corrected for modern readers and, for reasons of space, the typescript has been abridged.

RESPONSE TO THE WAR

The outbreak of war on 4 August 1914 shocked many Congregationalists who, like other Free Church people, would have preferred Britain to remain neutral. The mood changed after Lloyd George, the Chancellor of the Exchequer, addressed a large rally at The City Temple on 10 November 1914 where he persuaded his hearers to support the government. Congregationalists shared the general outrage at German excesses and many, like Trinity's young men, volunteered to fight.[3]

The early recruits in late 1914 consisted of both working men and the lower middle classes and above. Forty per cent of men engaged in financial services, commerce, the professions, hotels, restaurants, theatres etc. volunteered. In London 14.3 per cent (107,000) of men of eligible age had joined up by 12 November 1914, compared to 10.2 per cent in England, Wales and Scotland in general. One observer in October 1914 watched a great many 'recruits marching over Waterloo Bridge ... in their ordinary civilian clothes, mostly pale-faced city clerks'.[4]

From Trinity, among those who enlisted in 1914 were Leslie Bedwell, the brothers Frank and Harold Eagle, Ernest Bowler (whose left leg was amputated in 1915) and Graham Godden (who died on 6 December 1914). As army reservists, Frederick Butcher (killed in action in 1916) and Alfred Austin were soon dispatched to France.

TRINITY YOUNG MEN'S BIBLE CLASS

The class met for Bible study and for 'mutual help in the Christian life' on Sunday afternoons from 3pm to 4pm. Adopting a 'homely conversational' method, discussion followed a brief introduction by either the class leader or a member. Topics for one month in 1905 included the woman of Samaria, healing the ruler's son and the miracle of loaves and fishes, all from John's gospel and all introduced by class members. Questions and the 'free expression of opinion' were encouraged.[5]

The Angels' Voice recorded the class's annual meetings, its election of officers and its support for various missionary works, including

---

3   Catriona Pennell, *A Kingdom United: Popular Responses to the Outbreak of the First World War in Britain and Ireland* (Oxford, 2012), 1–3; Alan Argent, *The Transformation of Congregationalism 1900–2000* (Nottingham, 2013), 79–80.
4   Jerry White, *Zeppelin Nights: London in the First World War* (2014), 34–5, 37.
5   *The Trinity Magazine*, iii. nos 26 and 28 (Feb. and Apr. 1905) – copy held at TCC.

those of Walter and Mary Fairman with the North Africa Mission in Egypt and John Rowe with the China Inland Mission, and the work of the London Missionary Society in general. The LMS was the leading missionary body supported by Congregationalists, although the young people's wish to support the Fairmans and Rowe naturally sprang from family involvement with Trinity Chapel, Brixton.

EDUCATION

The young men of *The Angels' Voice* received an elementary education. On leaving school, generally at 14, they qualified to join Trinity's Young Men's Bible Class.

In 1870 school boards had been set up to provide elementary education. Provision for compulsory school attendance was made in 1881, followed in 1891 by an act establishing the principle of free education for all children. In London, as elsewhere, a family's social status invariably determined the school to which children went.[6]

The Brixton-born future Labour politician Herbert Morrison (1888–1965) attended Stockwell Road Board School aged five in 1893, where the classes consisted of perhaps 50 pupils. Caning was normal and Morrison received six strokes for sliding down the banisters. When he was 11 he moved to the nearby St Andrew's Church of England School and left aged 14 in 1902, with a love of reading but with his formal education complete. His schooldays resembled those of the members of Trinity's Bible Class who were taught the three Rs (reading, writing and arithmetic), physical education or 'drill', and perhaps how to pursue further education for themselves.

Alexander Paterson (1884–1947), living in a tenement and working for a year as a supernumerary assistant teacher, observed in 1911 that the average class in Bermondsey's elementary schools contained 'a few short of sixty' and that most boys left school aged between 13 and 14 years. Imparting the three Rs took over half the week's 24 teaching hours, while pupils also had a 'grounding in English, geography, and history', enabling a former schoolboy 'to read a newspaper or … vote with some idea of what he is doing'. Morrison felt that in his teens he was older than his years 'through the enforced need to grow up and do a man's job' and that his generation was composed of 'angry and impatient young men'. He continued, 'We could write, and above all we could read' and 'reading was my further education'.[7]

---

[6]   H. J. Dyos, *Victorian Suburb: A Study of the Growth of Camberwell* (Leicester, 1966), 163–8.

[7]   Herbert Morrison, *Herbert Morrison: An Autobiography by Lord Morrison of Lambeth* (1960), 18–20, 24; Bernard Donoghue and G. W. Jones, *Herbert Morrison: Portrait of a Politician* (1973), 7–8, 13; Alexander Paterson, *Across the Bridges or Life by the South London River-Side* (1928), vi, ix, 41–3, 51.

A. J. Balfour's Education Act of 1902 abolished the school boards, placing English and Welsh elementary schools under local education authorities, themselves controlled by the county and county borough councils.[8] In 1906 a further statute urged local authorities to provide meals for children at the elementary schools and in 1907 schools were authorised to hold medical examinations of their children. Fabian socialists in south London advocated these measures in the 1900s.[9] By 1911 Paterson noticed that doctors made regular inspections but did not necessarily provide treatment, so that children with poor eyesight were diagnosed but 18 months later still lacked spectacles.

In 1910 proposals to raise the school leaving age from 12 to 14 foundered, with critics weighing any benefits for children against their possible contribution to the family income. Some children therefore did not attend school beyond the age of 12, although, Paterson remarked, a schoolboy expected 'to become a man' aged 14 years. In 1918 H. A. L. Fisher's Education Act raised the school leaving age to 14 and abolished all fees in state elementary schools.[10]

BRIXTON'S RESIDENTS

In 1910 Brixton, 4 miles south from Charing Cross and 4½ miles south-east from the Bank of England, was a suburb. It was, wrote Herbert Morrison, 'virtually the edge of London'; beyond it were the homes of richer folk with 'stables, gardeners, and a retinue of servants'. Railway expansion from the 1860s onwards had encouraged housing developments, attracting many to Brixton. Each development drew workers from neighbourhoods nearer the centre, which fell into decline while Brixton prospered. The rich and affluent lived in the larger houses on the higher ground of the suburbs.

Charles Booth (1840–1916), the social investigator, published the results of his survey of London's population in multiple volumes between 1887 and 1902. The seven volumes of series three concentrate on the religious influences on Londoners.[11] Tulse Hill and Brixton Hill, south of Trinity, provided homes for 'the servant-keeping middle class' and 'well-to-do City people', some of them retired, as did also Angell Town, to the north of Trinity. To Trinity's west lies Acre Lane, leading to Clapham, and it and the adjoining King's Avenue comprised

---

8   For A. J. Balfour see *ODNB*.
9   See *AV* 2 (Dec. 1910), 18; Maud Pember Reeves, *Round About a Pound a Week* (2008), 215–17.
10   For H. A. L. Fisher see *ODNB*; H. A. L. Fisher, *An Unfinished Autobiography* (1940), 106–9; David Ogg, *Herbert Fisher 1865–1940: A Short Biography* (1947); K. O. Morgan, *Consensus and Identity: The Lloyd George Coalition Government 1918–1922* (1979). Paterson, *Across the Bridges*, 55, 68.
11   Morrison, *Autobiography*, 11; Booth, vi. 43, 61. For Booth see *ODNB*.

larger villas. Here in King's Avenue lived Dan C. Messent, while in Branksome Road, a street off Acre Lane with terraced houses nearer to Trinity, dwelt for a time *The Angels' Voice* editor, James Godden.[12]

The 'fairly comfortable' Brixton contrasted sharply with neighbouring areas like Walworth, north Lambeth and Kennington (where Charlie Chaplin lived in poverty). Young Chaplin (1889–1977) and his mother had a holiday in a friend's house 'in the fashionable district of Stockwell'. They lived for a week 'in the lap of luxury, with a house full of servants, pink and blue bedrooms, chintz curtains and white bear-rugs'. Chaplin and their hostess's gentleman friend walked 'the lady's two beautiful greyhound dogs' on Clapham Common. He recalled that Clapham had 'an elegant atmosphere'. A mile away in Brixton, Herbert Morrison lacked the 'privileges of wealth or education' but never starved, and, like Trinity's young men, he aspired to better things.[13]

The middle class might have lacked the working class's community spirit or the superior cohesiveness of the gentry but it tended to have 'a family-centred individualism'. The 'local roots' of the middle class were often more shallow than those of the working class, although Trinity's young men displayed a loyalty to Brixton and to Trinity.[14] Lower-middle-class youths entertained ambitions to rise socially; certainly the magazine and its editor teased their adolescent readers for any sign of social pretension. Exceptionally snobbery surfaced in remarks in *The Angels' Voice* no. 3, criticising F. Squires' Cockney accent, a rare instance of such an attitude.[15]

Charles Masterman (1873–1927) believed the growing middle classes were 'the creations not of the industrial, but of the commercial and business activities of London'. Masterman was writing after the London County Council elections of 1907 when the Progressive Party's defeat led to control by the conservative Municipal Reform Party. He identified the residents of the suburbs with individualism and the rejection of collectivist ideals. Yet *The Angels' Voice* is an expression of collectivist ideals in action, testifying to a network of social and religious support which enhanced these friends' lives and which refuted Masterman's criticism of suburban life.[16] Sir Walter Besant in 1912 also looked down on Brixton. He saw it as composed of 'exceedingly

12   Booth, vi. 89–91.

13   Charles Chaplin, *My Autobiography* (1964), 51–2; Donoghue and Jones, *Morrison*, xii, 5.

14   McLeod, 133–4. The cinema afforded mass entertainment 1920–55 and the Astoria, Brixton, resembling an Italian garden, with balconies, vines, trellises and statues of ancient Greeks, was a 'magnificent people's palace in which to live a dreamworld'. Jerry White, *London in the Twentieth Century: A City and its People* (2001), 336.

15   *AV* 3 (Jan. 1911), 31.

16   C. F. G. Masterman, *The Condition of England* (1909), 69–70. <http://digital.library.lse. ac.uk/collections/londoncountycouncilelection1907> accessed 24 Dec. 2014.

uninteresting and drab streets, where middle-class people ... make their homes' among 'the most nondescript architecture'. The streets consisted mainly of terraced houses, with a few detached and larger ones alongside them.[17] George Gissing (1857–1903), 'the novelist of the middle class', who defined his characters by their suburban homes, saw the new flats in 1890s Brixton as representing a modern 'type of vulgarity', while Brixton itself reflected a 'slightly unconventional style of life'.[18]

If Brixton was 'too regular in its architecture, too new in its associations, to suit the artist', it provided 'genteel' homes.[19] Like Trinity's young men, Herbert Morrison, born in nearby Ferndale Road in 1888, belonged to the lower middle class. His neighbours included policemen like his father, railway officials and commercial travellers, and Brixton also accommodated the 'more successful' entertainers of the day.[20] Charles Booth found Brixton's respectability 'a little oppressive', with street after street testifying to 'the virtue of the shopkeepers' who lived there 'in large numbers'.[21] In truth Brixton had a more diverse population than Booth allowed. Alongside the shopkeepers, clerks and artisans were 'doctors, ... theatrical and musical people, much shabby gentility and many lodgers, medical students ... and some labourers'. Their neighbours might be civil servants, solicitors and merchants, while printers and meat market workers used the all night railway to the City.[22] In contrast to Brixton's critics, Morrison's mother liked it so much that she refused to leave, preventing her policeman husband's promotion to sergeant.[23]

ARLINGFORD ROAD

Arlingford Road, situated near Trinity, included many among its residents who attended the church and its weekday activities. A detailed analysis of its residents offers a guide to the community.

---

[17] Walter Besant, *London South of the Thames* (1912), 169. Besant's survey of the architectural landmarks omitted Trinity.

[18] McLeod, 132–3.

[19] White, *Twentieth Century*, 17; Clarence Rook, *London Side-Lights* (1908), 28; Jerry White, *London in the Nineteenth Century: 'A Human Awful Wonder of God'* (2007), 84.

[20] Donoghue and Jones, *Morrison*, 3–5; David Robinson, *Chaplin: His Life and Art* (1985), 5.

[21] Booth's *Life and Labour of the People of London* (1902) emerged from interviews, questionnaires, reports from London School Board visitors, and from visitations. Cox, 28, 30.

[22] Cox, 30; Booth, vi. 43, 61; Booth MS Collection B–305, p. 129, B–326, p. 51, held at British Library of Economic and Political Science, London School of Economics. Hereafter these notebooks are referred to as A– and B–.

[23] Donoghue and Jones, *Morrison*, 4. Family gossip suggested that a move to Blackheath meant promotion.

Census records give details of employment and the relationships between residents in a household (those sharing meals and living accommodation). The 1911 census also included the amount of rooms occupied by each household.[24] In Arlingford Road most houses contained eight to ten rooms and were divided between two distinct households. Only 14 houses, among the total of 63 in the road, from its junction with Brailsford Road, were occupied by one family, whilst four contained three households and one was divided into four households. However, these Victorian houses allowed for spacious living. Out of 118 households in the 63 houses, only 25 fuller households had fewer rooms than the sum of people occupying them, while eight households employed live-in servants. The overall population in the houses surveyed was 448.

Out of 84 married couples, only five wives had a paid occupation. Predominantly, those of working age in the street who were employed were engaged in clerical and shop work, confirming the evidence of Herbert Morrison and other contemporaries, as the table below shows. Some five Arlingford Road residents ran their own businesses, employing others – a fried fishmonger, an accountant, a basket-maker, a dressmaker and a house decorator. Another 18 were self-employed, including gardeners, a barber, a jeweller and a cigar dealer. A few of Trinity's members living in Arlingford Road were managers like Messrs Snoswell (no. 76) and Johnston (no. 70), whereas Mr Bedwell (no. 22) was a commercial clerk. All Trinity's young men who lived in the road were either clerks or shop-workers, as were most of their sisters, though two young women were schoolteachers.

The following table classifies by occupation those living in Arlingford Road in 1911. Not all occupations, such as 'stand maker', are recognisable to modern readers.[25] The 'Other skilled workers' category encompasses a wide variety of employment – stand maker, farrier, piano part maker, engraver, gas engineer, jewellers, clock repairers, wheelwright, gun maker's assistant, cabinet maker, assistant electrician, upholsterers and basket makers. The insurance professionals include insurance agents. Also of note are occupations which are predominantly or entirely single sex. Among our sample, teaching, dressmaking and live-in domestic service are exclusively women's occupations. Conversely, printing, building, gardening, labouring, delivering, live-out domestic service and 'other skilled workers' are almost exclusively male.

---

[24] The 1911 census form instructed householders to 'count the kitchen ... not ... scullery, landing, lobby, closet, bathroom; nor warehouse, office, shop'.

[25] A stand was an open tub, for example used for washing. *Oxford English Dictionary.*

Arlingford Road in the 1911 census

Occupations	Household members				
	Male head	*Female head*	*Other male*	*Other female*	*Total*
Teachers, journalists, insurance professionals, accountants, company secretary	7	0	2	8	17
Clerks, typists, book-keepers, office boys	10	0	18	18	46
Shop assistants, sales, warehousemen	22	0	17	10	49
Clothing, dressmaking employees	0	5	0	11	16
Printing	6	1	1	0	8
Building trades, decorators	7	0	2	0	9
Other skilled workers	10	1	5	1	17
Variety/music hall performers/agent	2	0	1	1	4
Domestic servants working elsewhere (coachmen, chauffeurs), nurse	4	1	1	0	6
Servants resident in place of work	0	0	0	9	9
Cooks, restaurant staff, cloakroom attendant	2	2	4	3	11
Gardeners	6	0	1	0	7
Carman, postman, milkman, delivery workers, labourer, bill-poster, messenger	8	0	5	0	13
Total	84	10	57	61	212

BRIXTON'S AMENITIES

In 1877 the department store Bon Marché opened in Brixton, providing good products and saving a trip to the West End. By the 1900s Brixton's 'cheap street market' supplemented the 'several large stores' on Brixton Road. Only a few hundred yards from Trinity were Brixton's theatres and a 'modern music hall'. The Brixton Theatre and Opera House had opened in September 1896, adjoining the Tate Central Free Public Library. However, the Brixton Theatre, the Empress Theatre of Varieties and the music hall do not feature in *The Angels' Voice*, suggesting that they were not frequented by Bible Class members, or if they were, the editor chose not to comment on them. Alexander Paterson reported,

9

Attendance at a music-hall as a weekly practice is commonly held to denote a careless and irreligious life; and though ... some good men and steady lads ... frequent these places, ... the worst boys are the *habitués*, and the best boys do not go at all. At the best it is a poor entertainment, at the worst it is the gate to every temptation.[26]

The difficulty was that music halls, having 'evolved from drinking establishments', still depended on the sale of alcohol for much of their income. In the 1900s the legitimate theatre enjoyed a higher reputation than the music halls. In contrast to Trinity's young men, Herbert Morrison's mother took him to the music hall, to the Brixton Theatre and the Empress. 'On a very few evenings' in 1910, aged 22, he sat in the gallery of the theatre. By 1931, Brixton's population had so changed that cheaper seats replaced the theatre boxes which had once accommodated the better off.[27]

Trinity's young men would have noted the opening of the imposing Lambeth Town Hall (built 1906–08), at the corner of Brixton Hill and Acre Lane and immediately opposite the library. George Gissing left Exeter, after more than two years, to live in Brixton in 1893–94, drawn by the Tate Library (opened in 1892, close to Trinity and endowed by the sugar magnate and Streatham resident Sir Henry Tate 1819–99).[28]

Suburban social life often depended on the activities provided by a church or chapel. These might include badminton, socials, discussions and a literary society.[29] The inhabitants of the suburbs, like Brixton's chapel-goers, were required to shun impropriety, to observe conventions, be industrious, sober, if not teetotal, and self-restrained. *The Angels' Voice* commends the literary society, not always well supported, at Trinity Chapel.[30]

SIZE OF FAMILIES

Herbert Morrison's mother bore seven children in under ten years, which was not unusual.[31] In 1911 most of Trinity's families had several children. The Lansdowns had one son and two daughters, whereas many families had four or more children. The largest family was the Snoswells with 15 children, while the Rowes had 11 children and the

---

[26]   Paterson, *Across the Bridges*, 102; White *Zeppelin Nights*, 8.
[27]   Booth, vi. 90; McLeod, 132–3; White, *Nineteenth Century*, 94, 191, 245; White, *Twentieth Century*, 22.
[28]   Morrison, *Autobiography*, 21; Donoghue and Jones, *Morrison*, 6, 9; Robinson, *Chaplin*, 12; Bridget Cherry and Nikolaus Pevsner, *The Buildings of England, London 2: South* (1983), 357. For Gissing and Tate see *ODNB*.
[29]   McLeod, 135.
[30]   *AV* 3 (Jan. 1911), 29.
[31]   Donoghue and Jones, *Morrison*, 4.

Messents nine. Childhood mortality did not touch all families and the Berrys' loss of both their children was exceptional. Others had lost some of their children by 1911, e.g. one of the Snoswells and two of the Messents.[32]

TRANSPORT

Brixton's transport links were good, with London County Council trams running along Brixton Road to Westminster, Waterloo and Blackfriars Bridges; 'trams were frequent and cheap', although people 'walked far more then'. Charlie Chaplin recalled that 'even the horse-drawn tram-cars along Westminster Bridge Road went at a sedate pace'. Yet, as Harold W. Walker wrote of his Walthamstow childhood in 1912, 'all trams have ... hard cane' seats which 'tend to bruise one's bottom'. The trams stopped frequently and in bad weather passengers on the open top deck had to endure the rain, hail, snow or fog. The Edwardian omnibus shook its passengers 'to pieces', owing to its lack of suspension, but had 'more warmth and intimacy' than the tram.[33]

The London, Brighton & South Coast Railway ran to Victoria and London Bridge from East Brixton station. The South Eastern & Chatham Railway ran from Brixton to Victoria, the City and south-east London. The 'omnibuses' competed with trams on all the main roads, using several cross routes, from Camberwell to Clapham, and from Brixton to Herne Hill and Norwood.[34]

CONGREGATIONALISM

In 1911 the *Congregational Year Book* listed 4,721 churches and mission stations, 454,810 church members and 2,932 ministers for England and Wales. Of these, London had 347 churches and 56,827 members. Lancashire had 333 churches and 42,062 members; Yorkshire had 323 churches and 35,943 members; and Wales (including Monmouth and certain Welsh churches in England) had 1,350 churches and 166,858 members. These Welsh figures include both the English-speaking churches and the Welsh-speaking churches of the Union of Welsh

---

[32] The 1911 census recorded the number of children born to a mother and how many remained alive. Information for the Rowes comes from the 1901 census, because in 1911 the children from the first marriage had left home.

[33] Morrison, *Autobiography*, 22; Chaplin, *Autobiography*, 14. H. W. Walker, *Mainly Memories, 1906–1930* (1986), 60, 122. <http://www.walthamstowmemories.net/pdfs/walker13.pdf> accessed 1 Oct. 2014.

[34] *Bradshaw's General Railway and Steam Navigation Guide* (July 1913), 219, 254–5, 286, 291, 296; Booth, vi. 91.

Independents.[35] No county union of Congregational churches exceeded the figures for London.

In England

The origins of Congregationalism lay with impatient Protestants who wanted more reforms in the Elizabethan Church of England and, in frustration, separated from it. They developed underground churches, some going into exile in the Netherlands rather than conform and some settling in the 'wilderness' of New England. With the outbreak of civil war in 1642, these independent churches surfaced, and throughout the relative toleration of the war and interregnum they grew in number and influence. After the Restoration in 1660, they withdrew into comparative political inactivity until, in the nineteenth century, they began to demand equality with the established church.

In the 1900s Congregationalism in England was confident that it was coming into its own, free of the legal shackles that had accompanied religious nonconformity and excluded its adherents from privileges open to the establishment. Nonconformists welcomed this age when Victorian injustices would be overthrown. The chairman of the Congregational Union of England and Wales (CUEW) for 1901, Joseph Parker, expected that the Congregational churches and their fellow Free Churches (a title then preferred to 'nonconformist' or 'dissenter') would no longer be subordinate. Although Parker died in 1902, his attitudes remained influential.

In 1906 the Liberal Party, having come to power in December 1905, secured a landslide victory at the general election, with the support of most Free Church folk. Consequently the sum of nonconformist MPs was at its zenith, 180 or so, giving Congregationalists unparalleled political power.[36] The Free Churches also hoped for mutual co-operation and the CUEW enjoyed friendship with its fellows. In 1910, with two general elections in one year, Congregationalists remained buoyant. H. H. Asquith, Liberal prime minister 1908–16, relied on support from the Irish Nationalists and the Labour Party. In 1910 the popular orator and Congregational minister Charles Silvester Horne (1865–1914) had become CUEW chairman and also a Liberal MP.[37] The young men of Trinity's Bible Class might legitimately believe that their views were at the forefront of public opinion.

---

[35] *CYB* (1911), 602–4.
[36] Argent, *Transformation*, 40–1.
[37] *ODNB*.

In London

Preaching had great appeal in the Edwardian age. In 1903 the theologically liberal modernist R. J. Campbell, Parker's successor at The City Temple, Holborn Viaduct, preached to 7,000 on his first Sunday as minister there. The erudite R. F. Horton of Lyndhurst Road Congregational Church, Hampstead, attracted over 1,000 to a service. In 1902 Christ Church, Westminster Bridge Road, where the Baptist F. B. Meyer was minister, boasted the third largest attendance of London's Congregational chapels, with 752 at the morning service and 1,294 for evening worship. There the young Charlie Chaplin listened to Meyer's 'fervent and dramatic voice'. He was embarrassed by his mother's tears during these 'appealing ... orations' but knew her 'religious scruples' were sincere. Silvester Horne, minister of Whitefield's Tabernacle, Tottenham Court Road, from 1903, drew packed congregations. Herbert Morrison heard the 'great preachers whose thunderings from the pulpit crammed the churches', recalling Meyer and Campbell from that 'era of splendid preaching'. On Sunday evenings he attended whichever church then boasted a famous preacher.[38]

According to Masterman, Congregational ministers disdained to restate traditional doctrines of 'hell and heaven', as Baptist ministers did, but were 'abreast of modern culture'. Therefore, the Congregational minister proclaimed 'a less exacting gospel and faintly' trusted to 'the larger hope'.[39]

Charles Booth wrote in 1902 that for the Congregationalists the pulpit was

> the centre round which everything turns. Each church is self-governed and owes no outside allegiance. There is a working organization of deacons for financial and disciplinary purposes, and an inner circle of members forms the Church. The members choose their pastor, but are not necessarily united ... in ... a common doctrine. The congregation ... are a larger body, including many who ... have not yet taken up membership; but the whole assembly ... is simply the spontaneous expression of a Christian sentiment seeking leadership, mutual support, exercise, discipline, and work. On the one hand ... are the Church members with whom all ultimate power lies, and on the other ... the ... pastor, with whom rests the absolute leadership of all those who gather round him.[40]

---

[38] *ODNB*; McLeod, 140; A–47, p. 2; Cox, 144–5; Argent, *Transformation*, 38–42; Chaplin, *Autobiography*, 19, 40, 44; Morrison, *Autobiography*, 22; Donoghue and Jones, *Morrison*, 10.

[39.] Masterman, *The Condition of England*, 75.

[40] Booth, i. 120.

Booth observed that when London's Congregational churches required money they commonly held bazaars for, on principle, they did not 'beg from outsiders'.[41] In December 1909, Trinity's church meeting hoped to finance a recent mission, with the pastor and a deacon sitting in the vestry to receive 'thankofferings' from friends.[42]

Therefore Congregationalists appointed, and still appoint, deacons from their members to tackle administrative duties, finance and other concerns and to advise the minister/pastor. Unlike Church of England and Roman Catholic deacons, Congregational deacons are not members of the clergy. One of Booth's investigators described a Congregational deacon: 'slight in build, bearded, quiet, inclined to precision in speech, liberal in his point of view, an excellent specimen of the highly respectable, religiously-minded citizen, who is thoughtful of the poor'.[43]

In Brixton

Lambeth's 'wealthier Nonconformist chapels' were almost all either Congregational or Wesleyan. Of these, **Brixton Independent Chapel**, with its tall spire and grand building on the main road, was 'the most distinguished', having opened as recently as 1870.[44] Booth saw this as a 'great' church, 'outside the Establishment ... wherein the doctrines preached are unorthodox and heretical to the verge of Unitarianism'. It 'was always full' and had 'never been more prosperous' than in the 1900s. The worshippers came from the higher class, with 'the working classes' noticeably 'absent'. Booth added that 'Young people, and especially young men, attend in large numbers.'[45]

William Kent in his autobiography described his move in 1904 from the less assuming Congregational church at Vauxhall, Wheatsheaf Hall, originally a mission hall, to the sophisticated Brixton Independent Chapel. He worshipped at the latter for eight years, where few but the pastor spoke to him. He wrote, 'Sometimes I faltered when faced with the alternative of a good sermon and no handshake at Brixton Independent Church and a bad sermon and a handshake at Wheatsheaf Hall.'[46] At Wheatsheaf he found friends and activities, although the latter had little to do with Christianity, and there, like the young men at Trinity, Kent met young women, without offending propriety.[47]

---

41   Booth, i. 121.
42   TCC Meeting, 1 Dec. 1909.
43   McLeod, 137, 160; B–218, p. 161.
44   Cox, 142.
45   Booth, vi. 43.
46   William Kent, *Testament of a Victorian Youth* (1938), 220; Cox, 45.
47   McLeod, 145.

The theologically liberal Bernard Snell, pastor of Brixton Independent from 1891 to 1934, analysed his congregation: 'The shopkeeper class is scarcely touched; the people are rather civil servants, journalists, and theatrical people.'[48] His church was 'a gathering place' for 'intelligent and right-minded men and women'.[49] Snell's obituary recorded 'the splendour, the daring, the fire, and the intense passion of his preaching'. He had a 'magnificent presence and voice' and 'a well-stored mind and passionate conviction', giving his sermons 'an effectiveness that attracted multitudes and sent men and women away with new ardour in their souls'.[50]

Brixton Independent lasted until the Second World War, but during the First World War many of its people left town, fearful of Zeppelin raids, and not all returned at the war's end. Damaged by bombing in the Second World War and with its congregation again dispersed, it was sold and became Our Lady of the Rosary Roman Catholic Church.[51]

Other Congregational churches existed in the area. **Stockwell Green**, to the north-west, was the oldest, having been founded in 1796. Its distinguished minister between 1845 and 1877 was David Thomas (1813–94). His congregation included Catherine Mumford (1829–90) who married William Booth (1829–1912), later founder of the Salvation Army, there in 1855. Curiously, Wilson Carlile (1847–1942), who would found the Church of England's Church Army, also attended Thomas's ministry at Stockwell Green.[52]

Brixton Hill Congregational Church (founded 1829) sat astride Brixton Hill, one mile south from Brixton and nearer Streatham. East of Brixton, **Loughborough Park Congregational Church**, in Coldharbour Lane, leading to Camberwell, was founded in 1860. It survived until 1942 when it lacked a minister but still recorded 73 members.[53]

Trinity Chapel was described by Booth as 'rather hidden away', in Church Road (renamed St Matthew's Road by the London County Council in 1936), yards from the thoroughfares of Brixton Hill and Effra Road. In the early twentieth century this chapel (founded in 1828) was 'intended to be temporary' and a prominent stone building was planned on land fronting the main road.[54] Booth rated the congregation 'a strictly

---

48   Cox, 142. Booth, vi. 43; B–303, p. 69.
49   Brixton Free Press, *Brixton's Churches* (1904), 216.
50   *CYB* (1935), 289–90. For Snell and Brixton Independent see: Alan Argent, 'Some Memorials of Bernard J. Snell', *Congregational History Circle Magazine*, v. no 1 (Spring 2005), 5.
51   The building survives largely intact, after repairs.
52   For Thomas, Catherine Booth, William Booth and Carlile, see *ODNB*. Carlile's parents were devout Congregationalists.
53   *CYB* (1940), 367; (1942), 121.
54   Information from Len Reilly of Lambeth Archives. The main road in question was Effra Road. This large, ambitious structure was not built and the 1828 building remains in use.

Trinity Congregational Church, Brixton, in 2015.

middle-class body, a few being wealthy and the rest well-to-do and prosperous'.[55] Some of its servant-keeping members earned perhaps £200 to £350 a year, although a few earned more. One Congregational minister commented that servants exercised their independence by going 'to a different church to their employers'. Trinity was 'solidly comfortable rather than wealthy'.[56]

Booth's remarks about Trinity's social composition have been questioned by the church's own historian who noticed that new church members did not match his description. She discovered housemaids, a lady's help, a cashier, drapers' assistants, drapers and a cook became church members at this time. One older member had recalled Edwardians coming to Trinity in morning dress and in their own carriages.[57]

In 1902 the morning congregation was growing rather than the evening one – 'a sure sign' of becoming 'more fashionable' – in fact the recent religious census showed Trinity's 11am attendance as 196, with 215 attending at 6.45pm. Worship followed 'a formal liturgy' which was John Hunter's *Devotional Services for Public Worship*, by 1903 in its eighth edition, first made popular at The King's Weigh House [Congregational] Church in Mayfair. Such use of 'a formal liturgy'

55   Booth, vi. 66–7.
56   Cox, 26, 142, 144.
57   Y. A. Evans, 'History of Trinity' (typescript c.1978), held at the church.

signified prosperity. However, unusually for a Nonconformist church, Trinity's unsurpliced and psalm-chanting 'choir of men and boys' was paid. The minister, W. H. Bradford, revealed his social conscience in wanting to 'do something for the poor', though he felt them 'to be very far away' for they could not mix with his people.[58] Again Trinity's records do not support this contention for the communion funds were disbursed to poor church members. In 1901 one member, destitute at her death, left no money for her milk bill or for funeral expenses, which the church paid. Following his father's death, Alfred P. Austin, of Trinity's Young Men's Bible Class, spent ten years of his childhood in an orphanage, as did other members of his family.[59]

The boys of Trinity's Sunday School wore 'Eton jackets and college caps'. On Sunday evenings, the minister's house, adjoining the chapel, was 'open to the young people' and was 'often full'. Booth concluded, perhaps misled by Bradford, that Trinity was 'very strictly limited ... by class and taste in religious matters' but that it showed 'strength and steady growth'.[60]

In 1896 the brothers William J. Messent and Daniel C. Messent became church members. Both would strongly affect Trinity's life and work. Their father, Daniel Messent, was Trinity's treasurer 1887–1920. In 1898 Miss Bessie Johnston, who married Dan C. Messent in 1915, became a church member. In June 1897 Henry Snoswell was appointed Sunday school superintendent; his family would prove influential too. Dan C. Messent died of cancer in 1936; Mrs Dan (as she was known) lived until 1962.[61] Will Messent was Trinity's church secretary 1921–47 and then became secretary emeritus. He was replaced by Kathleen Pratt, who had been in Mrs Dan's Bible Class for young women. Will Messent lived while secretary at 21 College Road, Dulwich.[62]

Charles Booth saw both Brixton Independent and Trinity Chapel as among those Congregational churches where

> prosperity and religion go hand in hand. This they ... recognise, thanking God for His good gifts, and praying that they may use them rightly ... There is no ... sourness or severity ... Pleasure is not tabooed. The young are trusted and encouraged. Happiness is directly aimed at but is associated with ... duty: ... Their pastors preach this ideal ... They use their churches ... for any purpose

58 Booth, vi. 66–7.
59 Census returns for 1881 and 1891.
60 Booth, vi. 67, B–304, p. 103, B–303, p. 55; Richard Mudie-Smith (ed.), *The Religious Life of London* (1904), 227; H. W. Harris and Margaret Bryant, *The Churches and London: An outline survey of religious work in the metropolitan area. With a full directory of places of worship in the County of London* (1914), 405; Argent, *Transformation*, 221–2; Cox, 144; Evans, 'History of Trinity'.
61 Evans, 'History of Trinity'.
62 *CYB* (1921), 203; (1947), 171; (1948), 186.

... not actually irreligious. Concerts, popular lectures, debates on social or political questions; all find a place.[63]

By the 1900s church attendance in Lambeth had been declining for 50 years. The fall in Nonconformist attendance was most marked in Brixton.[64] Yet growing Nonconformist confidence led to the adoption of the term 'churches' for their chapels.[65] By the 1890s, Trinity Chapel had become Trinity Congregational Church to its members, though its building still bore the inscription 'Trinity Chapel', cut high into its stonework above the porch.

The parish of St Matthew's Brixton, in which Trinity Chapel geographically was situated, approximately 200 yards from St Matthew's Church, comprised some 11,032 souls in 1902.[66] Seating 2,000, St Matthew's attracted large numbers of young men to its evangelical services. Just off Brixton Hill was St Saviour's parish church which also drew numerous young people.[67] Trinity's Young Men's Bible Class faced competition in recruiting members.

Mathias Lansdown, Trinity's minister 1902–20, lived at The Manse, 21 Church Road, Brixton Hill. An experienced minister whose brother and nephew also became Congregational ministers, he was born in Cardiff and trained for the ministry in Bristol before serving his first pastorate at Looe in Cornwall from 1884 to 1886. He ministered at East Cliff, Bournemouth from 1886 to 1895, and Tolmer's Square, Euston, London from 1895 to 1902, before moving to Brixton. The death of his wife, Fanny (née Stripp), in 1920 may have prompted his leaving Trinity.

Throughout this time Trinity claimed that it could seat a congregation of 550, far in excess of the number of formal church members. The *Congregational Year Book* listed church members, Sunday School pupils, teachers and lay preachers and the figures for 1910–14 are listed below:

Congregational Year Book	Members	Scholars	Teachers	Lay preachers
1910	150	250	24	
1911	150	250	28	
1912	150	250	28	
1913	155	360	42	4
1914	158	375	43	4

[63]   Booth, i. 121–2.
[64]   Cox, 36–7.
[65]   Cox, 51.
[66]   Booth, vi. 5.
[67]   Booth, vi. 61, 63.

Trinity's church meeting, at which members discussed and decided on the church's work, met monthly. In 1911 the church secretary (an unpaid office filled by a senior deacon) was Charles H. Welch who lived nearby at 6 Morval Road. He died in November 1911, and in 1912 the church appointed Mr W. J. Gray Ramsay of 77 Brailsford Road, also only a short distance away.[68] The deacons listed then were Messrs Cran, Fisk, W. J. Messent, D. C. Messent and Welch. Six months later the deacons also included Messrs Budden, Ramsay, Snoswell, Howard Evans, Stanley Williams and George Williams.[69] Kathleen Pratt knew many of those mentioned in *The Angels' Voice*. She became Trinity's first female deacon during the Second World War when, she reported, the men were engaged in war work. Other churches probably promoted women to responsible positions then for similar reasons.

During Bradford's ministry at Trinity, 1895–1901, a twentieth-century fund was founded with the intention of erecting a new church building. Trinity was considered to be in a backwater, with the main thoroughfare a hundred yards further west. However, by 1911 the plan to build a new sanctuary in the gardens of 19 and 21 Church Road was abandoned. Daniel Messent senior had generously bought the houses and the land behind them. He now resumed ownership of the property and received £50 per annum for the minister's occupation of the manse, i.e. no. 21.

In March 1910 a 'sale of work' included a series of 'living wax works', a lantern display, refreshments and sweets, provisions and a men's stall. It was opened by the Dowager Lady Lawrence and the pastor invited friends 'likely to be interested in' Sir Alexander and Lady Lawrence to attend.[70] The sale, after expenses, yielded £45.[71] Sir Harry Samuel (MP for Norwood 1910–22) and Lady Samuel opened the three-day bazaar planned for late February and early March 1913, and the Mayor of Lambeth was also present.[72]

On 2 August 1911, a Mr Redmond was appointed the chapel organist at a salary of £15 per annum. Dan C. Messent continued as choirmaster, enabling him to influence the young men as choristers and as Bible Class members.[73]

---

[68]   TCC Meeting, 31 Jan. 1912

[69]   TCC Meeting, 1 Dec. 1909, 1 June 1910, 29 June 1910.

[70]   Probably this was Sir Alexander Lawrence (4th Bt), the defeated Liberal Party candidate for Norwood in Jan. 1910. See: *Who Was Who*, <http://www.ukwhoswho.com/view/article/oupww/whoswho/U212645>, accessed 24 Oct. 2014.

[71]   TCC Meeting, 2 Mar. 1910, 1 June 1910.

[72]   TCC Meeting, 27 Nov. 1912, 22 Jan. 1913. For the Conservative politician Sir Harry Samuel, see *The Times*, 27 Apr. 1934.

[73]   TCC Meeting, 2 Aug. 1911.

Composition of the Bible Class

In August 1913 James Godden analysed the Bible Class membership in terms of age. He identified three groups. The first consisted of four older men: the leader, Dan C. Messent (33 years), the class organist, R. Charles Moxley, Alfred P. Austin and Albert H. Evans, all of whom were the 'remnant of a former generation'. Secondly he listed 'the main body of the class', including himself (he was 19), 'who partook in its formation or its development'. Lastly he identified the 'welcome influx of younger blood' who had repaired 'an unavoidable wastage', meaning those whose age, attitudes or employment had led them to leave the class. Some might have left on marriage, reinforcing the sense that the Bible Class was for bachelors.

Separating his four 'Patriarchs', Godden still noted that 14 members were older than 21 years. Of the remainder, 17 were aged 15 to 20 years. The 'main body' of the class had 'an average age of 22', while the 'newer members' averaged 17 years old. These two groups had a combined average age of 20. When the four 'elders' were included, he determined that they may easily call themselves 'an adult class'.[74] Clearly age the range was wide, with men in their late 20s and early to mid-30s, like Messent and Evans, mingling with teenagers, though the mix seemed to work.

Women at Trinity

While *The Angels' Voice* was created by the Young Men's Bible Class, nevertheless references to women at Trinity abounded and, in later issues, some women were even contributors, principally as artists. The church's records indicate several women's meetings and activities. Throughout much of the nineteenth century, Trinity had a Dorcas and Benevolent Society, providing warm clothes and household necessities for needy women and lending clean linen to prospective mothers in confinement. Its records ceased in 1898.[75] The Sunday school teachers numbered men and women, with the latter slightly in the majority.[76] Among the groups represented at Trinity's anniversary in 1912 were the Girls' Guild and Classes, the Women's/Mothers' Meeting and the Ladies' Working Party.[77]

The young men and women were well aware of each other, with the Girls' Bible Class meeting in the adjacent room to the Young Men's Class and with the two classes following a similar syllabus. Of course,

---

[74] *AV* 11 (Aug. 1913), 12.
[75] TCC Dorcas and Benevolent Society minute book 1846–98, *passim*; TCC Dorcas and Benevolent Society account book 1846–97, *passim*.
[76] TCC Sunday School Teachers Meeting minute book 1891–1914, *passim*.
[77] *AV* 8 (July 1912), 44; TCC Meeting, 29 May 1912; TCC Deacons, 13 May 1912.

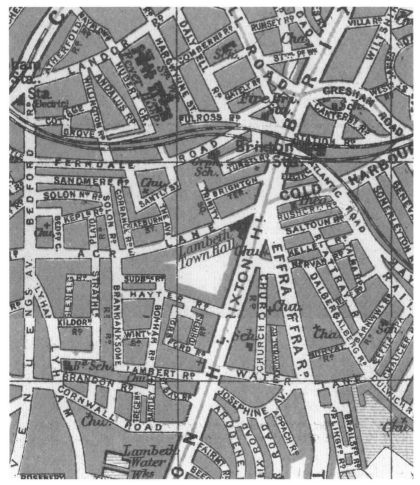

Brixton pre-1914

many of the girls were sisters of the young men and others would become their wives. The term 'girls' may imply some condescension, although female suffrage was aired in *The Angel's Voice*.[78] Other Trinity records refer rather to Young Women's classes, suggesting that condescension was not universal.[79] The minutes also reveal that women shared in decision making, both proposing and seconding resolutions in church meetings.[80]

[78] *AV* 12 (Sept. 1913), 12.
[79] TCC Deacons, 13 May 1912.
[80] TCC Minutes, *passim*.

GROWING UP IN PRE-1914 LONDON

The Angels' Voice opens a window on lower-middle-class youths growing up in pre-1914 London.

In Bermondsey in 1911 Alexander Paterson, having graduated from Oxford, tested his belief that Christianity could achieve social reform. He found that City office boys were attracted to petty gambling, with sweepstakes on horse races. Yet he observed that 'few boys' were seen in public houses (excessive drinking came at a later age). Paterson held that the 'real antidote to all boyish failings' lay in 'some form of education and discipline' like boys' clubs and Saturday cricket and football. He observed that 'barely 1 per cent' attended Sunday School 'after the emancipating age' of 14 years. The south London boy noted that the Christian 'does not drink, or swear, or gamble, and goes to concerts, but never to a music-hall'.[81] Probably Trinity's Bible Class members knew these attitudes, even if they did not share them. The Baptist F. B. Meyer at Christ Church, Westminster Bridge Road, was not alone in condemning gambling and its temptations.[82]

THE CONTENTS OF *THE ANGELS' VOICE*

Sport

By 1900 there were 200,000 amateur footballers in England. Lambeth's Nonconformist chapels sponsored numerous football clubs before the First World War, as is evident from Trinity's regular matches against other church clubs.[83] A similar story could be told of cricket and women's hockey.[84] Cycling influenced women's emancipation, giving the 'New Woman' increased mobility and encouraging simpler dress, free of corsets and long skirts. One contributor to *The Angels' Voice* wrote of his Sunday morning cycling to Redhill and his evening church attendance.[85] In addition Trinity's young men and women used Brixton's roller-skating rink (opened 1910) on the corner of Brixton Water Lane and Tulse Hill.[86]

---

[81]　Paterson, *Across the Bridges*, 112, 114–17.

[82]　D. W. Bebbington, *The Nonconformist Conscience: Chapel and Politics, 1870–1914* (1982), 51.

[83]　Many of the Bible Class members supported Chelsea FC. *AV* 13 (Oct. 1913), 33. Cox, 59; White, *Nineteenth Century*, 263; John Arlott, 'Sport', in *Edwardian England 1901–1914*, ed. Simon Nowell-Smith (1964), 470, 478.

[84]　Trinity's cricket team is first mentioned in *AV* 7 (Nov. 1911), 44. In 1896 the Ladies' Hockey Association was set up. Hockey enabled women, even with long skirts, to play in clubs, free from men's control. Arlott, 'Sport', 450, 452, 469.

[85]　'Cycling' in *Encyclopaedia Britannica Online Academic Edition* (2014), <http://www.britannica.com/EBchecked/topic/147973/cycling> accessed 3 Sept. 2014. *AV* 5 (Mar. 1911), 5–6.

[86]　<http://www.urban75.org/blog/brixton-roller-skating-rink-memories-from-the-late–1950s/> accessed 14 Mar. 2015.

Booth found that several Lambeth churchmen railed 'against cycling and other forms of Sabbath breaking and unrest'. The vicar of St James, Camberwell, complained that 'church-going is dying; families used to come; now the younger ones are off bicycling'. However, in their survey of London churches Harris and Bryant described 'an active church' as having cycling, football, rambling and swimming clubs, as well as a literary society and even an orchestra.[87]

Socialism

Most readers of *The Angels' Voice* were Liberals in sympathy. Conversely, one socialist contributor, 'Politician', raged against the Liberals. This was probably Algernon Carpenter who composed 'articles written in red' that 'Are violent enough to awaken the dead'. Carpenter also advocated land nationalisation.[88] In the late Victorian era the trade unions and 'proponents of the new-fangled socialism' organised 'many demonstrations, marches and strikes in London'.[89] Given that the Independent Labour Party's first parliamentary candidate stood in 1895, and that in 1910 the party's 40 MPs supported the Liberal government, the socialist writer in *The Angels' Voice* could not be easily dismissed.

As mentioned, Trinity's young men considered themselves superior to their female counterparts, although Carpenter gave support to women's suffrage during a ramble and this was reported in issue 10. In a later issue, the magazine printed an anonymous article acknowledging women's grievances but concluding that they were fitted for domestic duties while men should manage 'the general business of the community'.[90]

At this time the future Labour politician Fenner Brockway (1888–1988), the son of Congregational missionary parents, moved to London. There he regularly heard Silvester Horne's preaching and R. J. Campbell at The City Temple but found socialism more appealing. Having joined the Independent Labour Party, by 1912 he was editor of the ILP newspaper, *Labour Leader*.[91]

The south London working-class MP John Burns (1858–1943) was castigated by 'Politician' in *The Angels' Voice*. As Labour MP for Battersea from 1892, Burns advocated change through parliament. In 1905, under the Liberal government, he became president of the Local

---

[87] Cox, 39–40; Booth, vi. 63; B–272, p. 67, B–305, p. 103; Harris and Bryant, *Churches and London*, 168–9.

[88] *AV* 3 (Jan. 1911), 31; *AV* 13 (Oct. 1913), 37. 'Algy's' physique is lampooned in *AV* 10 (July 1913), 34.

[89] Donaghue and Jones, *Morrison*, 4.

[90] *AV* 10 (July 1913), 19; *AV* 12 (Sept. 1913), 20–2.

[91] Fenner Brockway, *Inside the Left: Thirty Years of Platform, Press, Prison and Parliament* (1942), 12–18; *ODNB*.

Government Board and in 1914 was president of the Board of Trade. As the 'first working man to achieve cabinet rank', he was seen by some socialists, like 'Politician', as a class traitor.[92]

(Albert) Victor Grayson (b. 1881), referred to in *The Angels' Voice*, trained to become a Unitarian minister but devotion to the Independent Labour Party led to his withdrawal from his theological course. In 1907 he was elected MP for the Colne Valley and in 1908 twice flouted parliamentary convention by demanding a debate on unemployment. He lost his seat in January 1910. In the second 1910 election he stood for Kennington, 2 miles from Brixton, and was again defeated. 'Politician' may have known him then. Having served in the First World War, he disappeared without trace in September 1920.[93]

Rambles

The Angels' Voice reports three rambles, naming the participants.[94] Before 1914 Surrey was still rural, although south London was creeping closer. In 1910 the publisher Methuen issued a small, pocket-sized book by J. Charles Cox (1843–1919) on *Rambles in Surrey*. This carried 24 illustrations, with several black-and-white photographs and a map on the inner front board. It was re-issued in 1911 and further editions followed. Cox wrote the volume on Surrey in Methuen's series of 'The Little Guides'. This book had a detailed map inside its back cover. Trinity's young men probably planned their rambles on the North Downs with such guides before them. Cox had rivals, like Eric Parker whose *Highways and Byways in Surrey* was illustrated by Hugh Thomson (Macmillan 1908) and Louis J. Jennings whose *Field Paths and Green Lanes in Surrey and Sussex* (John Murray) appeared in 1907.

In addition *The Angels' Voice* recorded a party of schoolboys, led by Harry Reeves, observing British birds and purloining their eggs, which activity Reeves attempted to justify on scientific grounds. Such egg collecting became illegal in Britain in 1954.[95]

Smoking

In the 1880s the invention of a machine in the USA to roll cigarettes and enable mass production made cigarettes cheap and available to those, principally men, who wanted to smoke, a desire encouraged by

---

92 Martin Pugh, *Speak for Britain! A New History of the Labour Party* (2011), 32, 54; *ODNB*.
93 *ODNB*; Brockway, *Inside the Left*, 24–5; Pugh, *Speak for Britain*, 6–7.
94 *AV* 8 (July 1912), 6, 36; *AV* 10 (July 1913), 14.
95 See 'Birdsnesting' in *Encyclopaedia Britannica* (1911); <http://www.rspb.org.uk/forprofessionals/policy/wildbirdslaw/wildbirdcrime/egg_collection.aspx>, accessed 16 Mar. 2015.

advertising. Indeed smoking cigarettes was considered sophisticated in Edwardian England. In 1895 about 5 per cent of tobacco imports went to cigarette manufacture. By 1914 this had risen to 40 per cent.[96]

From the Canary Islands, Henry Rowe wrote that tobacco was 'fairly cheap', for 'one can get a good cigar for ½d'. He ventured that 'If this price ruled in England', more men would be 'swanking outside Trinity Church on Sunday evening'.[97] The awareness that smoking led to cancer came much later and, in the years of this study, lung cancer was rare. Given that smoking often began during adolescence, the frequency of its mention in *The Angels' Voice* may be understood.

Alcohol

The few mentions of alcohol, temperance and teetotalism in *The Angels' Voice* suggest that these subjects mattered little to these young men. The attitude to those members who drank was gently critical rather than censorious. For instance, 'the Major' [Charles Moxley] was teased while on a ramble with E.H. B[owler] when he returned 'filled to bursting point'. Moxley was told that if he drank frequently he would be 'tight'. Bowler, like Godden, was teetotal.[98]

Nonetheless drink did concern Congregationalists. In 1909 Charles Masterman noted that the Hampstead Congregational minister R. F. Horton believed 'drink is the chief cause of the indifference to Christianity of the working classes', although Horton added the scarcity of good preaching as a contributing factor. Masterman dismissed the former because alcohol consumption did not keep the Scottish or Irish from church attendance. He also wondered if good preachers drew believers away from churches with poor preachers; that is, good preachers did not increase church attendance but merely caused movements within the body of believers.[99]

From her study of Lambeth families, Maud Pember Reeves found that many working-class men earned so little that they could not afford to drink, and consequently did not. In addition many 'were non-drinkers, and some did not even smoke'. She scorned those writers and preachers 'with uneasy consciences' who 'label all poverty as the result of drink, extravagance, or laziness'. That a man suffering 'from poverty is supposed to drink' is 'the easy explanation', she wrote.[100]

Temperance and teetotalism were responses to the perceived moral decline of the working classes resulting from alcohol consumption.

---

[96] A. J. Taylor, 'The Economy', in *Edwardian England*, ed. Nowell-Smith, 128–9.
[97] *AV* 10 (July 1913), 11.
[98] *AV* 8 (July 1912), 9; *AV* 5 (Mar. 1911), 13.
[99] Masterman, *The Condition of England* 271; G. Haw (ed.), *Christianity and the Working Classes* (1906). For R. F. Horton, see *ODNB*.
[100] Pember Reeves, *Pound a Week*, 8–9, 66–7.

Indeed widespread drinking was an urgent health problem in the 1900s and both Baptists and Congregationalists had total abstinence societies. However, some prominent Congregational ministers, like James Guinness Rogers, never became teetotallers and the Congregational layman Sir Albert Spicer renounced alcohol only after the king did so during the First World War. Abstinence was normal for contemporary Congregationalists and Trinity's young men would have known this.[101]

Charlie Chaplin often saw vaudeville entertainers, like his father, enter Kennington's pubs. His parents separated because, according to his mother, his father 'drank too much' and she feared 'his drunkenness and violence'. As a boy Chaplin, repeatedly hungry, knew his father and his father's mistress (in whose care he was placed for a while) were regularly drunk. He judged that his father was 'ruined by drink', for he 'died of alcoholic excess' aged 37. The death certificate gave the cause of death as 'cirrhosis of the liver', although Chaplin called it dropsy.[102]

To overcome the reliance of many on the 'demon drink', alternatives to the public house were promoted, like Temperance Halls where members related their testimonies and signed the pledge to renounce drink. The Labour Party had close links to temperance until 1914.[103] The Band of Hope, which gained support from the churches, stressed temperance meetings aimed at the young.[104]

Holidays

Trips to Boulogne

A small party, including James Godden, travelled by cross-Channel ferry to Boulogne at Easter 1910, led by the 'great A. H. E.' (Evans). Their steamer took 1½ hours to cross the Channel. The service from Folkestone to Boulogne, operated since 1843 by the South Eastern Railway, experienced a passenger upsurge after the Franco-Prussian War of 1870–71. English tourists feared catching foreign diseases and worried about language difficulties. Yet by 1910 French hotels often employed English speakers and guide books were available. Herbert Morrison went on a day trip from Ramsgate to Boulogne, his first time abroad, and was sick on the return journey. Three trippers from Trinity returned on the August bank holiday of 1910 and spent time in Wimereux. In reviewing the possibilities for 1911, the cost of a trip to

---

[101]   Bebbington, *Nonconformist Conscience*, 46–7.
[102]   Chaplin, *Autobiography*, 9, 15, 16, 37–8; Robinson, *Chaplin*, 27, 36.
[103]   James Munson, *The Nonconformists: In Search of a Lost Culture* (1991), 195–6.
[104]   Bebbington, *Nonconformist Conscience*, 6, 47.

France was 12*s*. and for August bank holiday 1913 the return fare on the South Eastern & Chatham Railway was only 10*s*.[105]

Belgium 1912

The Angels' Voice made no mention of passports, which were not generally required for international travel until the First World War.[106] The 1912 expedition of James Godden and a companion (probably A. H. Evans) involved travel on Belgian railways and accommodation in inexpensive lodgings. They spent nine days away for less than £4.[107]

Having crossed the Channel from Dover to Ostend, they went to Bruges where they found lodgings for the night. They paid nearly 5 francs[108] for bed, breakfast and dinner (their midday meal) in a hotel near the Belfry; its location meant they were kept awake by chiming bells. In Antwerp they stayed in relative comfort, paying an extravagant 7 francs a day. Later they visited Liège, Dinant and Brussels. On the boat home they determined to return in 1913 with some of Trinity's keenest ramblers and in July 1912 proposed this in *The Angels' Voice*.[109]

In early 1913 Moxley travelled overnight from Victoria (via Dover and Ostend) to Ghent for the Ghent International Exhibition.

Jersey (September 1913) and a voyage

In 1913 a party of six, including Alfred P. Austin and Stanley Rowe, holidayed in Jersey for two weeks. A. H. Evans intended to join them and Walter Cramp hoped to be there for the second week. They took the London & South Western Railway from Waterloo to Southampton, and on the 8-hour voyage Stanley Rowe felt queasy, though none were sea sick.

They appreciated Jersey's beaches but noted also the potato and tomato farming, the orchards, nurseries and fishing. From their St Helier lodgings they made several day trips in horse-drawn brakes or carriages. The holidaymakers observed that all bathing in Jersey, with one or two early morning exceptions, was for men and women together. For this vacation a 'Holiday Fund' proved a great help, especially to younger class members. A similar fund was intended for 1914.

---

[105] See John Hendy, *Folkestone for the Continent 1843–2001* (Ramsey, Isle of Man, 2014), and <http://folkestoneharbour.com/pages/history.html> accessed 1 Oct. 2014; Donoghue and Jones, *Morrison*, 14; *AV* 1 (Nov. 1910), 3–12; *AV* 3 (Jan. 1011), 22; *AV* 10 (July 1913), 37.

[106] The first modern British passport resulted from the British Nationality and Status of Aliens Act, 1914. Leo Benedictus, 'A Brief History of the Passport', *The Guardian*, 17 Nov. 2006.

[107] £4 in 1912 approximated to £400 in 2014. <http://www.bankofengland.co.uk/education/ Pages/resources/inflationtools/calculator/flash/default.aspx> accessed 5 Apr. 2015.

[108] In 1912 the exchange rate was 22.35 Belgian francs to £1 sterling. Information by e-mail from A. Di Zinno of the National Bank of Belgium.

[109] *AV* 8 (July 1912), 33.

Lewis Messent sailed from Southampton to Genoa on the steamship *Prinz Eitel Friedrich* in September 1913 with some non-Trinity friends.[110] The extant copies of *The Angels' Voice* mean that only the latter half of his account of these 15 days survives.

Other recreations

One report in December 1913 recorded the visit to a colliery by class members who had cycled from London. In Wrexham they arranged to see the coalface. On 22 September 1934, in the same north Wales coalfield, Gresford colliery suffered an explosion and the loss of 265 lives.[111]

In addition, a contributor (probably George Harper) wrote in 1913 of his first flight in a biplane a year previously. He was so taken with the experience that in the interim he had made several further flights.[112]

Working abroad: Canary Islands, Switzerland, India, Australia

Henry Rowe[113] moved to the **Canary Islands** where the average temperature is 21°C. He would have noted the small amount of rainfall, the volcanoes, forests, ravines, cliffs and clear waters. In the 1900s the islands had a small British community which included a Seamen's Institute run by Harold and (Lizzie) May Hiley for the British and Foreign Sailors Society. Rowe wrote of the abundant fruit and how this affected the islanders' diet. He wrote that the whole population was concerned with either shipping or fruit growing.

In November 1913 the arrival of the emigrant Munro family in **Australia** was noted in *The Angels' Voice*. They were described as settling down to 'farm or bush life'. Approximately 390,000 new settlers arrived in Australia between 1905 and 1914, principally from Britain, increasing the population to almost 5 million.[114]

Alec Noble wrote for *The Angels' Voice* from **Switzerland**. The population of Zurich in 1910 was 215,488 (Noble's figure of 185,000 was out of date). Of Zurich's total in 1910, 70,329 were foreign nationals resident within the city. About 500 of these were from Great Britain and Ireland.[115]

---

[110] *AV* 5 (Dec. 1913), 12; TNA, Board of Trade passenger lists, BT 27/825.
[111] *Hansard*, 23 Feb. 1937.
[112] See *AV* 15 (Dec. 1913), 47–9.
[113] *AV* 10 (July 1913), 19.
[114] <http://www.immi.gov.au/media/publications/statistics/federation/timeline1.pdf > accessed 8 Mar. 2015.
[115] Calculated from the national statistic that 0.75% of foreign nationals in Switzerland were from Great Britain and Ireland. See <http://www.statistik.zh.ch/internet/justiz_inneres/statistik/de/daten/daten_bevoelkerung_soziales/bevoelkerung.html> and <http://www.bfs.admin.ch/bfs/portal/fr/index/150/03/02/00/02.html> both accessed 29 Oct. 2014.

Will Crosley spent about a year in **India**, returning home by Christmas 1913. He worked there on board a ship, the RMS *Elephanta*.[116] By later standards, the language and tone of his article are racist, although, with few opportunities for Europeans to mix with others, such language was perhaps more acceptable to his contemporaries. Crosley was noted in July 1912 as 'the angriest member of our class', which may imply more than merely a pun on his surname.[117]

Fred Berry and typhoid

Early in its life *The Angels' Voice* reported the funeral of one Bible Class member, Fred Berry, who died from typhoid in November 1910. His youth and delicate constitution made him vulnerable to this contagious bacterial infection for which no effective treatment then existed. It is contracted by consuming food or water contaminated by infected faeces from another victim, allowing bacteria to spread throughout the body and typhoid to develop.

Typhoid fever remains common where sanitation is limited and clean water is scarce.[118] After London's 'great stink' of 1858, a new sewerage system was constructed by 1875 which reduced the incidence of typhoid and other water-borne diseases.[119] An article in the *British Medical Journal* in 1896 stated that London's water supply was slightly contaminated – even 'one germ may infect' a susceptible person.[120]

In 1910 the typhoid death rate was low, at 0.4 and 0.5 per 10,000 for London and Lambeth respectively. The medical officer of health for Lambeth in 1910 recorded 17 deaths out of 77 cases reported. During the early twentieth century, cases of typhoid in Lambeth steadily declined, with marked fluctuations. Fred Berry's illness was not part of a wider outbreak, even though a larger number of cases occurred in 1910 than in the years immediately before and after.[121]

[116] *AV* 13 (Oct. 1913), 4.

[117] *AV* 8 (July 1912), 53.

[118] NHS Choices website: <http://www.nhs.uk/Conditions/Typhoid-fever/Pages/Introduction. aspx>, accessed 25 Oct. 2014.

[119] M. J. Daunton, 'London's "Great Stink" and Victorian Urban Planning', <http://www.bbc. co.uk/history/trail/victorian_britain/social_conditions/victorian_urban_planning_04.shtml>, accessed 25 Oct. 2014; White, *Nineteenth Century*, 53–5.

[120] 'London Typhoid and London Water', *British Medical Journal* (25 Apr. 1896), 1046–7.

[121] Joseph Priestley, *Report on the Vital and Sanitary Statistics of the Borough of Lambeth During the Year 1910* (1911), 27, 42, appendix 44–5. In 1901 there were 147 cases and 23 deaths in Lambeth; 1902, 213 cases, 38 deaths; 1907, 56 cases, 5 deaths; 1908, 63 cases, 8 deaths; 1909, 49 cases, 9 deaths; 1912, 61 cases, 13 deaths; 1913, 38 cases, 7 deaths. Priestley, *Report 1912* (1913), 34–5, 40–1; Priestley, *Report 1917* (1918), 24, 28. Reports from <http:// wellcomelibrary.org/moh/search/>, accessed 5 Aug. 2015.

Drawings, cartoons and journalism

James Godden knew that good artistic representations in *The Angels'
Voice* significantly improved its appearance. He wrote that 'None
of the artists are ... in our own class, although several ... are well-
known Trinitarians; there are still some whom few of us know.'[122] On
occasions, despite his teasing of the 'long-haired chums', Godden
recruited women artists. His comment in December 1913, 'Our cover
artist we particularly thank for her sustained and practical interest',
perhaps signified the magazine's following among Trinity's females.[123]
Godden also stated that Mr E. Munro had 'the welcome power of
raking up drawings for the mag', suggesting either that Munro found
suitable illustrations or provided his own drawings.[124]

The artists included Harry Reeves,[125] M. Gladwin,[126] Percy von
Rittershausen,[127] F. L. R. (probably Frank Leonard Rowe),[128] F. R.
(perhaps also Frank Rowe), E. T. J. (Elizabeth Taylor Johnston)[129] and
I. M. (Isabella Messent).[130] Other artists more difficult to trace are C.
V. M.,[131] H. E. C.[132] and Ri– (last initial illegible).[133]

The most celebrated Congregational journalist of the period was
W. T. Stead, the campaigning editor of the *Pall Mall Gazette*, who,
with Bramwell Booth, had exposed the easy procuring of young girls.
Stead died on the *Titanic*.[134] In addition, many Congregationalists then
regularly subscribed to the weekly *The Christian World*. Both may
have influenced Godden's appetite for journalism.

THE FIRST WORLD WAR AND AFTER

At least 20 of those mentioned in *The Angels' Voice* were in the armed
forces during the First World War and several were killed. Probably
most of Trinity's young men served. This cannot be confirmed because
many records were destroyed by Second World War bombing. Several
families suffered grievously, like the Rowes who lost Henry and the
Snoswells with two sons killed. In addition, Frederick Butcher, Montague

---

122   *AV* 6 (Apr. 1911), 26.
123   *AV* 15 (Dec. 1913), 3.
124   *AV* 7 (Nov. 1911), 48.
125   As noted by the editor in *AV* 3 (Jan. 1912), 1. Drawings at: *AV* 3 (Jan. 1913), 4, 12; *AV* 5 (Mar. 1911), 4 etc.
126   *AV* 7 (Nov. 1911), 42.
127   *AV* 3 (Jan. 1911), 19.
128   *AV* 12 (Sept. 1913), 23.
129   *AV* 6 (Apr. 1911), 24; *AV* 7 (Nov. 1911), 25.
130   *AV* 3 (Jan. 1911), 24; *AV* 7 (Nov. 1911), 11.
131   *AV* 7 (Nov. 1911), 19, 31; *AV* 10 (July 1913), 1.
132   *AV* 7 (Nov. 1911), 39, 61.
133   *AV* 2 (Dec. 1910), 25.
134   For Stead and Booth see *ODNB*.

Davies, Edward Lynch and the editor's brother, Graham Godden, lost their lives, as did William Johnston. Trinity's war memorial, erected in 1921, recorded 21 names.[135] However, Austen Stripp, the nephew of Mrs Lansdown and a Trinity church member since 1909, and Frank Walter Eagle, a Trinity junior footballer, died in the war but are curiously absent from the memorial. A possible match to one mentioned in *The Angels' Voice* and who died in the war is (Charles) Frederick Biggin, also missing from the memorial.

Both during and after the war several of the young men married, often at Trinity. Among these marriages was that of Isabella Messent and David Johnston in 1923. This followed their siblings' marriages: William Messent and Rachel Johnston (1907) and Dan C. Messent and Elizabeth T. Johnston (1915).[136]

The Munros' emigration to Australia has already been noted. Later emigrants, also to Australia, were Henry Messent, Frank Rowe (later returned to the UK) and Laurence Snoswell.

Few remained permanently in Brixton. Frank Perkins, Frank Jones and Charles Moxley were notable exceptions. Perkins continued his employment in the family piano manufacturers and scrupulously attended Trinity. Jones became a deacon and Trinity's treasurer by the 1950s. Moxley lived in Trent Road until his death in 1949.

Most Messents, apart from Henry, worked in the family butchery business. The entries in Trinity's marriage registers give snapshots of some of the men's careers soon after *The Angels' Voice* ended. Harry Reeves in 1915 was an insurance society's sub manager, whilst Ernest Bowler, who lost his leg in 1915, had returned to advertising as a clerk by 1916. Cyril Bedwell was a buyer (export trade) in 1917, and in 1919 Richard Chippindale was a paper agent's manager. In 1921 Walter Cramp was a 'managing clerk to stockbrokers'. Algernon Carpenter was a boot salesman in 1924. Wider sources reveal that Norman Bedwell qualified as an accountant and was treasurer of Herne Hill Congregational Church for 20 years. Others had diverse careers, many having been shop and office workers before the war. Their occupations include farmer (Stanley Rowe), fruit grower (Harry Lansdown), furrier (Percy von Rittershausen), merchant trading in the Far East (Will Crosley), master mariner (Harold Eagle), Congregational lay evangelist (Harold Hiley), Congregational minister (James Rofe). John Rowe continued with the China Inland Mission dying there in 1933.[137]

Their pre-war larks and diversions left lasting memories, recorded strikingly in *The Angel's Voice*, and their friendships were sustained

---

[135] TCC Deacons, 21 Mar. 1921.
[136] TCC Marriage, *passim*.
[137] For wider sources see these names in Appendix.

by annual reunions at Trinity. As they aged, no doubt some memories faded. Yet *The Angel's Voice* allows readers for whom the magazine was not intended to recover the emphases and accents of that pre-1914 generation. For this we may be deeply grateful.

Number 1, November 1910

The Angels' Voice

VOL: I NO. I

Editor:– J. Godden
Sub Editor:– E. Bowler

[p. 1]

THE ANGELS' VOICE.

VOL. I.   November 5TH 1910   No. I.

SMALLEST CIRCULATION

EDITORIAL

Dear Readers,

Our editorial pen is a very new one and its unsympathetic nib scratches madly over the paper without any result. We would willingly stop but custom forces us to say something; besides the magazine must be introduced. Everything points to its brilliant future. Its contributors are unsurpassed for sterling quality and their talent is apparently inexhaustible. Indeed this is an epoch-making departure.

Be careful all ye Voicites, for these gems of art and literature are to be passed down to future generations, a process which would be impossible if our only copy were torn and soiled by unfeeling Goths.

Our task is done and we must leave you to the enjoyment of this rich literary feast with the heartfelt wish that it will not give you mental indigestion.

    Eds.

[p. 2]

[Sketch of a tramp, with an umbrella. He is a Burlington Bertie type, holding a telephone earpiece.]

[p. 3]

BOULOGNE BY EXCURSION

It was Easter Sunday and all attempts to form a rambling party for the Bank Holiday had failed. Everyone we approached had apparently

33

found it easy to decide how to spend the next day, but right up to the last minute we could not make up our minds where to go. Just as we were separating for the night the idea of Boulogne occurred to us, and almost at once our plans for the next day were settled.

On the following morning we met at Charing Cross in good time and secured corner seats.[1] The journey was quick and interesting, but our expectation of the things to come prevented us from paying much attention to the surrounding country.

The boats on which the crossing is made are fine large turbine steamers and reduce the sea voyage to about one and a half hours. Several people on board were evidently experienced travellers, but the majority were like ourselves, very raw, possibly more so as they had not been coached by the great A.H.E.[2] The sun shone with exceptional power and the sea was so smooth that even those most liable to the travellers' bogey[3] were not affected.

[p. 4]

The boat stops some distance out of the Boulogne harbour and turns round so as to be ready to go straight out on the return journey ... The jetty is crowded with people ... whilst in the background the dome of the cathedral stands out prominently against the sky and away on either side are the tall, huddling houses, perched on the hill-sides which make one feel at once that England is far behind.

All are eager to commence their day's sight-seeing and there is a rush for the quay, where a line of officials direct the crowd through the customs. Our wily guide had previously shared out his wax-vestas,[4] giving us six each, that being the maximum number allowed to pass duty free. Most of the excursionists walk right round the harbour to the town, but for those who know where to find it there is a ferry. We took advantage of this and crossed quickly and comfortably to the landing-stage on the quai Gambetta. This quai is a promenade to which many timorous English souls keep all day, and come away with the firm impression that Boulogne is French only in name.

We changed some money at a shop on the front and made our way to the cathedral, noticing with great interest the different fashions and customs which were so new to us.

[p. 5]

[Two postcards – one of exterior of cathedral and one of the town gatehouse.]

---

[1]   Ships to Boulogne departed from Folkestone and Ramsgate.
[2]   Albert Howard Evans was almost always referred to by his initials.
[3]   Sea-sickness.
[4]   Wax vestas were short wax matches.

[p. 6]

It was a holiday, being Easter, and all the women of the lower classes were wearing linen head-dresses like the one in the picture. The gendarmes or police ... wear a bright red and blue uniform, very loose and very baggy, whilst their boots far surpass a London policeman's in size and thickness of sole. The priests are perhaps the most novel of all and their beaver hats and long gowns give them a very solemn appearance.

The cathedral is situated in the centre of the citadel. This is the most ancient part of the town and is surrounded by high and wide walls cut by interesting old gate-ways. Those shown in the pictures are at opposite ends of the little town and in the street which connects them to the sacred building. We walked through the Port de Calais and entered the cathedral. This is a comparatively modern building although its site and associations are so interesting in their antiquity. The legend which gives the necessary touch of the miraculous is as following –

Long ago an exquisite statue of the Virgin with the Infant Christ drifted to Boulogne in an open boat, and ... the Virgin appeared to her worshippers in the church and told them to build a cathedral in which her miraculous statue might be placed. This cathedral, despite its sanctity, suffered a great deal at various times, and after being rebuilt and considerably altered,

[p. 7]

[Two postcards. One shows a woman with a large head-dress and the other shows the dome of the cathedral from outside.]

[p. 8]

was finally declared to be common property during the Revolution. All but one hand of the statue had been destroyed and the cathedral was now sold to a private company and pulled down.

In the present cathedral the remaining hand of the statue is, as a rule, suspended round the neck of the Virgin, but Easter being a special day, it was in a metal case so that the superstitious might kiss it. The picture of the cathedral shows its entire length, but large curtains are usually hung across the building behind the high altar, completely separating the lady chapel from the nave. Right at the end the Virgin's image and the altar dedicated to her may be seen ... This altar is extremely beautiful, and here most of the casual worshippers pay their devotions. All the small chapels are worth visiting and one is continually reminded of Boulogne's connection with the sea by the numerous statues standing in boats.

As we were going out, all our thoughts of the solemnity of the place were destroyed by a little choir boy who rushed in, plunged his fist into the basin, spilling half the holy water, and clattered away down the aisle as fast as he could go, crossing himself.

A change had come in the weather while we were in the cathedral, the dry streets were now pools and the rain was still

[p. 9]

[Two postcards of cathedral interior.]

[p. 10]

falling fast. We ran for shelter under the Port de Calais and waited. It was there that we saw the first instance of a dog being used for draught purposes. The animal was harnessed to the axle of a hand barrow and saved his owner a large part of the pulling.

When the rain stopped we took a walk round the ramparts ... In ... a stroll about the town we came across several remarkable things ... In the High Street was a butcher's shop with the suggestive sign of a horse's head, while at the railway station we noticed some cattle trucks marked "8 horses or 40 men", and were really quite scandalised until it was explained to us that they were for military transport.

About five o'clock we went into a shop and ordered coffee and cakes. The waitress was supposed ... to speak English but all we could understand was "brid-an-booter".

After tea we took a short tram ride and then made our way to the boat to await the departure.

On our next visit we went by tram to Wimereux, a small sea-side resort some little way along the coast. This line of trams have open trucks behind with seats running from side to side. The conductor has to scramble along a narrow foot-board and tears the flimsy tickets out of a book, with a stick of rubber.

[p. 11]

[Postcard of Wimereux – La Plage et les Chalets, with holiday-makers on the beach.]

[p. 12]

The sands ... were crowded with tents, bathers and little girls in boys clothes. On our way back to the High Street we passed a fellow about fifteen or sixteen in a bathing costume, towel and shoes. I'm afraid we must have offended him with our stares ... . Mr A.H.E. was full of the praises of a certain confectioner's shop in the village, and was enthusiastic enough to pay half a franc or about five pence for a cup of tea.

On the return journey to Boulogne we saw Napoleon's column, ... erected ... where he gathered together his proud army for the invasion of England but was foiled by the old sea-dogs who never gave him quite enough time to invade our island country.

After this ride we had dinner at a hotel near the quai. The cooking was excellent and the drinks were somewhat novel. Before we had finished a gentleman and his wife who had been fishing, came in proudly showing an eel ... The proprietor rushed up and amid many gesticulations ... was asked to cook it for dinner. We left just in time to catch the boat and went on board after a most interesting ... day. Regretfully we watched the French coast growing more ... indistinct, and ... soon we arrived back in London, eagerly looking forward to our next glimpse of life abroad.

J.G.G.[5]

[p. 13]

[Postcard of Wimereux – La Colonne de la Grande Armée, with Napoleon on top.]

[p. 14]

THE PROFESSIONAL AMATEUR

1. I'm known throughout this mighty land
For intellectual power
Besides I never show my hand
Or hasten on the hour
I'm never early, never late
But reach my end as sure as fate.

2. From this you will agree with me
I'm eminently fitted
To teach; and that my aim shall be
Before this page I've quitted
I'll show the things to do with crime
Which I have studied such a time.

3. First note the Burglar as he prowls
Towards the wealth utopian,
The faithful watch-dog never growls,

---

[5]   J. G. Godden, the editor.

He's drugged with chinese opium,
His boots around his neck he wears,
To make no noise upon the stairs.

4. To catch this kind are traps galore
Like cloth with bird-lime spread on
The wise put tin-tacks on the floor
For tender feet to tread on,
And if you hear his startled shriek
You'll have to laugh all through the week.

The burglars caught if I am there
(An amateur would blunder)
It only needs a little care,
To make the vulgar wonder.
N.B. In an abstruse research
Apply to ME outside the Church.

P Irkins[6]

Criticisms, suggestions, complaints, or indeed letters on any topic whatever will be welcomed by the staff.

We should especially like fresh ideas for conducting this magazine.

[p. 15]

COMPETITION
ENTRIES MUST REACH US BY DEC 10
NOVEL DEVELOPMENT OF THE LIMERICK
VALUABLE PRIZE OFFERED

The editor and his assistant after studying the question for three weeks have finally arrived at the decision that a competition requiring skill and some measure of ingenuity would be a desirable adjunct to this magazine.

In accordance with the expert advice we have received, it will be an entirely new phase of the Limerick.

In this interesting and original competition, the last line of a Limerick verse is given. Competitors have only to compose four lines according to the well-known Limerick metre and fit our "last line".

The results will be judged by two eminent Trinitarians, whose decision will be final.

In order that there may be no misunderstanding we give a few simple rules:–

---

[6] This is Frank Perkins who was teased for being an amateur detective.

1st Only one attempt allowed to each competitor.

2nd An entrance fee of one penny must accompany each attempt.[7]

3rd A nom-de-plume must be written on the back of the verse and the real name given on another piece of paper.

For Competition No. 1. we give the following "last line":–

"So that fellow's now up a tree".

[p. 16]

COMPETITION
(contd)

The successful competitor will be announced in our New Years issue.

The reason for each competition lasting two months is that it will be very near the publication of the next issue before some subscribers have read the November Number.

A competition however will appear in each issue.

NOTICES

We have almost come to the end of our study of St. Marks Gospel and a new syllabus must be arranged. This will probably take the form of a series of independent discussions on Biblical questions. Papers will be read by members of the class opening the subject for discussion ...

Early in December the Literary Society are holding ... a Dickens Recital by a very well-known friend at Trinity. If you are not quite certain of his name, "Ask your parents and I am sure they will be pleased to tell you".

The Football Fixture Cards are now ready ...

[p. 17]

OUR FOOTBALL PAGE

SPORT What an important item in our lives. The boy at school, the student at College or University, the young fellow just starting business, the experienced commercial man, the statesman and the Monarch on the Throne, in fact all who are healthy both in mind and body are stirred by its magic.

---

[7] The pre-decimal currency of Great Britain, prevailing until 1971, consisted of pounds, shillings and pence. Twelve pence made a shilling and 20 shillings, or 240 pence, a pound. The penny was composed of four farthings until 31 December 1960 and, until 31 July 1969, halfpenny coins also circulated. A guinea was 21 shillings.

If we turn up "Webster"[8] we find that "sport" is an abbreviation of disport, i.e. to amuse or enjoy oneself. Sport therefore is a means to an end and not the end in itself, and its function is to help to keep both mind and body healthy. Anything short of this is a travesty.

... it is imperative that our sports ... should be indulged in heartily and intelligently. The man who uses his brain in his sports ... gets most benefit from them. At the same time a judicious restraint should be exercised for we must not let our heartiness carry us away, nor our thoughts be continually centered on pastimes, but rather see to it that our sports be our <u>servants</u> and not our <u>masters</u>, subservient and not dominant.

REPORTS AND COMMENTS

Our season opened on Oct. 1st. on the Rosendale Sports Ground[9] where we met ... the "Crusaders". The games with our Clapham rivals are always looked keenly forward to by

[p. 18]

all, as the similarity of the aims and interests of both Clubs render the meetings particularly pleasant.

The Play was ... scrappy ... ; both sides indulging in the kick and rush tactics so foreign to good Football. During the first half our opponents had much the best of the play, but after halftime our men pulled themselves together and the tables were turned. ...

The ball travelled from goal to goal until ... our backs left an opening for a shot which it was impossible to save. Our opponents had again to score before Trinity's turn came, but just before half time, Harry Lansdown put in a shot which hit the cross-bar and dropping to earth, twisted into the net.

Being one down we started the second half well and kept the ball in the "Crusaders" territory, but ... our forwards could not net the ball until Jack Bishop put in a fine centre right across the goal mouth which tempted Wilson, their right back to punch it out. Stanley Rowe who took the penalty kick scored the equalising goal just a few minutes before time.

RESULT:– Crusaders 2
Trinity 2

---

8   Noah Webster's *American Dictionary of the English Language* first appeared in 1828. Webster's *New International Dictionary* was published in 1909.
9   Rosendale Road, Herne Hill.

[p. 19]

TRINITY v. LYNDHURST OLD BOYS (Oct. 8th)

This was our first home fixture. Two changes were made in the team; Mr. Castle substituting for Guy Barrett ... and Frank Jones appearing for the first time this season. Owing to Fred York having given his leg a nasty twist on the previous Saturday, Henry Rowe had to take the 'outside' position: Frank Jones playing at half back.

The game was a bit one-sided, largely due to the good work of Mr. Castle who kept his forwards well to-gether. Towards the end our opponents tired considerably and adopting the one back game effectually spoiled the remainder of the match.

RESULT:– Lyndhurst O.B. 0
Trinity 8

TRINITY v. MUNDANIA ATHLETIC CLUB

Our Baptist friends at Dulwich have a splendidly organised Club ... We always look forward to meeting them.

Saturday, October 15th found us on their ground – Casino House – ... W. Cramp made his first appearance for us.[10]

In the first half of the game we did well. Our forwards ... led by R. S. Rowe played good football with the result that ... we scored two goals, one the work of Harry Lansdown and the other a good ground shot by J. Bishop. On changing over at half time the score

[p. 20]

was 2–1 in our favour.

We commenced with two determined attacks on our opponents' goal and got within an ace of scoring on each occasion, but soon losing the upper hand, ... Mundania pressed continuously ... One remarkably fine save was made by our goal keeper Fred Handy who threw himself full length along the goal mouth ...

In spite of a literal bombardment we managed to prevent the 'Muns' from equalising until just before time, when a ... collapse took place, our defence failing three times in almost as many minutes. ... Fred Handy is exonerated. He had no chance to save either shots, but the incident shows us the necessity of practice on the part of our defence ...

RESULT:– Mundania 4. Trinity 2.

---

[10]   Casino House, on Herne Hill near Casino Avenue, was demolished in 1906 but games were played on its grounds. <http://www.dulwichsociety.com/newsletters/62-summer–2009/429-casino-house>, accessed 15 Mar. 2015.

TRINITY v. St. ANDREWS STOCKWELL. Oct. 22nd. '10

Played at Burbage Road[11] before a fair number of spectators, this proved an exciting game and resulted in a draw, both sides scoring one goal.

[p. 21]

Jack Bishop having received a nasty shin wound on the previous Saturday stood down, but Guy Barrett after two weeks absence again appeared at centre.

St. Andrews were very aggressive ... Fred Handy in goal was splendid. His play on several occasions evoking applause from both friend and foe ...

A marked improvement was noticed in the play of the backs, there was not so much 'fiddling about' in front of the goal ... One thing is very evident and that is that Will Fagan and Harry Jones do too much toe work; ... toe and instep ... alone can control the ball ... Trinity's defence with this correction would be grand.

RESULT:– Trinity 1
Stockwell 1

TRINITY v. LARCOM FOOTBALL CLUB
(October 31st)

Played at Beckenham Hill this match proved very disappointing. Faced by opponents who had little collective knowledge of the game, Trinity should have romped home.

[p. 22]

Instead of which they only won by two goals to nil.

The fault lay primarily with the forwards who continually worked the ball up to the goal, but ... either failed to try to net the ball at all or ... put in some miserably weak shots. Harry Lansdown, Guy Barrett and Lewis Messent were especially guilty ... , although it may be said for Harry Lansdown that he did hit both post and cross-bar ...

A compensating feature ... was the decided improvement in the passing. Several times the ball travelled from man to man in a pleasingly neat manner and it seemed a great pity that such good mid-field play should be rendered useless by ... imbecility in front of the goal. ...

RESULT:– Trinity 2
Larcom 0

---

11   Burbage Road leads from Herne Hill to Dulwich.

42

The Sports Editor will be pleased to hear from ... readers ... All such letters shall have his consideration and publication by us if serious.

[p. 23]

[Drawing of a coat of arms held by two young ladies, one either side of the shield. The banner below reads:] Faint heart never won fair lady.

[p. 24]

HERALDRY
COAT OF ARMS OF
Mr. Bedwell.

SHIELD 1st. Death of Nelson, black edged to denote disastrous effect on listeners.
2nd. On a green field a bat taking Middle and Leg proper.* (SWANK)
3rd. On a field of the same colour, a referee's whistle proper. (Same note as 2nd.)
4th. On a gory field two heads colliding proper. (Oblivion produced)

SUPPORTERS Two Platonic Friends.

CREST Mad bull (Hungry calf?) charging proper

MOTTO Faint heart never won fair lady.

*Proper is the heraldic term for natural colours.

[p. 25]

FORM IV[12]

I found it one morning on my breakfast plate
And read slowly through it, then scratched my pate
I'd never seen anything like it before,
It wasn't a summons, but simply FORM IV.

To fill in the answers I tried on and off,
But the questions were such that I started to cough,
For how could I satisfy all it's demands
When the deeds I required were not in my hands.

---

[12]   Form IV related to valuation of property and resulted from Lloyd George's Finance Act of 1910. *Hansard*, 23 Nov. 1911; <http://www.nationalarchives.gov.uk/records/research-guides/valuation-office-records.htm#18240>, accessed 1 Apr. 2015. For Lloyd George see *ODNB*.

To my lawyer I went and explained the position,
His face turned quite grave in accord with tradition,
And knowing quite well he had all the deeds
Dismissed me and said he'd attend to my needs.

In course of a day or two, three at the most
I received back my form by registered post,
With instructions to sign in the places he'd marked.
It does not seem difficult now! I remarked.

The duty was really no trouble at all.
I could see no occasion whatever to bawl,
Or to kick up a fuss as many have done
They seem to be worried before they've begun.

Having signed in two places and filled in the date
I posted it at the expense of the State
And thus did I settle the quests of the law,
T'was really so simple that little FORM IV.
                    A.P.A.[13]

Chulalongkorn I, King of Siam, who has recently died, possessed some extraordinary titles ... 'Lord of the White Elephant', 'Brother of the Moon', 'Half Brother of the Sun', 'Possessor of Four Golden Umbrellas', etc. etc. etc.[14]
It would be interesting to know what relationship either direct or indirect this illustrious monarch bears to Brockwell Park.

[p. 26]

[Two photographs.]
The Editor
Harvest Festival

[p. 27]

THE HARVEST FESTIVAL

This is perhaps one of the most pleasing of our church services, and certainly the interest was not reduced this year. A generous quantity of edge tables and fruit was provided and its excellent arrangement is very well shown in the picture.

---

[13]   A. P. Austin.
[14]   Chulalongkorn (1853–1910), King of Siam, died 23 October 1910. D. K. Wyatt, *Thailand: A Short History* (1982), 313.

The editor, James G. Godden

THE EDITOR

Our second photograph shows a member of a hard and callous tribe. He is a firm believer of the survival of the fittest, and mercilessly slays all the weaker productions which come within reach of his terrible blue pencil ...

PARAGRAPH

The young thing ... richly deserves a paragraph. It is plain ... that it is not one of us, yet it occupies a seat in our pews with evident self-satisfaction ... we find nothing which would entitle it to such an honour.

Apparently its feminine relations send it to us ... We wish they would keep their own nuisances.[15]

---

[15] This young man, not then a Bible Class member, had sat in the Bible Class pews. He was probably R. George Giggs whose aunts lived in the same house, 65 Arlingford Road. See *AV* 2 (Dec 1910), 19, *AV* 3 (Jan. 1911), 31; 1911 Census.

[p. 28]

OUR POLITICAL PAGE
WHY I AM A SOCIALIST

In these articles I am conscious that my ideas will not meet with universal approval. It may be that they will be severely criticised: in that case either side cannot fail to learn something. But now let us turn to the subject as shown by the heading.

I am a Socialist because I believe Socialism is needed. One looks round for a remedy for the evils which exist to-day but none is found unless it be Socialism. Liberals and Tories declare that they have done their best: but it is a very poor best and not much to be proud of. Reforms have done next to nothing: the system cannot be effectually reformed.

But why have the Liberals and the Tories failed? ... It is because they have dealt only with results: things will be just as bad a hundred years hence unless a root remedy is found. To cure the disease you must seek the cause. This cause is Competition. Abolish competition and the problem solves itself. If the State can carry on the Postal Telegraph services, and corporations make gas and manage the water supply, I maintain that mines and railways could be similarly worked, instead of being owned by private companies.[16] But, you ask, would not this result in a monopoly,

[p. 29]

producing a worse condition of affairs than exists to-day: No; for it would not be monopoly at all, but co-operation. Monopoly is the plundering of the many by the few. Co-operation is the mutual helpfulness of all.

We have lately been favoured with ... Liberal Ministers ... drawing attention to the unequal division of wealth: proclaiming that the idle rich are a burden upon the community and generally admitting the case for Socialism: but they are not going to put matters right. The two great parties existing to-day seem to forget that the defects in our social systems are identical with those existing in other countries, and what is the use of applying remedies which have failed in other countries? But they do apply them. ... If we had Tariff Reform tomorrow, it would make no difference. If we abolished the House of Lords, and left the Liberal party in power for fifty years, things would not be much better. No, Socialism is the only way. That is why I am a Socialist.

Politician.

---

[16]   Until the 1960s gas in Britain was produced from coal.

Our 'Politician' is ... rather enthusiastic, he also seems prepared for the worst with regard to public opinion. We sincerely hope that his fears will be realised and that some argumentitive [sic] person will write to us discussing the above article. We can assure him of a hearty welcome from the majority of our readers ...

[p. 30]

LIST OF SUBSCRIBERS

The magazine is to be circulated in the order in which the names appear below, and no alterations are to be made. The limit of time for one subscriber is two days. i.e. If received on Wednesday it must be passed on on Friday. In the case of more than one subscriber living in the same house or very near together, the magazine is only to be kept for three days. Any reader who can pass the magazine on in one day will be greatly helping ...

Each reader is to write the day of the month and the name of the day on which he receives the magazine against his own name.

Mr. D. C. Messent.
Mr. W. J. Messent.
L. Messent.

Mr. Moxley.

S. Rowe.
H. Rowe.
F. Rowe.

W. Crosly. [sic]

F. York.
C. Smith.

H. Lansdown.
H. Stripp.

G. Harper.
F. Jones.
L. Snoswell.
G. Giggs.
A. Carpenter.
F. Butcher.
A. Calloway.
H. Beagley.
A. Marriott.

[The above names are typed but in pencil are also] A. Holman, P. Shearer, C. Bedwell, Mr. Evans, Mr. Austin, G. Barrett.

THE ANGELS' VOICE

VOL: I NO. 2

Editor:– J. Godden
Sub Editor:– E. Bowler

[p. 1]

THE ANGELS' VOICE.

VOL. I.   December 3rd 1910   No. 2.

SMALLEST CIRCULATION

EDITORIAL

Dear Readers,

We thank you. The reception accorded to Vol. I. No. I. was most gratifying, and constitutes one of the chief encouragements in the production of the second issue.

From our infancy it has always been pointed out to us that the first step is much the hardest. We are sure that the inventor of such a phrase could never have had any experience in an editor's work. In writing our first Editorial we thought the limit of hard work had been reached, but No. 2. has been a revelation to us and it is with a sinking feeling that we look forward to No. 3.

Voicites! Have compassion on us and by … your contributions relieve us from all anxiety save that which is unavoidably connected with our position.

Let the magazine be an outlaw from the tea-table, do not imagine that if you butter it you better it.

And now having kept your restless glance a sufficient time on our worthless page, it is free to roam at will through the succeeding articles. We will detain it no longer.

                                                            Eds.

[p. 2]

ANNUAL MEETING
TRINITY BIBLE CLASS

One of the most interesting meetings ... was held in the larger room upstairs on November 24th 1910. Members ... began to arrive at 7–45 and shortly before 8 o'clock light refreshments were handed round. The Chairman arrived promptly at 8 and after half an hour of pleasant social intercourse the business of the evening commenced.

The man of the hour was undoubtedly our Secretary. His clear and concise report ... roused ... hearty applause. He suggested that a fitting memorial should be erected in our class in memory of our late friend Fred Berry.

... Mr. D. C. Messent heartily endorsed this suggestion, and the meeting also showed its approval by unanimously adopting the report.

Mr. Lansdown then called upon the treasurer ... , and Lewis Messent placed before us a few easily comprehended figures which showed ... a falling off of 4/6 as compared with last years receipts, although the balance was larger owing to our reduced expenditure ... we were entertained by a most vigourous [sic] speech from Mr. Bedwell and ... by his munificent gift of one farthing, to be entirely devoted to the wiping off of an old fraction.

[p. 3]

This and the subsequent reports were unanimously adopted.

Our Football Captain ... recommended the class magazine ... and advised all ... to become subscribers. (Applause and pointed remarks).

The election of officers was a quiet affair, all being re-elected with the exception of the Prayer Meeting Secretary, Cyril Bedwell, who resigned the position owing to his taking up Sunday School work downstairs. Stanley Rowe was unanimously elected in his place. The treasurer stated that he would like two auditors to examine the accounts. Guy Barrett and Will Crosley were asked to undertake the work and both accepted.

It was here that the only exciting election took place. Two committeemen had to be appointed besides those who would have seats EX OFFICIO (C. B.). Nominations were asked for and C. Bedwell, E. H. Bowler, W. Crosley and F. Jones were proposed.

C. Bedwell obtained a majority but the chairman declared no election in the case of W. Crosley and F. Jones. On a second poll each received twelve votes so the matter was decided by lot and W. Crosley duly elected.

The routine business being over the meeting was thrown open for remarks. Mr. D. C. Messent promptly seized the opportunity of reminding some ... not ... to use the class-room as a lounge or as he remarked, to take six chairs one for each foot.

[p. 4]

Mr. Lansdown immediately followed asking our co-operation in keeping free the exit from the church, especially during communion services, as the loud conversation disturbed those inside.

...

Mr. Lansdown then closed with prayer ...
(For particulars of the merriment outside we refer you to G-y C-y)[1]

POLITICAL

The Editor,
   Angels' Voice.
      London.

Dear Mr. Editor,
I am quite in accord with your footnote to the Political Article of the November issue. The writer is very enthusiastic, and indeed most optimistic over the good results which his 'socialism' would achieve, but he has not told us what it really is. I suppose this is an impossible task ...

Yours truly,
Rasselas.[2]

Contributions of all kinds wanted for the special

NEW YEARS ISSUE

[p. 5]

[Drawing of a coat of arms. The banner below reads:] Many A True Word Spoken in Jest

---

[1]   Does this refer to noisy conversations between <u>Guy</u> Barrett and Will <u>Crosley</u>?
[2]   Samuel Johnson's *Rasselas the Prince of Abyssinia* (1759) concerns a young man's attempt to find the source of happiness.

[p. 6]

HERALDRY

Achievement of Arms of
Earnest Harvey-Bowler Esq., [sic]

Escutcheon

In chief, a BOWLER hat proper.
Dexter (right) A fancy waistcoat improper.
Sinister (left) A clowns face.
(Probably from a Wax Works Show)

Crest

A fleet runner proper.

Supporters

Two Jesters proper.

Motto

"There's many a true word spoken in jest".
(Not in this case)

...

Don't forget our former invitations, but criticise, suggest or commend any points which may appeal to you.

Can you draw? If so send a specimen along.

Can you write? Make up something really entertaining and send it to us.

Are you discontented? We invite you to suggest a remedy, but only written communications are accepted or will have our attention.

[p. 7]

FOOTBALL

Some people laud cricket and others praise "goff",
Whilst some funny mortals at all games would scoff;
But still there's a pastime which brings forth some pluck:
It's played in such weather as best suits a duck.

The wetter the rain, the more slipp'ry the mud,
More greasy the ball and the harder the thud.
The better they like it do manly young men,
For fun such as this only comes now and then.

Supposing one does stop the ball with one's face,
Or get bundled over – it's not a disgrace;
And what does it matter to you or to me
If someone gets crocked by a biff on the knee?

52

It's all in the game so your grumbling's no good,
    And you soon get quite used to the grass as a food;
While if there's no grass in the place you're shoved over,
    There's mud! No one wants or expects to get clover.

You keep the ball rolling the best way you can,
    Of course with the object of "besting" your man:
At times you'll succeed and at others you won't;
    If you do, you do well: otherwise, well you don't.

[p. 8]

There's shouting, and bustling with orders galore
    To pass the ball somewhere; if not there's a roar
Of derision from those whom your enemies favour,
    And also some words with your own Captain's flavour.

But when on occasion you do something smart
    You clear the defence, and then like a dart
Make straight for the goal, take aim and then shoot.
    Have you netted the ball? No! Then blame your old boot.

But there's one thing to mention; now who's the official
    That struts up and down? He's the Knight of the Whistle,
    Whose duty it is to control the whole game,
Until he gets winded, or blinded, or lame.

Poor Ref! All your duties one cannot call jolly:
    To anger the crowd would be absolute folly.
Just please the spectators and players as well,
    And your safe, otherwise none your sad fate can tell.

Two men there are also the Ref. To assist
    Whose duties may roughly be said to consist
In pointing out whose is the ball when it's on,
    And judging "off sides" there's a grave doubt upon.

And thus is the game titled "Football" now played;
    The bold at its rigours are never dismayed.
The exercise quickly all business care lightens,
    It tightens the loose 'uns and loosens the Titans.

                          A. P. A.

[p. 9]

[Photograph of a suited young man with tie and waistcoat, with arms folded across his chest, looking to his right.]

[p. 10]

IN MEMORIAM

During the past month Fred Berry has passed away. He died peacefully at 11.45 on Saturday night, November 5th. For seven weeks he suffered great weakness, emancipated by the ravages of that terrible fever, typhoid, he was reduced to so low a state as to be ... entirely dependent upon those around him ... He seems however to have begun to improve, the fever was leaving him and great hopes were entertained for his recovery, but unfortunately serious complications set in ... and our friend passed away.

I have just returned from the funeral deeply moved and profoundly impressed, thoughts that it is impossible to commit to paper, crop up in ones mind. The changes of life come upon us almost unawares. A week ago and who would have thought the events of to-day possible.

[p. 11]

Thus are we again reminded that we know not what a day may bring forth.

It is a solemn experience to bid farewell to the mortal remains of a friend, this we all felt this afternoon. Twenty three of us gathered around the grave; a sorrowful band. Others would have been there had it been possible for the whole class mourned a friend; but twenty three presented themselves in affectionate memory of him and in loving sympathy with those so painfully bereaved.

The cortège was timed to start from No. 98 Acre Lane at 2.50, but circumstances prevented it leaving till half an hour later. It was arranged that on the way to the cemetery the remains should be taken up Church Road, thus passing the gates ... where we so frequently congregated together in groups both before and after either Class or services. It was fitting that just outside these gates the Hearse should stop a few

[p. 12]

seconds, and Fred's remains for the last time were on the spot that knew him so well.

On arriving at Nunhead Cemetery the coffin was met by a number of friends who despite the bitterness of the day – for it was very cold – ... had patiently waited.

54

The little Cemetery Chapel was full; and will those of us who were present ever forget that service? The ... comforting words with which the Burial Service commences "I know that my Redeemer liveth", followed by other Scriptures reminding us of that glorious Resurrection hope that we have in Christ; then again the few carefully chosen ... words given by our minister, Mr. Lansdown, drawn from the incident of the Raising of the Widow of Nain's Son,[3] and last of all our Pastor's prayer that God would comfort those bereaved, and that all present

[p. 13]

might by the Grace of God, so live that when we receive the call we may be ready.

We will draw the curtain of respectful sympathy before the sad scene by the grave side, but the Committal being over we filed past and looked down into that place where Fred's body must lie awaiting the Resurrection.

The floral tokens were very numerous; a landau full of them followed. At the house the floor of the drawing room was covered ... and they overflowed as it were, on to the landing. As I stood looking at all these beautiful flowers ... I noted that the wreath from our Class was placed in the centre, and the thought came into my mind that it was not inappropriate that it should occupy that position, for it seemed to me that in the goodness of God, possibly the influence of our friendship and undoubtedly the lessons learnt from the study of God's Word played their part in the moulding and shaping of the character of

[p. 14]

him whose death called forth so many tokens of affection.

Fred had a gentle disposition ... I shall always remember him as one from whom hard or harsh words were never received. He was a thorough gentleman in the truest sense of the word.

He was deprived, on account of his being naturally delicate, from taking part in ... sports ... Occasionally he accompanied us on our Rambles ...

I knew Fred for about eight years. He joined our choir as a boy about Xmas 1904 and left it at the end of September 1906. He was a member of Mr. Ramsay's class before the late Sunday School Secretary went to Canada and the States, and when I took over that class he came under my care. He was one of those who helped to form the present Young Men's Bible

---

3. Luke 7:11–17.

[p. 15]

Class, remaining a regular attendant right up to the time of his fatal illness.

For two years he held the position of Assistant Secretary to the Trinity Literary Society and also took an active part in ... other societies connected with the Church.

What shall I write in conclusion. Such an experience ... should ... lead even the youngest of us to remember the frailty, brevity and uncertainty of life, and to see to it that while opportunity exists we will be up and doing for "The time cometh when no man can work". It should remind us that we have a life to live and not to idle away, we have hours, days and years granted to us, the use of which we shall have to account for ...

[p. 16]

we shall be impressed with the supreme importance of life and its responsibilities, we shall remember that we have characters to mould and dispositions to train. We must ... take a grip of ourselves and try to shape our lives according to the Great Pattern.

No man is a man unless he has control over himself in everything and there is only one thing that can help us ... and that is Christianity.

Let us therefore ... strengthen the bond of Friendship already so strong amongst us, and may we above all never neglect the assembling of ourselves together for the study of God's Word, remembering that the Psalmist of old said, "Wherewithal shall a young man cleanse his way? By taking heed thereto according to Thy Word."

D.C.M.[4]

[p. 17]

OUR POLITICAL PAGE
WHY THE LIBERAL PARTY IS DOOMED

The reason why I have chosen to deal with the Liberal Party this month is two-fold. In the first place the majority of the readers of this magazine are Liberals, and secondly because the Liberal Party claims to be the "Peoples Party"; but in reality are very little better than the Tories. At the time of going to "press", the King has been advised to dissolve Parliament, and by the time this reaches the reader ... the Liberals ... will be rushing through the constituencies asking the electors not to forget the party which has done so much for them. Let us see what they have done and what they have not done. The present

4. Daniel C. Messent.

Government has not done anything worth mentioning, but that is the typical Liberal state.

I suppose the greatest novelty the last Government invented was the Budget. We were told that this Budget was the beginning of the great revolution which would sweep away the great landlords and restore the land to the people. The strange thing is that we were not told how the land would get back to the people; it did not take a single acre from the landlord, but left it where it was – a monopoly. However the land taxes are a step in the right direction. Tax the land heavily and the Socialists will do the rest.

[p. 18]

I will give the Liberals credit ... They have passed a distinctly useful Workman's Compensation Act, also a Small Holdings Act. The Children's Charter ... is one they may be congratulated upon. Again they passed after mutilations, the School Feeding Act which the Labour Party had demanded. It did not mean much however for it only said that the Local Councils might feed the children if they pleased; and that only on school days, so I suppose they could starve during the holidays. But such is Liberalism.

Then, there was the Old Age Pension Act. Ever since the Act was passed the Liberals have been shouting "WE gave Old Age Pensions". Yes, but why! It must be remembered that the Socialists have been demanding these pensions for years, but the Liberal Party always refused them. When they saw that it was dangerous to do so much longer, they gave in. But mark this; ... they had no intention of giving them to all who needed and had a right to them. Can I prove it? Certainly. If they had been sincere they would never have fixed the age at 70, and they would never have tried to pass it at five shillings a week, seven and six for two. Fancy treating people in this bargaining fashion. All who are receiving these pensions to-day have to thank the Socialists and not the Liberals.

After many years the Liberal Party has woken up to the fact that the House of Lords is a useless assembly ... My opinion is that the Veto Bill is not worth a general election. The Lords have no right there

[p. 19]

and ought to be abolished.

When are the Liberals going to do something for the Unemployed? It is no use making grants of money; one might as well try to empty the Atlantic with a tea-spoon; and to throw the Labour Exchanges at them is an insult. Some day the people will take the political machine in their own hands; they will mould their own destinies. Some day they will learn what Socialism means: then the Liberal Party will have to go.

POLITICIAN

PARAGRAPH

"Double one, please miss".
"Certainly, two".
"Oh, is that you Ethel?"
"Yes".
"Well you might stop trying to be funny, I want double one".
"Why don't you ask for 'double donkey' and be sincere?"
"How do you know I want to call some one a donkey?"
"Well you're not quite as sweet as usual so I suppose Something's the matter."
"Sorry, but this fellow gets on my nerves"
"Oh! What's he done?"
"Do you remember me telling you about our mag?"
"Yes".
"Well he kept it for three days and when he brought it down at last, he didn't apologise like any ordinary fellow would but just said in the rudest and coolest manner possible, that he wasn't going to put himself out for the mag. Rotten action, I call it. Don't you?"
"Rather! Surely it wasn't one of the old gang?"
"Oh no! It's a new chap they call Giggs. I want to rag him a bit".
"Alright! I hope now you make him feel ashamed … you're through".

[p. 20]

Xtemporaneous

99

There is a beast which books call lynx,
    With staring eyes just like a sphinx.
In daylight it sits still and blinx
    At night it's up to many jinx.

Some fellows love the saucy minx
    That whirls around the skating rinx,
And dresses up in pretty pinx,
    And shoes at which the whole room blinx.

The tippler who strong whiskey drinx,
    Until at everyone he winx,
Into sweet oblivion sinx;
    And finds next morn he's lost his linx.

'Tis time to stop this game methinx,
The once bright fire now slowly sinx;
Jack Frost is creeping through the chinx;
Besides, I've wasted all my inx.

Jag.[5]

Xtremely Xcruciating.
Ed.

[p. 21]

FOOTBALL

REPORTS AND COMMENTS

Trinity v. Christchurch 2nd XI

Every year ... we have regularly met our Streatham Friends. The two elevens being ... well matched, good games ensue and the results are about equally divided. We met at Burbage Road and kicked off at 3-30. The weather was very frosty and a fog hung over the ground, at times rendering the touch lines invisible from the centre. However things cleared up a bit just before half time, but afterwards it became thicker than ever and the match had to be abandoned.

Trinity v. St. George-the-Martyr

Nov. 12th. 1910.
This match was played at Raynes Park and resulted in a win for Trinity. The play was very even throughout, both goals being in constant danger ... Fred Handy played another good game in goal and Will Fagan and Harry Jones showed improvement at back.
Trinity were favoured by ... the Referee ...

[p. 22]

At least two of their goals were undoubtedly the result of "off-side" efforts and should never have been allowed, but as this official was provided by the home club, no complaints need be made.
The pleasing feature of the match was that Guy Barrett ... "found his form". His football up to now has been singularly ineffectual ... ; but in this game he played well ... with the result that he shot four goals in this way, the fifth being the outcome of a nice piece of individual work on his part that was quite legitimate.

---

[5]   James Godden.

...

St. Georges are a fast team and with more combination would have easily won. As the light failed they pressed continually, Trinity having hard work to prevent them scoring, but at length the whistle blew and Trinity were left victors.

RESULT:– St. George-the-Martyr 4.
Trinity 5.

[p. 23]

TRINITY v. St. ANDREWS

Nov. 19th.
Playing at home on an ideal afternoon for football, Trinity could only draw.

St. Andrews being the heavier and more sturdy team it was somewhat unexpected that the trend of play should be in Trinity's favour, and had the home forwards taken ... their opportunities the result would have been different ...

J. Bishop not turning out, the home forward line was again disorganised. It is a great pity that Trinity's outside right does not regularly play ... H. S. Rowe ... always does his best and sometimes puts in some really good centres, yet he is obviously not suited to the outside position, his place being at half back. Harry Lansdown at inside left was good; he nearly always is. Although on the slow side, he is by far with the exception of Fred Handy, the most scientific of our players; he passes well and given a little more pace would become a really good footballer ...

[p. 24]

...

RESULT:– ST. ANDREWS 1.
TRINITY 1.

TRINITY v. CLAPHAM VILLA

November 26th

After a long trudge through thick mud which reminded one of walking across a ploughed field, Trinity found themselves at the bottom of Green Lane, Norbury, where they were to meet the "Villa". Their team was distinctly an emergency one. G. Barrett, J. Bishop, F. Handy and L. Messent all being on the sick list. In their places the Club tried F. Edmonds, F. Biggins, C. Bedwell and F. York.

Of the recruits, C. Bedwell played a useful game in goal; but in F. Biggins Trinity have a very promising player. Although very light he played a useful game at outside right, being quick and very unselfish …

The Clapham Club turned out with two men short and decided to play the one back game, so reducing Trinity's chances of scoring.

The "Villa" were the first to score, but Trinity soon followed through their Captain and … he later scored once more …

      RESULT:– Trinity 2.
         Clapham Villa 1.

[p. 25]

[Sketch of a sailor, emerging from a pub called] Ye Blue Pig. [signature partially legible:] Ri/[?]. XII/10

JACK ASHORE

[p. 26]

COMPETITION

WONDERFULLY EASY
VALUABLE PRIZE

It was with great regret that we were informed of the difficulty of our first competition. Many sleepless nights … have been spent in the endeavour to fulfil its terms … accordingly everything has been altered and made much easier. The nature of Competition 2 is totally different …

You are all acquainted with the title of this magazine:-

THE ANGELS VOICE

It consists of fourteen letters of which twelve are different. With these fourteen letters you have to make as many words as possible.

The same letter must not be repeated in one word, except the letter "e". This … may be used three times. The words need not have any connection with each other. Each word must contain at least five letters. Plurals and proper names are allowed.

The rules are … :-
1. Only one entry allowed each person.
2. Name must be signed at bottom of list.
3. An entrance fee of one penny (stamp) must accompany each entry.
4. Lists not accepted after January 9th.
   …

[p. 27]

List of Subscribers

The Magazine is to be circulated in the order in which the names appear below ...

The time limit for one subscriber is TWO days.

In the case of more than one subscriber being closely connected the magazine must not be kept for more than three days.

Anyone passing this on in less than his appointed time confers a benefit on his fellow subscribers ...

Please give the particulars asked for in the columns.

NAME	DATE RECEIVED	DATE PASSED ON
Mr. D. C. Messent.		
Mr. L. Messent.		
Mr. W. Messent.		
S. Rowe.	Recd evening Dec. 4th	even. Dec. 5th
H. Rowe.		
F. Rowe.		
W. Crosly. [sic]	5th	afternoon Dec. 7th
F. York.	7th	
C. Smith.	8th	evening Dec. 8th
A. Austin.	9th	morning Dec. 11th
H. Lansdown.	11th	Dec. 14th
B. Stripp.		
G. Barrett.	Afternoon Jan. 15th	

[p. 28]
G. Harper
F. Jones
A. Jones
A. Carpenter
F. Butcher
H. Butcher
Calloway
W. Cramp
L. Snoswell
Giggs
A. Holman
P. Shearer
C. Bedwell
C. Moxley
W. Evans
Bealey
Marriott

1911

THE ANGELS' VOICE

VOL: I NO. 3

[p. 1]

CONTENTS

Editorial	I
Drawing	
The Childrens Tea	2
Sketch	
Soliloquy Poem	6
Political	6
Sketch	
Football Reports	7
Painting	
A Complaint	13
Drawing	
Trinity Trips for 1911 – Where?	14
Drawing	
An Appreciation	16
Political	18
Whisper Page	
Bible Class and Literary Society	19
Silhouette	
Our Boys. Poem	20
Coat of Arms	
Paragraph	23
Our Political Page	24
The Angels' Voice	26

[p. 2]

[Another red cover with painted image of angel.]

[p. 3]

THE ANGELS' VOICE

I

VOL. I.   NO. 3.

January 7th 1911.
SPECIAL NEW YEARS ISSUE

EDITORIAL

Dear Readers,

We were both pained and surprised to discover that last months issue was being passed from hand to hand without any protective covering and was also being doubled up and thrust into side pockets. We should have thought that at least a piece of brown paper might have been substituted by whoever decided to dispense with the envelope and ... a crease down the centre does not improve the appearance of the magazine. All this makes us feel that our special New Year's Number is not quite safe in your hands. It ... demands very gentle handling. Much of it's charm is due to it's artistic features. The cover artist is to be particularly congratulated on a striking piece of work, and Mr. Harry Reeves has signalized his advent into the ranks of our regular contributors by some excellent sketches.

Before our space is filled we must add just one more plea, the time-worn editorial plea for copy – and so farewell.

Eds.

[p. 4]

[Drawing of two muses reading a scroll of *The Angels' Voice*. Signed:] HR.[1]
Art (to sister Literature):– 'This is a welcome addition to our ranks, sister. It even eclipses its predecessor.'

[p. 5]

THE CHILDRENS TEA

2

We all regret the passing of Christmas ... but after our own festival is over, those for whom the season has had few joys catch a glimpse of the departing spirit. We are not so busy with our own pleasures and

---

[1]   Harry Reeves.

Art (to sister Literature): 'This is a welcome addition to our ranks, sister. It even eclipses its predecessor.'

at last have leisure to attend to those who must trust to us for whatever joy the season brings them.

Our Class ... subscribed a sovereign to the Poor Childrens Tea which took place in the lecture hall on the thirtieth of last month. On the way to the school room I passed several disappointed mothers taking small children back home and it was their remarks which told me how eager the demand must have been for tickets. Outside the gate there was another group of mothers, furious because their offspring could not gain admittance, whilst on the grass was a small crowd of dirty children who hung on to my coat-tails wailing out "Pleaser, they forgeter gimme a ticket sir." "Let's come in guv'nor" and suchlike begging petitions.

Once inside ... two rows of noisy feeding children ... attacked the food ... with an eagerness which proclaimed their scanty meals on ordinary

[p. 6]

3

occasions. No sooner had I got to the end of the room than I was pounced upon to fetch a policeman who alone could satisfactorily deal with the trouble outside. However … he could not be found. After twenty minutes search I returned to the hall, took off my coat and prepared to do – - – nothing. I merely strolled up and down in the hope of catching some naïve remarks which might help to enliven this account; but everywhere the unceasing cry was "Pleaser me sir, I ain't 'ad none yet sir" and the smiling waitresses could hardly serve up the cake quick enough. Towards the end there was some excitement … which afterwards turned out to be an anxious father arguing that his two boys ought to have been admitted. After much talking … they were allowed … in although they would not be able to make a very hearty meal of what was left. When every crumb was at last eaten the air had become so thick … that more delicate people would have felt ill. Had not fresh air been introduced … we should have inevitably fallen asleep. Accordingly the children were all sent outside to romp about and, incidentally, to catch colds; a thing I succeeded in doing without any special effort whilst acting as shepherd or guardian 'Angel'.

[p. 7]

4

Once inside again all the tables had been removed and in their places were rows of seats which were soon filled with children listening to a musical entertainment. One of the lady helpers, a certain Miss Haley [sic],[2] sang an extremely sweet little song until the accompaniment stopped, without warning and for no apparent cause, but this unintended effect passed unnoticed by the children who applauded heartily. Mr. Lionel Jones deserves some commendation for the admirable manipulation of his gramophone whilst a hand bell entertainment provoked thunders of applause … The most remarkable feature of the evening … was a comic song with actions, given by … our respected friend Mr. Williams. His imitation of the various instruments of a band … profoundly stirred his audience. The children themselves sang a few carols, but though the noise was appalling … , it made no impression after the humorous song we had heard a short time previously.

When the … musical talent was completely exhausted all eyes became fixed on the Christmas Tree. The distribution of the toys it bore took some considerable time and … the watchful stewards had a hard task to suppress …

[p. 8]

5

… the surreptitious blowing of whistles and trumpets. At last the toy distribution was over and a parting gift of a few sweets had been given to each one.

---

[2]   Presumably a misspelt reference to 'Trissie' Hayley.

All was now silence for the last few words and ... those present were asked to express their thanks ... ; the children showed their approval by a medley of noise. Tin whistles, cardboard trumpets, tin trumpets, dog whistles, squeaking animals, mouth organs ... were brought into service, besides hands, voices and feet ... Proud mothers now led their children away and those who were arriving for their practice afterwards told me that one could hear whistles and trumpets, animals and organs throughout the neighbouring streets.

WHISPERS

Do you want to tell the editor anything?

If so, just write it on a piece of paper and seal it in a vacant envelope (if there is one left) on our Whisper Page.

...

[p. 9]

[Drawing of a policeman watching a waitress jump into the air carrying a large jelly or trifle.]

Temptation.

[p. 10]

SOLILOQUY

6

How I regret the day I left the happy realms of school
To go and wear my trousers out upon an office stool.

The masters, worthy men; indeed: none worthier than these,
Hard laboured long to teach me how to earn my bread and
cheese.

As a boy, unluckily, I used to crib my work,
But now I'm paid for what I do I find I mustn't shirk.

I used to think myself so wise, in City ways, I mean.
The office boy now kids me on. Oh! Why am I so green?

Some day however, I suppose the tables will be turned;
The vicissitudes of life all past, I'll rest on what I've earned.

Jag.

POLITICAL

Dear Mr. Editor,
    "Politician" appears to be a very keen advocate of that most dreamy
of creeds, Socialism. Now there is some sense in which nowadays all
right thinking men are Socialists or ... have Socialistic tendencies, but
I am quite convinced that only the most visionary ... can hold with
the views expressed by Grayson & Co.[3] While human nature is what
it is, Socialism is totally impracticable, perfectly impossible, absolute
nonsense.

LIBERAL

[p. 11]

[Drawing of a young man with oiled hair trying to uncork a bottle.]
[Signed] HR.
'A small page drawing' for "THE ANGELS' VOICE"

---

[3]   For Victor Grayson (b. 1881) see *ODNB*.

[p. 12]

FOOTBALL REPORTS

7

TRINITY v. CASINO.
December 3rd

Owing to a week of continual rain, the pitch in Burbage Road was practically under water. Had reason prevailed the match would have been scratched but ... the captains decided to play.

The game resembled Water Polo rather than football, for dashing through large puddles of water ... did not add dignity to the field if it afforded amusement to a crowd of onlookers.

Casino ... under favourable conditions would give Trinity a hard game. As it was the play was very even.

The home club again played F. Biggens and H. S. Rowe on the right wing and a good pair they proved. H. S. Rowe put in some first class work and nothing but the terrible condition of the ground prevented him from scoring ... two good goals, whilst Biggens confirmed all our expectations, one or two of his feints being particularly smart.

Guy Barrett at centre would have done better had he shot instead of attempting to literally rush the ball through the goal-keeper. Harry Lansdown missed two

[p. 13]

8

good opportunities of scoring but on the whole played well.

... Fred Handy made two good saves in spite of ... a small lake in the goal mouth. The backs were steady and played well considering the heaviness of the ground ...

The only goal of the match was scored by Vice-Captain Barrett.

RESULT:–   CASINO 0
TRINITY 1

TRINITY v. ST. ANDREWS, KENNINGTON.
DECEMBER 10th.

The return match with this club was to have been played at Crofton Park but unavoidably had to be scratched.

[p. 14]

TRINITY v. CASINO

9

December 17th

The return match with this club was played on the Rosendale Sports Ground, Trinity again winning.

The pitch being very heavy, the play was not fast and principally in the Casino territory. Little happened worth recording, both sides being only mediocre.

... For Trinity Guy Barrett shot one and Lewis Messent two goals.

RESULT:– Casino   1.
Trinity   3.

TRINITY v. WREN RESERVES
December 24th. 1910

Unfortunately this match had to be scratched, neither side turning up in sufficient numbers owing to the proximity of Xmas.

TRINITY v. CRUSADERS
Boxing Morning

Seldom had the Trinity team been seen to less advantage ... The more was the pity for a fair number of friends had gathered on the Rosendale Road

[p. 15]

10

Ground hoping to see a good game ...

Both teams were out at full strength; the Crusaders being the heavier set had the advantage as the ground was very heavy ...

Undoubtedly the best men on the field were the Clapham backs and goal-keeper who kept up an impregnable defence ...

On the Trinity side, F. Handy in goal, W. Fagan at back, and H. Rowe at left half were the only men up to anything like their usual form ...

The forward line was execrable. Harry Lansdown was in one of his slowest moods ... whilst W. Cramp was more often ... in the half back ground than in his proper forward position. Guy Barrett at centre was the best of the five ... Fred Biggins

[p. 16]

II

played a gallant little game at outside right, surrounded by men twice his size, but he committed the unpardonable offence of robbing his captain of a shot which could scarcely have failed to score …

RESULT:– Crusaders   3
            Trinity   0

TRINITY v. 83rd OLD BOYS
December 31st. 1910

With a weakened team through the absence of W. Fagan, Trinity met their old rivals on the Burbage Road Ground.

The Company[4] soon began to press … but for … F. Handy and the backs, Trinity would have soon have been in considerable arrears.

The 83rd. were the first to score through a penalty …

[p. 17]

12

It was not until half time that Trinity equalised by Guy Barrett who had been finessing … too much, scoring a good goal. This nettled the Clapham men who soon regained the lead …

RESULT:– 83rd Co. Old Boys.   2.
            Trinity   1.

Only by a miracle has our Sub. Editor been spared to us. The cause of our great anxiety was the arrival of a funny story. It came by post and was not signed. The Sub. Editor … was very greatly distressed owing to his inability to find the funny part. The author … had a peculiar fancy for drifting: The ship drifts with the storm, and after the wreck, the hero drifts to an island. In fact everything in the story drifts somewhere, and it is remarkable … how often the author drifts from the point. It was actually read half a dozen times in the vain attempt to catch the drift of the story so we finally threw it … into the river and watched it drift away.

… our Sub. Editor is much too valuable to be wasted in the examination of such experimental trash.

---

4   The 83rd London Company of the Boys' Brigade was based at St James' Church, Park Hill, Clapham.

[p. 18]

[Coloured drawing of village roofs in snow.]
[Signed] P.v.R.[5]

[p. 19]

A COMPLAINT

13

To The Editor.

With reference to the last issue ... , I find that I have been the subject of an attack from some "rotter" ...

The offensive remark is, "EX OFFICIO" (C.B.[6]). I mentioned the words which are the cause of the trouble, three times in ... my speech. Why I am so harshly dealt with, I do not know ... since such a speech as was made by the treasurer, --- ... pure swank[7] on his part ... --- passes unheeded.

Yours faithfully,

EX OFFICIO.

We cannot see what Ex Officio has to grumble at. He apparently wishes his speech to be classed with another which he describes as 'pure swank', and share the same treatment. Such speeches are seldom noticed in journalism, but striking points in great speeches are invariably ... emphasized.

This however, ... will hardly satisfy E.O. for such an outcry could only have been raised by an uneasy conscience ... a sure sign of transgression.

Ed.

[p. 20]

[Drawing of two female nymphs – one child like, the other a young woman.]

---

5   Percy von Rittershausen, younger brother of Ferdinand.
6   Ex Officio and C.B. is Cyril Bedwell, *AV* 3 (Jan. 1911), 42.
7   The term swank, often used by these young people, referred to ostentatious behaviour and a pretended superiority. *Oxford English Dictionary.*

[p. 21]

TRINITY TRIPS FOR 1911 – WHERE?

14

A subject such as this re-calls to memory many a jolly ramble through Surrey woodlands and hearty al-fresco feeds finer than the dubious provender served up under French aliases in London … But I go back to the time when a former Trinity Bible Class followed the sheep paths across the four miles of chalk cliffs between Dover and the South Foreland Lighthouse, and in the frequent rests watched the shipping five hundred feet below. A short time ago I turned out some old photographs of one of these expeditions. How intently did we listen to the keepers lecture in the lantern of the lighthouse, and with what becoming modesty did the members of the party decline my suggestion that they should be photographed with the notice board of the prison on the cliff as a background? What impromptu speeches and lively chorouses [sic] we had on the way home?

In … 1910 we have done little in the way of trips. True, three of us had five hours together in France on the August Bank Holiday but that was hardly large enough for an "official" trip. Why should we not have one good trip this year, if not to France, which would cost about 12/-,[8] then to the coast which would come to about half that figure. Dover and Folkestone cliffs are well worth a visit and so is

[p. 22]

15

Eastbourne with Beachy Head …

How many spend in six months on cigarettes and other useless things sufficient to give them … a glimpse of a country other than their own? Will those who agree … write to the Editor … In a few months perhaps the editor would find a corner in our … influential periodical for those who want holiday companions and might give the date of their holidays. It may seem rather premature to write like this for the January number but judging from past experience it will all be practical policy by the time my turn arrives to read the paper.

A.H.E.

The above suggestions with regard to holidays seem likely to be very helpful in bringing together … holiday companions.

…

Ed.

---

[8]   12 shillings.

[p. 23]

[Drawing of tramps – two bathing in a river and one on the bank.]
[Signed] IM[9]

"Come on, 'Enery, it's fine. Off wiv yer clo's" "Yus, an' get 'em stole!"

[p. 24]

16

AN APPRECIATION

This is the third issue of the "Angels' Voice" and I feel it incumbent upon me that it should contain a word of appreciation.

The ... magazine was originally conceived in the fertile brain of our Class Secretary who spent weeks carefully thinking out his plans and gathering ... assistants ...

Everything ready, a meeting was especially convened before which he laid his suggestions; they were taken up most enthusiastically and the first number appeared with a subscribers list of well over twenty names.

...

The periodical far surpasses our expectations. The quality of the contributions and the ... pains taken ... show how well qualified [Godden] is for the position he holds ...

BUT, towards the continued success of this enterprise all must contribute, else ... our Mag. will be a thing of the past.

I do therefore very earnestly urge that all show their appreciation of the Editors energy and zeal by assisting

[p. 25]

17

him to keep alive ... the "Voice".

All must feel it laid upon them to contribute a short article, or criticism at some time or other, then shall our Monthly serve the purpose for which it was established.

D.C.M.

---

9   Presumably Isabella Messent.

MUSICAL ARITHMETIC

56
190
451
933
<u>182</u>
1812   This little sum adds up to the tune of '1812'.
No wonder tots are popular among lovers of music.

                                         Jag.

AN ORIGINAL GIFT

The vicar of Hadthorpe was discussing ... a recent harvest festival.
Referring to the willingness ... to contribute ... he said:–
"The incident which touched me most however, was when little
Maggie Hodgkins came up and laid an egg on the altar".

All contributions gratefully received.

                                         Ed.

[p. 26]

POLITICAL

18

To
     The Editor
Dear Sir,
I notice that your 'Politician' started with the terrifying heading:–
"Why the Liberal Party is doomed". but after reading through the
article twice, I cannot see how or why they are 'doomed'.
You give no reasons or proofs.
About the Budget: Who said it was the beginning of a great
revolution which would sweep away the great landlords and restore
the land to the people? I cannot remember ever having heard that ...
As for the article on the Old Age Pensions Act, I consider it absolute
nonsense. I challenge you to name a dozen Socialists who demanded
them any more persistently than other ... people. When the Old Age
Pensions Act was passed, there were not half a dozen Socialists in the
House (including that semi-lunatic Grayson). When have the Liberals
'refused them'? The Tories promised them, the Liberals said nothing
about them till they gave them. But when did the Socialists 'make it
dangerous to refuse any longer'?

You sneer at the Labour Exchanges and the proposed Unemployment Insurance, but can you give a ... more feasible solution to this great question? No. Socialists are no more than a set of dreamers and do not show any way by which they may benefit mankind.

Welshman.

[p. 27]

WHISPERS

[Consists of 6 tiny white envelopes with their flaps facing the reader.]

[p. 28]

19

THE BIBLE CLASS AND THE
LITERARY SOCIETY

Dear Sir,

A member of the Literary Society Committee recently observed ... that ... the Bible Class was not ... well represented at the Literary Society meetings, and I felt bound to admit it was true. That is a pity because our Literary Society programme is an excellent one and it gives good opportunities to those who desire to learn to speak in public. It enables those who have conquered the nervousness of addressing their fellow members in class to ... address a somewhat wider audience.

I know that evening classes commendably occupy the time of some of our members, but there are many others who could spend pleasant and ... profitable evenings with the Literary Society.

The programme for the new year includes an "Inquiry Evening" dealing with general questions and answers, a discussion on "Is the present generation better than the Past" and a mock trial carried out on the lines of a former success.

Yours faithfully,
HOMO.

[p. 29]

[A silhouette of two figures – one male and one female – both dressed as clowns.]

"OUR BOYS"

20

B stands for Barrett, as good as they make 'em;
But don't touch his knees, if you do, you may break 'em.

What can you say of a fellow like Bedwell
Who always declares that at work he's not fed well.

Biggins possesses a passable sister.
Doubtless you know it, perhaps you have ---- her.

Black is a youth with a voice deep as thunder.
The length of his whiskers give all cause to wonder.

Butcher the senior, also his brother
Go to the rink to fall over each other.

Bowler though last is not least of the B's.
He acts as the sub. to the first of the G's.

C stands for Crosley, a nice gentle creature
Whose wonderful length is his prominent feature.

Carpenters articles written in red
Are violent enough to awaken the dead.

C stands for Calloway who as you know,
Emmigrates so that his riches may grow.

G stands for Godden, the Sec. and the Ed.
Whom one could'nt class with the starving unfed.

Giggs is the beggar of paragraph fame.
We hope that in future he'll keep free from blame.

H stands for Harper who rode at a cab
And smashed it to atoms with one single dab.

Holman is said to put grease on his hair
In case we forget that a parting is there.

Handy who shows off his talent as "keeper",
Rests in the mud if he cannot roll deeper.

[p. 31]

Jones and his brothers are really first rate
Although they appear on the field rather late.

L is the letter for Lansdown the laugher.
With care he will rival his pa as a chaffer.

M stands for Messent besides many others,
So first we will deal with these two famous brothers.

Mr. D. C. is our popular leader,
And if we believe him a very light feeder.

Messent the younger looks after our money.
His views upon auditors seem rather funny.

Poor Major Moxley is always in pain[10]
With gout caught through watching us play in the rain.

Marriott's r's are pronounced in Scotch fashion
Whilst all his orations are given with passion.

M stands for Munro whom p'raps you don't know:
It's true he is small but in time he will grow.

Morse is a fellow who quietly rests
Like dear little mice in their warm cosy nests.

Perkins is great as a criminal tracker,
But as for the mag. he's a horrible slacker.

R introduces the great name of Rowe.
The eldest is known for his spirit and go.

Rowe number two, bowls a curious brake,
Which seldom fails five or six wickets to take.

Last of this group we place Rowe number three
Who still sings his hymns in a sweet minor key.

Squires' voice is such that its accent may teach
To what awful depths Cockneyism may reach.

[10]   Charles Moxley was known throughout as the 'Major'.

Our dear old friend Shearer once joined in the rush
And dressed himself up in bright buttons and plush.

Snoswell of late has bestowed his affection
On some sweet young thing of the feminine section.

[p. 32]

22

No one has ever heard Smith make a noise.
It's easy to see he's not one of the bhoys.

S stands for Stripp with his nice curly hair
Which owes its perfection to unceasing care.

Y stands for York who's a lad among lads
And numbers 'Gesif' amongst some of his fads.[11]

Those I've not mentioned, we don't see I think
Often enough to require further ink.

Jag.

We have received a long letter, rather too long to publish in full, but a football criticism may be interesting.

'the main fault seems to be the lamentable lack of ... combination ... , it is not difficult to see why the Team is not so capable as it might be. A set of forwards should study each other's play and come to some understanding with regard to what method to adopt ... Like wise the half backs ... The backs are somewhat differently placed, they have to oppose all sudden rushes and deal with the enemies tactics. Proper combination is the best setting for brilliant individual play.'

[p. 33]

[Drawing of a coat of arms. The banner below reads:] Consumptor Ignis.

11. Presumably 'Gesif' means 'guess if'.

[p. 34]

HERALDRY

23

Coat of Arms of F. Perkins Esq.

Escutcheon:–
    1st. An immaculate boot proper.
    2nd. A nap hand proper.
    3rd. Detectives hand book, proper.
    4th. "Voice" contribution withheld (shockingly improper)
Crest:–
Jar of tobacco crossed by two cheap pipes, proper.
Supporters:–
No one can be found to undertake the job.
Motto:–
      "Consumptor Ignis"
Literal translation, "Devourer of fire".
Probable meaning, "Consumer of vile shag".

PARAGRAPH

Of course, you can't definitely attach the blame to anyone, but the fact remains and we were not the only ones to notice it; the church was extremely cold on that occasion and perhaps accounted for the small attendance at the New Years Services. The fires should certainly have been kept alight and the actions of its stoker bordered on criminal negligence. A repitition [sic] in slightly colder weather, would inevitably find us frozen to our seats, however warm and fiery the sermon might be.

[p. 35]

MUTUAL

[Drawing of two women, one in traditional Dutch clothes, hooped skirt, flyaway head dress and clogs, the other a woman of fashion with pince-nez.]
    What a sight you are!

[p. 36]

OUR POLITICAL PAGE.

24

LOOKING BACKWARD --- AND FORWARD

The year 1910 has ended, = ended amid the dust of political confusion, = and it is a suitable time for the Socialist to ... see how his Socialism stands. I have looked around and find that the idea of Socialism is spreading ... The Anti-Socialists are active; they are appealing to the wealthy owners of vested interests to contribute to their funds ... to carry on their characteristic campaign of misrepresentation and slander. We are delighted ... ; it is a tribute to the progress we are making.

Yes, the old parties are fighting a losing battle, their shady tricks will not stand the light of Socialism and they descend to base means ...

At the last Parliamentary Elections forty two Labour members were returned, as against forty in the last Parliament. This is even better than it looks for one or two of the Liberal-Labour men were defeated; so the Labour Party in the House of Commons is more Socialistic than ever.

The Independent Socialists however did not come off quite so well from this point of view

[p. 37]

25

but ... the number of votes polled was encouraging. The appearance of these Independent Socialists made the Liberals nervous, and by the way some of them talked, one would have thought that England belonged to the Liberal Party.

During the past year the branches and membership of the Social Democratic Party and the Independent Labour Party have been on the increase; and in the municipal elections ... a "Socialist Revival" set in. Very few seats were lost, and an encouraging number gained ...

Concurrently with a revolt in the I.L.P. headed by four members of the National Administrative Council who desire a more active Socialist Policy to be pursued ... , there has grown a desire on the part of the S.D.P. for a common understanding with the I.L.P. and the Fabians.[12] A preliminary Conference has been held, and ... the Conference is a good omen.

Mr. Lloyd George says there is no Socialist movement of any weight in Great Britain. On the Continent, he thinks existing institutions have reason to fear its growth.

---

[12]   Independent Labour Party and Social Democratic Party.

26

Of course, this gust of Liberal east wind deceives no one. Mr. Asquith[13] it appears is greatly concerned about it, seeing that he refuses to reverse the Osborne Judgement.[14] All he does is to promise legislation to enable the Unions to make a voluntary levy – which they can already do.

The year 1911 may witness some startling developments. It may see the formation of a United Socialist Party. A Socialist daily paper is to be started this year, so we shall no longer be dependent upon a cowardly capitalist press. The result will be that the movement will grow wonderfully.

I am looking forward to the day when the Irish will have Home Rule and the balance of power rests with the Socialists – real ones.[15] Then we shall see what we shall see.

They are attempting to crush Socialism in Germany ... but it is all useless. Before long Socialism in Germany will sweep all before it and England of course will follow.

POLITICIAN.

Politician wishes us to state that he does not understand Rasselas' letter asking for a definition of Socialism. In the first issue he said that it was the nationalisation of the means of production and distribution, which would not create a monopoly, but the mutual co-operation of all.

Ed.

The Angels' Voice

28

It is a strange thing but an absolute fact that new things always call up old memories. This was particularly the case when I first heard the title of our magazine. It at once took me back to a summers evening on Blackheath. Not far off was a small crowd deeply interested in some object lying on the ground ... the centre of attraction was a beautiful (?) woman. No one had attempted to do anything for the poor creature although her eyes occasionally opened with such a pathetic gaze, and her lips moved as if she were trying to speak. But ... a policeman arrived and ... he at once grasped the situation, went down on his

---

13 For H. H. Asquith see *ODNB*.
14 The Liberal W. V. Osborne challenged the General Railway Workers' Union which used its funds to fund Labour MPs. The House of Lords ruled in his favour. Pugh, *Speak for Britain*, 86. For Osborne see *ODNB*.
15 The Irish Nationalists at Westminster traditionally supported the Liberals.

knee and taking the womans hand on his arm, commenced to loosen the clothing round her neck; whilst ... someone went for a doctor. In the meantime this poor wretch was murmuring "The Angels Voice, The Angels Voice, I hear the Angels Voices".

A doctor was difficult to find and as usual the crowd passed its time in abusing the poor bobby. "The matter should be reported in the proper quarter". The Home Secretary's name was mentioned, etc. etc. A sympathetic gentleman suggested brandy, but as the policeman pointed out, it was dangerous to

[p. 40]

29

to give brandy to an unconscious person.

More abuses for bobby.

Opinions were freely expressed that the poor woman would shortly breathe her last. "The Angels Voices" could now and again be heard, though as someone remarked, the articulation was fainter.

At this point a young man ... began to examine the woman's eyes and pulse. He handed his card to the constable and was careful to explain that though he was not yet a registered practitioner, he soon hoped to pass his final exam.

His face became serious and he pronounced her to be in a fit although he could not say exactly what kind. He suggested a little brandy would revive her and the sympathetic brandy merchant at once produced some. This 'cognac' had a wonderful effect. The patients eyes rolled, "the angels voice" came stronger, and the constable seemed a great deal happier to think that he would not be held responsible for the woman's death. More brandy was fetched ... but at the same time the doctor arrived. He quickly examined the sufferer and turning to the policeman said: "she's horribly drunk, you'll want the ambulance." The crowd dispersed like the mist before the rising sun. The 'coming' doctor was gone, and the "Angels Voice" is no longer the dream of a drunken woman, but the actuality of spirited youth.

[p. 41]

	Date Received	Date Passed On
Mr. D. C. Messent		
Mr. W. Messent		
L. Messent		
S. Rowe		
H. Rowe		
F. Rowe		

W. Crosley

F. York

C. Smith

H. Lansdown
H. Stripp

Harper
H. Jones
A. Jones
F. Jones

A. Holman
P. Shearer

A. Carpenter

L. Snoswell
W. Cramp

G. Giggs

Butcher. F & H.

A. Austin
R. v. Ritterhausen [sic]

Mr. C. Moxley

Mr. A. H. Evans

A. Marriott

H. Beagley
C. Bedwell (E.O.)

Please sign and pass on in the usual manner. The time limit for the groups in brackets is three days.

THE ANGELS' VOICE

VOL. I NO. 5

[p. 1]

THE ANGELS' VOICE.

I

VOL. I.   No. 5
March 4th. 1911

EDITORIAL

Dear Readers,

There is strife in the Editorial Office … there always has been, but this month it has broken out in vigorous argument. The Editor wishes to give his readers a page full of words, beautifully and skilfully arranged, leaving an idea but saying nothing. The Sub-Editor, on the other hand, maintains that the Editorial should do no more than serve the functions of a notice board. Hence you find neither in this issue, but only a faithful account of what is actually taking place. Besides this affair has so wasted our time that we have not been able to prepare your usual entertainment. We hope that the coming month will suffice to mend the breach so that once more you may revel in the product of our united efforts.

Notice! Notice!

We must have the magazine at class every Sunday to open

WHISPERS

[p. 2]

OUR LONG HAIRED CHUMS AT PLAY

2

Not long ago I went to see the girls, Trinity girls, our old acquaintances, play hockey. My chief aim was … to tell you all about it, but now … I find there is nothing to write about.

For the most part it was a solemn and dignified pastime, the players after making a few futile hops, for one could hard-say they ran, without gross exaggeration, would rest and consult in mysterious tones. The only signs of activity … were occasional whirlwinds of sticks, legs, arms, hair, and ribbons; … excited females rushing round and round a little ball just like a frisky puppy trying to catch its tail. This never lasted long and always resolved itself into the brilliant dashes, but if so I was asleep at the time through watching their former play.

There was one great exception, and that not a player but the referee.[1] I meant to have asked who he was, but no opportunity occurred so I had to watch his graceful movements in silence. He leaped from side to side calm and confident, avoiding the ball with marvellous skill, while at frequent intervals he blew his whistle, whereat each player seemed glad, for it meant a halt and consequently a rest.

[p. 3]

3

Oh! they are a lazy lethargic collection. I only hope we have a chance to play them some day.

Of course with another ref. He loves his own team far too much.

PARAGRAPH

"Is it hard work bringing out the mag?"

"I should think it is; you see we don't get much support."

"Is that so? I should have thought you would get plenty of articles for a magazine like this."

"Well we were promised a lot … but I suppose they got mislaid in the post. At any rate, they have not yet arrived. Our fellows are so very slack, they walk about with long faces just as though they were thinking … but I'm quite certain it's not the magazine they're thinking about."

"Do you speak to them about it?"

"I should think we do. Our voices go quite hoarse in trying to make them write an article. Some of them want to know what they've got to write about, and others say they've paid their three pence just as if they paid us to keep the thing going.

Why! we do as much as that ourselves besides having to do some work at it as well. They're a slack lot, we find that out every day, but of course they'll lose something in the end."

---

1. Moxley refereed the ladies' hockey. *AV* 7 (Nov. 1911), 46.

[p. 4]

[Drawing of a young woman's head with back-combed hair.]
[Signed] HR.

[p. 5]

SUNDAY CYCLING

4

(To the Editor)

Sir,

Permit me to encroach on your valuable time and space by troubling you with these lines in support of "Scorch's" article on Sunday Cycling.

To my mind there is nothing more healthy to both mind and body than a good Sunday morning spin after a week's hard work in the office or workshop. The average young fellow who possesses a bicycle has to WORK ... all the week, so why should he not enjoy God's Nature on the only day ... available, viz. Sunday?

It may be suggested that cycling on Sundays is detrimental to his religious education. This is all twaddle. Nowhere can the splendour of the Creator's work be better realised than in the open country away ... and what occasion is more appropriate than a bright Sunday morning, when all the world is at peace. I sympathise with those poor benighted mortals who have never been out on a Sunday morning, say on Redhill Common, and have never had the ringing of the church bells carried up to them on the breeze from the town below. Lying on the grass and gazing into the blue sky above, who can help thinking of higher things, and

[p. 6]

5

admitting that the wonders of the Creation are beyond comprehension? I think ... there is no person in a more contented frame of mind than the cyclist who has spent his Sunday morning in this manner; and when he turns up at church in the evening, he is more able to grasp the full meaning when the minister happens to touch on the beauties of Nature ...

Take the German Sunday for instance. The German goes to his church in the EARLY morning – HE does not have to have his services at eleven because he can't get up earlier – and after service takes his lunch basket and goes pic-nicking for the day; or he goes cycling, boating, shooting, riding, motoring, fishing, in fact he indulges in all manner of sports and pastimes. And what does he gain by it? Everything. He learns to appreciate all the good things, which were bestowed upon him FOR HIM TO ENJOY; and he does not look upon them as evils placed in his way to tempt him. What does he lose by it? ABSOLUTELY NOTHING. The average German is as God-fearing a man as may be found on the face of the earth.

The argument may be put forward that all this sort of thing could be done on Saturdays. But how can we go cycling on Saturdays when we think it our duty to play football – ... cricket in the summer – ... even if we do not really care about playing.

[p. 7]

6

Then again we were told some time ago that it is our duty to keep ourselves physically healthy. This can be done by cycling or playing football, but it is hardly healthy to go cycling on Saturday afternoons and evenings with motors ... pervading the atmosphere with petrol fumes. Saturday afternoon therefore, can be profitably devoted to games, but for the young fellow who works all the weeks round, SUNDAY MORNING is undoubtedly the time to go cycling; before motors have appeared on the road, and when the air is sweet and pure.

Of course it is not essential to stop away from church in the morning. A healthy young fellow thinks nothing of getting up at 5 am. and going for a few hours before breakfast, being in ample time to get ready for church. I myself, however, would much prefer to make a forenoon of it.

I admit there are two kinds of cyclists. There is the cyclist referred to above, who goes out with the intention of doing himself some good, and the BIKIST who has a bicycle out at 6d an hour and is a general source of annoyance to the public. The second sort need not be dealt with, he condemns himself.

Trusting you will find space enough to air these views, even though you do not agree with them yourself, I remain,

Yours faithfully, SUNDAY CYCLIST.

We don't agree.
Won't someone take up the other side.

[p. 8]

7

SUFFICIENT ... ...
... ... UNTO ETC.

Silently the days slip by
And at the end of each I sigh,
For though I really do not try,
    Some foolish thing I've done.

I hear my varied audience speak.
"You think there could be no such freak"?
"Well listen to a sample week
   And form your judgement then".

Sunday has an air refined
And too much food should be declined;
But ne'ertheless when I had dined
   I got up feeling stuffed.

Monday morn at half past eight
I scrambled out two hours late,
And missed my train, a thing I hate,
   The guv'nor gets so wild.

Tuesday being rather gay,
I chased the girl across the way.
Her piquant manner made me stay,
   So I was late again.

[p. 9]

8

Coming home on Wednesday night
A vagrant told me of his plight.
I wept; and much to his delight,
   I parted out a bob.[2]

Thursday, in a Council Tram,
(This shows you what an ass I am)
I meekly rose and like a lamb,
   I gave a girl my seat.

Friday evening 'twas I think,
I'd buns with ginger beer to drink.
That night I dreamt about the rink
   And woke up on the floor.

The last of the seven is simply sublime
For Saturday gives me a little free time,
But ass that I am this possession I wasted
   In watching the girls of the Guild getting basted.

---

[2]   Bob is slang for a shilling.

Now I expect you're convinced of my folly,
But that doesn't stop me from feeling quite jolly,
Whilst "Open confession is good for the soul"
So after these verses I ought to be whole.

Jag.

[p. 10]

9

POLITICAL

(To the Editor)

Dear Sir,

If I may again take up my space in your magazine, I should like to defend my criticism of "Politician's" article in the December issue.

He still adheres to his statement that the Liberal Party as a whole, claim that the Budget ... is the beginning of a great revolution which will sweep away the landlords, and restore the land to the people. I say this is not so. What they do claim is a part of the great profits which these landlords make out of the land, but which they do not really earn, either by working themselves or spending their own money in developing it.

I may be very ignorant but I must admit that I did not know that every Socialist orator ... has ... demanded Old Age Pensions more persistantly [sic] than the leaders of any other section of the people.

Next about his statement that in 1894 the Liberal Government opposed an Old Age Pension Bill. In answer to a letter to the Editor of the "Daily News" on the subject, I received a reply that "In 1894 a bill was brought in by a private member – Col. Palmer of Gravesend – the second reading was agreed to by 205 to 136, but the Bill was taken no further". As the Liberals were in power, how was it that the bill got a second reading, and was agreed to on that reading, if the Liberals

[p. 11]

10

seriously opposed it?

He says "All Socialists favour pensions", so do all Liberals. What they wanted was a good sound scheme and a time when the country was ... willing to pay for the Pensions – that time has arrived and so have the Pensions.

In conclusion, "Politician's" idea that the Liberals spent £8,776,000 a year on pensions, and have now by the removal of the pauper disqualifications, greatly increased that expenditure, merely to keep the Socialists in check is I think, very silly.

Yours faithfully,

WELSHMAN.

The next issue of our magazine will be the last of Volume No. 1. Such an issue naturally marks an important step ... We do not aim at a special number profusely illustrated and of special length, but we wish ... to satisfy individual tastes. It is a difficult task and quite impossible of complete accomplishment but much may be done in that direction if our instructions are carefully followed.

After page 18 you will find provision made for you to give us your opinion. We wish you to write what you think has been the most enjoyable article we have published, and ... a few which you think come close after. If you think anything should have been left out, place it at the end of your list with a cross at either end.

[p. 12]

[An advertising handbill.]
SHERRY 18/-
Henekey's Olde Wine House, 22 & 23 High Holborn, London.

[p. 13]

II

THE EXPLANATION

of the previous page.

We owe you an explanation for it certainly seems strange that such an advertisement should appear in our magazine; but ... rest assured ... it was not put in for the purpose of assisting the "trade".

It would be a difficult task ... to justify such an action as the whole of our staff is strictly tee-total. It would be still more difficult to smile on ... whoever it is thus reveals his Bacchanalian tastes, although we cannot point the accusing finger with certainty.

The little parchment slip ... was not picked up in the street, nor in the grounds of the church. It was not even introduced by one of the congregation, but was found in the choir itself.

I can almost hear your astonished thought ... that we have one who could stray in our very midst. The guilt is reduced to one of seven persons. Six are suffering under unjust suspicion, and the seventh is still lying concealed.

This is certainly a case for Detective Perkins. IF he can undertake the investigation with a clear conscience, it proves that he is innocent, whilst his efforts IF success-

[p. 14]

12

ful will do the same for five others. We should like him to take this up, it would be so interesting to watch his behaviour, for ... it was found under his seat, and ... ... Well! We have our particular fancy.

The wise man of the day ... tells you never to have your Photo taken. How much trouble would have been saved if people were not so eager to spend their money in this way. This especially applies to criminals, for a photo is such a sure clue to the poor man's identity. Suppose for instance, I (John Clark) were to err in a moment of weakness. At once some officious person would place the Police in a position to obtain my portrait. This would at once be added to the Royal Al-Fresco National Portrait Gallery which includes the notice boards outside every Police Station ... Just fancy how I should regret my reckless extravagance whilst I read:–

"Wanted, John Clark, a young man of markedly high intelligence;

"low forehead, also low collar. Last seen wearing patent boots

"on which by this time the patent has expired (see over). Has a small speck etc. etc. etc.

It would be horrible, and all the more so because of an accurate picture of myself at the top. Now I should regret the three pence spent on the merry sands of Southend-by-Limpid-Sea.

Ah! Take my advice, shun the camera, for ever. But if you must ... .

(the rest is too bad for publication. Ed.)

[p. 15, p. 16 and p. 17 are divided by lines into ten sections on each page, in each section being an individual's response to the editor's request for an appreciation of the magazine.

D. C. Messent, L. Messent, S. Rowe, H. Rowe, F. Rowe, W. Crosley, F. York, C. Smith, H. Lansdown, A. Austin, F. v. Rittershausen, H. Jones, A. Jones, F. Jones, A. Carpenter, F. Butcher, H. Butcher, A. Holman and P. Shearer all complete their own little box with comments. Mr W. J. Messent's box is described as:] TO LET – AT PRESENT THE OWNER OF THIS SPACE HAS BOTH HANDS FULL

[p. 18]

13

THE WHISPERING GALLERY

Whisper: – "It is whispered that Mr. James Godden attended a lecture on Africa held at Trinity on Tuesday, January 24th, without paying for admission. We invite him to forward his cheque, or cash, for 6d. to the Secretary of the Literary Soc, failing which we shall have to seriously consider whether or not it is advisable to put the matter into other hands for ... ultimate collection.

Echo :– our readers will at once notice that whoever it is mak- [sic] this accusation has quite forgotten to give us his name. The charge ... would place the accused in a most awkward position were it not for the accurate way in which the Society's accounts are kept. Should anyone suspect that there is any truth whatever in this gross libel, Mr. W. J. Messent will ... satisfy them by refering [sic] to his 'vest pocket loose-leaf ledger'.

As a last word we should like to say how reprehensible is the writer of anonymous accusations. It is the index of a cowardly and sour nature.

Whisper:– "When will the results of the competitions appear?

P.S. Don't put Detective Perkins on the scent to unravel the mystery of the 'Disguised Handwriting'.

Echo:– at last some member of our class has taken an interest in the competitions. He wants to know the result. We cannot

[p. 19]

14

understand this idle curiosity seeing we have not yet received his entry.

He finishes with the request that we will not put Dect. Perkins on the scent of his disguised handwriting. We assure this youth that Perkins has a much bigger case on hand at present, and would not think of solving so small a mystery when even the Editor has managed it.

Whisper:– "It is the general impression that in the Poem entitled "When you want to swear" the lines referring to a small lump being used as a collar stud, would have been better sub-edited.

Echo:– this whisperer was one of the first persons to read the magazine and as his whisper was taken out at the end of the first week, we should like to know how it can be the general impression. We always thought that a general impression was the opinion of the majority and not of one particular person.

Whisper:– "It is whispered that the Deacons desire that certain young men wait till until they get away from the front of the church before lighting up their cigarettes etc. etc. etc.

Echo:– We have particular authority for stating that this matter if attended to, would give great satisfaction to many of the Trinity public.

[p. 20]

[A photograph of a man with top hat, cane and bow-tie – suggests a theatrical performance.]
[Signed]
Le Vicomte des Guibolles[3]
Alfred P. Austin.

[p. 21]

15

THE PHOTO
AND REFLECTIONS THEREON

It is quite a long time since we have received a photograph for publication, so your appetites will be sufficiently keen to enjoy the one in this issue. We doubt if anyone could recognise our eminent friend were it not for the autograph ... in the corner. It is ... well known that he belongs to the jabber-loving[4] section of our community and so we feel no especial surprise at his branching out thus under the theatrical managers wing. The only thing that does surprise us, is that he should represent so undignified a rascal. From accounts gathered from outside sources he acted admirably and with realistic expression. But all authorities acknowledge that it is impossible to act a part satisfactorily without ... feeling its emotions. The evidence ... tends to show that our friend is a scamp at heart; or else the most accomplished, barefaced hypocrite that has ever appeared before the footlights. He is forgiven much of this, however, for sending us the tell-tale photo which has done its share towards filling our interesting periodical. The example is a good one and although these serious pages can hardly smile upon such frivolity, the giving of the Photograph we hold up to others as a shining example in these days of tardy contributors.

Ed.

[p. 22]

16

A COMPLAINT

I think that the poem in the last issue of the "Voice", entitled "The Captain's Mess" is rather more personal than is necessary. Reading a paper at a class meeting, satisfactorily is not one of the easiest of tasks. Of course, if we were all gifted with the same literary attainments as

---

3   Guibolles – informal French for legs.
4   Jabber – to talk rapidly and indistinctly. *Oxford English Dictionary*.

our worthy editor and his confrere the sub, it would be a different thing. But, when a fellow tries his best, as I have no doubt Mr. Marriott did, to be "commented" upon to the extent of the poem referred to, at least demands an apology.[5]

FAIRNESS
ANOTHER OF 'EM

I think that the Editor has shown very bad taste in allowing the poem entitled "The Captain's Mess" to be published in the magazine. As a poem it is alright, but the sentiment is bad. I strongly resent any such attacks ... on a person who has doubtless expended much time ... in preparing a paper to read on a Sunday afternoon. Not only is it bad form, but it practically prevents the gentleman from writing another paper and it will also make anyone else think twice before writing one, if they know that they also are likely to be so severely criticised.

OTHERWISE SATISFIED.

We have made a brief reply on Page 30.

[p. 23]

[Drawing of a coat of arms. The banner below reads:] The early bird catches the worm.

[p. 24]

17

HERALDRY

Coat of Arms of:–
Mr. D. C. Messent.

ESCUTCHEON,

Dexter. On a green field (Burbage Road?) a tennis racquet and ball proper.

Sinister. 1st. Quarter. On yellow parchment, a book-worm crawling proper.

2nd. Quarter. A greasy football against a piece of blue shirt proper.

CREST,

A glass of water and plate of stale bread proper.

(To be used for dieting only)

SUPPORTERS,

A knife and steel, rampant, proper.

---

5   The poem referred to appeared in *AV* 4, now no longer extant.

Motto,
    "The early bird catches the worm".
    (If this is true, Mr. D. C. M.
    should be responsible for the high death
    rate amongst the Clapham Park worms.)
    20th. Century Version of "What"?
    Scintillate, scintillate, globule vivific.
    Fain would I fathom thy nature specific.
    Loftily poised in ether capacious,
    Strongly resembling a gem, carbonaceous.
    Oh! No! we wouldn't do such a thing.

[p. 25]

[Is a page with five small envelopes and the word WHISPERS repeated several times on the page. Only one envelope contained any paper. It is a small MS, handwritten in ink, entitled] "A far far better way.

A professor who was always ready for a joke, was asked by a student one day, if he would like a good tip for catching rabbits.

"Why, yes," replied the professor, "What is it"?

"Well", said the student, "you crouch down behind a thick stone wall, & make a noise like a turnip".

"That may be," said the prof., with a twinkle in his eye, "but a better way than that would be for you to go & sit quietly in a bed of cabbage-heads & look natural".[6]

[p. 26]

18

SOCIALISM AGAIN!!

The Literary Society held at least one most interesting meeting last month, and the discussion would have been full of interest to our readers although, unfortunately, not many attended. It was a review of Guy Thornes book, "The Socialist"[7]. Our staff "Politician" was of course present and the sight of his taking copious notes, filled me with glee and expectation. I was not disappointed. He got up and made the first speech that a member of our class has ever delivered before the Literary Society. He aired his well-known political opinions in the manner with which you are all so well acquainted and then unostentatiously re-seated himself.

---

6   So the whispers were little notes (unsigned, in this case) passed around among the magazine's readers.

7   Guy Thorne was the pseudonym of Cyril Arthur Edward Ranger Gull (1875–1923). His novel *The Socialist* appeared in 1909. See British Library catalogue.

The worst behaved member was as usual, Mr. D. C. Messent. During the evening he created a great deal of diversion by shouting "Hear! Hear!", every time an unlucky speaker ... was at a loss for something more to say; so it was only just that when at last he found himself in a similar predicament he should be still further confused by a hearty "Hear! Hear!", close at hand. Needless to say the Society laughed aloud.

The tit-bit of the evening however, was, "academical acceptation". Now I appeal to my readers. Do you think our Major could furnish that phrase out of his own head or was it no more than a shameless crib? Again, would the Major understand

[p. 27]

19

what he was saying when his last resonant phrase concluded with "anathama" [sic].

He must have books which we, poor mortals, have never heard of, and dictionaries of hitherto unknown conciseness.

It shames us what an earnest student he must be and it would I think, be worth our while to attend these meetings a little oftener, if only for the benefit to be derived from his deep discourses.

REF

The arrangements for a discussion are all in hand and the only thing that remains is for you ... to attend. We do not wish to write much, as by the time some ... read this the discussion will be no more than a pleasant memory. But to those whom we may be able to reach thus, we urge the necessity of a large attendance, even if some have to somewhat dis-arrange their usual programme in order to be present.

Mr. Reeves has again favoured us with ... his fine drawings ... But; he is now getting beyond the frivolities of youth and he should by this time be able to refrain from planting a sly wink on the face of so beautiful a lady.

PLEASE do not forget your contributions.

[p. 28]

TRINITY v. Lyndhurst Old Boys. 20
February 4th 1911

The return match with this club was arranged to be played at Lee ... Unfortunately "Lyndhurst" ignored the fixture ...

TRINITY v. CRUSADERS.
February 11th.

One looked forward to reporting a favourable result ... Everything looked so promising; Trinity were on their own ground ... they were also at the top of their form in the previous fixture. The only element of doubt was ... the absence of Guy Barrett ... but with Stanley Rowe deputizing for him, it was felt that what the Captain lacked in science he made up for in dash, so the substitution was not expected to weaken the attack.

Anticipations held good up to a certain point but after that things went away, for although Trinity scored three goals there could hardly be claimed as the result of the teams combined play ...

[p. 29]

21

The forwards were very disappointing. With the exception of R. S. Rowe at centre they seemed to lack enthusiasm . Rowe would possibly have done better had he ... insisted upon his wings waking up, for L. H. Messent at outside right, and Holman at outside left, were very weak, whilst neither Biggens at inside right or Lansdown at inside left were up to their usual form.

The weakest spot ... was the half back line ... Perhaps the worst offender was J. Godden, it is likely that his shortcomings accounted for the poor work of the wing in front of him.

The backs were for the most part steady, but ... they became very ragged and it was during this period that two very weak efforts by H. Jones opened the way for the "Crusaders" to put in two unsaveable shots.

Fred Handy in goal was good.

...

[p. 30]

22

Much disappointment was felt that Trinity ... failed to beat their old rivals in this the last of the three meetings ... this season. In the first match ... at Rosendale Road the result was a draw, two all. In the second also played at Rosendale Road ... Trinity lost three – nil, and in this last fixture Trinity were again defeated.

CRUSADERS 4
TRINITY   3

February 18th 1911
No match was fixed for this date.

TRINITY v. ASHBURTON PARK[8]
February 25th

Owing to the late notification ... Trinity travelled down to Croydon two men short. Fred Handy and Biggens

[p. 31]

23

were the absentees and their places were filled by C. F. Bedwell and Mr. Messent, the latter keeping goal. Will Fagan and Lewis Messent were unable to turn out ... but Trinity was assisted for the first time by Harold Austin, a Faversham man, whose services were much appreciated ...

From the previous encounter at Burbage Road it was generally anticipated that Ashburton would be quite formidable ... Their forwards were especially aggressive and came near to scoring several times but were checked by the Captain who gave a splendid display of good sound back work.

The Trinity forwards were weak with the exception of Guy Barrett who did some good work. The half back line was an improvement upon last week. Frank Jones was much too prone to centre within the penalty area, but otherwise he played a good game. Of the backs, S. Rowe was much the better. Some of his kicks were terrific, one especially deserves mention for it was the cause of Ashburtons second goal. The ball was coming along at a good pace with their forwards well after it and when quite near the goal S. Rowe gave what should have been a splendid clearing kick. Unfortunately it hit one of the Ashburton men and rebounded with terrific force into the corner of the goal.

Towards the end of the game "Ashburton" came near to scoring several times but at length the whistle blew and the game ended in a draw.

Ashburton Park 2
Trinity   2

[p. 32]

A Threat!
[Drawing of a boy hanging from a tree by one arm above an inoffensive-looking dog.]
(Boy) to farmer when caught stealing apples "Say mister if you don't call off that dog of yours, I – I'll drop on him."

---

[8]   Ashburton Park is in Woodside, east of Croydon. See Cherry and Pevsner, *Buildings of England London 2*, 236.

[p. 33]

24

FAMILIAR SOUNDS WE HEAR IN LONDON

When travelling on the Bakerloo
   Has it ever struck or confronted you
How often you hear such words as these,
   "No smoking allowed in the lift please".

Or perhaps you're commencing your ride from the Bank
   On the smart C.L.R. where the officers swank;
The train waiting, coloured a coco de l'Epp,⁹
   It's then that you hear it, "Please mind the step".

And when you've arrived at the station required,
   Each up-to-date ad. being duly admired;
You prepare to go out, but just as you shift
   You hear it again, "This way to the lift".

Then up goes the lift and before it has stopped
   While some clumsy beggar has on your feet hopped –
You take up your stand and then patiently wait,
   When loud bawls a voice, "Stand clear of the gate".

Suppose we rise above the level
   Of tubes and underground dishevel,
To take a glance at London's streets
   And note the things we often meets.

[p. 34]

25

You very soon spot a huge motor bus,
   You know the smell and the noisy fuss.
From Charing Cross to Fenchurch Street
   A penny fare gives you the treat.

Just as you journey down the Strand
   You pass the good old horse bus, and
You hear the old conductor say,
   "Bank! Bank!, a penny all the way".

---

9   C.L.R. refers to the Central London Railway, whose eastern terminus was at Bank. It was a forerunner of the Central line on the London Underground. The 'coaches were painted chocolate with a cream band': H. F. Howson, *London's Underground* (Shepperton, 1981), 36. Presumably 'coco de l'epp' is a description of the C. L. R. livery.

And here a crowd has blocked the street
   Someone has been knocked off his feet;
When suddenly a policeman's knees
   Stick in your back: "Pass on here please".

An exchange of greeting one often hears
   'Twixt omnibus drivers well on in years.
"What cher, beer barrel", says one who knows.
   The reply is just this, "What! strawberry nose!"

The wit of these men is often immense,
   And drivers of motors get told to go hence.
The driver of horses gets one on his own,
   "Garn! take it home, old Eau de Cologne!"

[p. 35]

26

Perhaps you've a bike getting old in the tooth.
   It creaks every time you get on it, forsooth!
And when passing by a young limb of the soil
   You hear pretty often, and loud, "Any oil!"

These phrases are just a few samples selected
   At random, to cheer you if you feel dejected;
There's plenty more really (perhaps not so choice)
   But these few will do for the "Angels' Voice".

A.P.A.

Talking of slackness, the magazine is not the only field in which it finds scope. The tired and weary feeling has taken such a hold on some of our members, that it is too fatiguing for them to shake hands more than twice on Sundays. Possibly Saturday night rambles are responsible for this distressing symptom.

Be sure your sins will find you out, Mr. A. H. Evans. You cannot go to a Whist Drive and have a sausage roll, two pieces of cake, a glass of lemonade and two sticks of toffee … without other people knowing it. It is … rather embarrassing …

We must have contributions please. Don't forget them as hitherto.

27

OUR POLITICAL PAGE
The Unemployed Problem

It will be remembered that "Welshman" accused me of sneering at the Labour Exchanges and the 'proposed' Unemployed Insurance. I will deal with the latter first. Surely ... the Unemployment Insurance Scheme will benefit but a small portion of the people. The Liberal Government has no intention ... of making this insurance universal. Then again they are not applying a root remedy ... only dealing with results.

Now let me deal with the Labour Exchanges Fraud. These Exchanges are no solution of the unemployed problem. They tend rather to aggravate it. I suppose "Welshman" will admit that they do not make WORK. What then do they do? They supply blackleg and sweated labour to the employer who wants it. Proof? Certainly. A cigar makers delegate at a meeting of the London Trades Council stated that in his trade girls had been discharged for no apparent reason, and then their positions – at two to three shillings a week less – had been notified at the Labour Exchange. Another delegate ... stated that both in London and in the provinces the worst rat holes ... were being supplied by the Labour Exchanges. Compositors have been asked for through the Exchanges at thirty shillings a week against the union rate of thirty-nine.

28

A delegate at a sheet-metal-workers conference, said the Exchanges were the biggest curse that ever existed. Several delegates at a boot and shoe trade conference ... stated that they were only a medium for sweating employers to obtain cheap labour. Has "Welshman" never heard of Bradford, where the master of the Labour Exchange went ... to get 'orders' for blacklegs from an employer whose men were on strike?

It is well to remember that these Exchanges were the outcome of a solemn promise by Mr. Asquith made in 1908, to go to the root of the unemployed problem next session. A striking example of how NOT to do it.

The Liberal Party have never been sincere about this question ... On October 14th. 1908, Victor Grayson, ... sick and tired of the Parliamentary bluff of the Liberals, Tories, and even of Labourites, weary of the whole paraphernalia of Parliamentary procedure, jumped up unexpectedly and moved the adjournment of the House to consider the unemployed problem, instead of discussing trivialities. The Speaker would not allow this, but Grayson ... refused to sit down. Both sides of the House yelled "Order", "Sit down"!! in spite of this he continued to declaim that

[p. 38]

29

people were starving, and he turned to the Liberals and stung them with the taunt that they were "well fed". At last he was suspended for one sitting. Mr. Grayson ... on the next day ... made a similar but more successful ... scene, in again protesting to the House for not attending to the unemployed question. This time he was suspended, with bell, book and candle, for the remainder of the session. Please remember that Grayson only did this when constitutional means had failed. The point ... is that the Liberals laughed. Laughed at the peoples starving! Laughed at the unemployed! No wonder Grayson poured forth volumes of invective upon them. But I think I cannot do better than leave it at that – a tribute to Liberalism – they laughed.

But to return to Labour Exchanges – Welshman has not a word to say in their favour, but asks if I can give a better way ... In the first place I would point out that unemployment is a direct outcome of the capitalist mode of production and will last as long as Capitalism exists. The only thing we can do is try to lessen it. I will give the following remedies ... :

[p. 39]

30

Improve your Labour Exchanges by (1) supplying no labour except under conditions that the wages and hours of employment are in conformity with the trade union conditions. (2) Preparing a list of sweating employers and refuse to supply them with labour under any circumstances whatever. (3) Supplying no blackleg labour.

If a universal eight hour day were enforced, it would have the effect of spreading the work out. Then ... if you cannot manage your affairs without leaving a wide margin of unemployed, it is your duty to look after them. Therefore I claim for the Unemployed the right to work; or maintenance without pauperisation. Evidently the Liberals are not prepared to do any of these things. Instead they pour forth floods of empty sympathy.

POLITICIAN

THE CAPTAINS MESS

We have something more than a shrewd suspicion that the writers of these two protests were present on the occasion referred to.

Those who witnessed the incident have not seen anything offensive in the poem, and we ourselves do not consider that it was any more personal than the circumstances warranted.

On reflection we do not consider that we owe an apology for its publication.

THE ANGELS' VOICE

VOL. I.No. 6

[p. 1]

THE "ANGELS' VOICE"

VOL. I.No. 6
April 8th 1911.

EDITORIAL

Dear Readers,
This number has been greatly affected by printing disturbances ...
and in consequence we are a little late.

Still, we <u>have</u> brought the magazine out, although unfortunately
for the last time. Circumstances make it necessary for some other
hands to continue the work ... There is everything in the favour of
our successors, for by now the "Voice" is old established, whilst the
balance to be carried forward does away with all financial difficulties.

Here is the editors address:–
80 Holsworthy Square,
Grays Inn road,
W.C.

Any "Angel" who feels inclined to adopt the magazine has only to
write when he will receive the stock and money in hand with a huge
supply of invaluable advice.

We now take an official farewell, not final, for we hope to commence
Volume II, before many years have passed.[1]

Ed.

[p. 2]

CLEOPATRA'S NEEDLE.

The Thames Embankment is the noblest thoroughfare ... but it is
certainly not the place for such a wonderful treasure as Cleopatra's

---

[1]   Clearly Godden intended to quit as editor. However, after a hiatus from April to November,
the magazine continued with him still at the helm.

Needle ... It is in an out-of-the-way position, and is not appreciated as it should be.

This splendid obelisk once cast its shadow over the Nile, when wild beasts and wild men still roamed our land although Egypt was in a state of wonderful civilisation. The Egyptian kings claimed to be gods and the obelisks were columns on which they cut their titles and virtues.

Cleopatra's Needle is not valuable because of what it tells us but merely as a relic. It was used by two kings at widely different dates. The centre column of hieroglyphics were carved first, and two hundred years afterwards another Pharaoh used the blank edges for himself.

A few points not usually known about the Egyptian obelisks are very interesting. They were never built up but were always quarried out complete, and afterwards finished so accurately that no support was ever needed to make them stand upright ... The needle as we see it now is lacking in one feature: a cap of thick golden plates. The great obelisks were always decorated

[p. 3]

thus, but of course some conquering army has long since stripped off the precious metal.

The column we possess is one of a pair which were set up on either side of the entrance to the great temple to the sun at Heliopolis or the City of the Sun. they were erected 1500 years before Christ and according to that are 3400 years old.

If Cleopatra's needle could speak ... It could tell us of the famine in Canaan, when Abraham took refuge in Egypt ... of the imprisonment and slavery of Joseph, of his prosperity and marriage. It could also tell of the wonderful meeting of Jacob and Joseph ...

Fifteen centuries later these obelisks were floated down the Nile to Alexandria and there re-erected, but about three hundred years ago one fell and was buried deeply in the sand and rubbish until ... the ruler of Egypt offered it to the British Government. In 1877 Sir Erasmus Wilson,[2] a famous doctor, offered a shipowner £10,000 to bring the obelisk over, but this was no easy task. The column is 68½ feet long and weighs 186 tons. However, a huge steel tube was built round it, and when all was ready it was dragged into the water, and taken in tow by a steamship named the "Olga".

[p. 4]

This vessel drew the cylinder by a huge steel cable, a quarter of a mile long.

---

[2]   For Erasmus Wilson see *ODNB*.

In the Bay of Biscay a terrible storm forced the "Olga" to cut the cable; but as there were eight men aboard the "Cleopatra" a boat was sent to their assistance. However ... the boat was swept away and eight men drowned. "The great column which had looked down on nearly two thousand years of Bible history was afloat at the mercy of the waves."

A day or two later, another steamer found the "Cleopatra" and her captain took the great cylinder in tow ...

... it was bought safely to London, where the finder was rewarded £200. There was much ... argument as to a suitable site, but it was finally erected in its present handsome, though unsuitable position.

There it now stands, the largest worked stone in England, and almost the biggest obelisk in the world.

[a little drawing, presumably the outline of the aforementioned iron cylinder]

"ALPHA"

Please notice that there is no alteration in the time limit. This last number should be passed round as quickly as possible so that each may read the invitation to take on the magazine before a month has passed.

[p. 5]

[A picture of the Thames with St Paul's in the background and a tug pulling two barges in the foreground. This is a printed copy of a painting by E. Fletcher.]

[p. 6]

[Drawing of a coat of arms – shield with young lady's face in centre, held by two young ladies, one either side. The banner below reads:] It's love that makes the world go round. HR.

[p. 7]

HERALDRY
THE COAT OF ARMS OF:–
FREDERICK YORK ESQUIRE.

ESCUTCHEON:–
  A pretty girl proper

CREST:–
  A pretty girl proper
SUPPORTERS:–
  Dexter: A pretty girl proper
  Sinister: A pretty girl proper

MOTTO:–

"It's love that makes the world go round"
(If this motto is true, it will doubtless explain why the honourable gentleman is so giddy.)

[p. 8]

A REPLY TO SUNDAY CYCLIST

Dear Sir,

The article on Sunday Cycling appearing in your last issue is very subtle, but … very unconvincing. This hackneyed and threadbare old subject debated upon continuously for years, almost tires one.

The greatest argument against Sunday Cycling for <u>mere pleasure</u> … is this: That a decent and moral young man … in the habit of going for a Sunday morning spin … , we need not call him a Christian. Well, our respectable … friend through the Grace of God becomes … converted … his view upon life … has changed because he has met with Christ and recognised … his SAVIOUR. Henceforth he must be governed not by "What <u>MAY</u> I do?, but by … "What <u>MUST</u> I do?"

Now this … conversion, will necessitate certain things that he had hitherto indulged in being dropped. His conscience will teach him which, but it is as certain

[p. 9]

as day follows night that amongst the first things to go will be his Sunday trips. It is always so, it must inevitably be so.

Now may I ask the simple question that if Sunday Cycling is not wrong but on the contrary quite beneficial, why should this be; for I suppose none will deny that my illustration is true to experience. Probably your correspondent will say that he sees the reason why the young man should lop off his Sunday spin. May I respectfully reply that … you may take it as an axiom that conscience never calls upon us to make useless sacrifices.

The attitude "Sunday Cyclist" takes up must of necessity lead him to an erroneous conclusion for he approaches the subject from the wrong standpoint.

Throughout the whole article he seeks to lead us to dote on self. One would think that SELF was the primary if not the only consideration in this matter. This is not … the Christian standpoint. He also … desires us to … adopt the continental Sabbath, and … tells us that the Germans " … appreciate all the good things that are sent for them to enjoy", for they spend their Sundays, cycling, boating, shooting, riding, motoring, fishing … Surely this is more

[p. 10]

than we "Voicites" can ... stand. We cannot accept this in the face of science, history and experience ... We view with alarm the modern tendency, not simply from the religious but from the national standpoint, for we are patriots and know on the best Secular authority, leave alone what God's Word teaches, that the good old English Sunday has had much to do with the building up of our glorious Empire.

The old adage that a "Sabbath well spent brings a week of content" is truer to-day than ever ... But I hear Sunday Cyclist saying, "Yes, quite right, I agree, but it is on the "well spent" that you and I disagree." Then I say to him, "Please tell me what constitutes a "well spent" Sabbath, and he gives a remarkable reply ... "Early morning services got over in such time as to allow of the major part of the day being spent in obedience to our Lord's injunction", but, I interrupt him, "That was our Lord's injunction. He says, "Remember the Sabbath Day to keep it Holy". He acknowledges that Sunday is not an ordinary day but one upon which man should think especially of his Creator.

Note how he would carry out this injunction. His ideal German invokes the aid of all his favourite sports ... and "Sunday Cyclist" seems to desire that we should emulate their example.

It is no good ... objecting to this con-

[p. 11]

struction of his words, it is the only logical conclusion that a practical man can come to after carefully reading his letter. Does he recognise what would be the effect of the general acceptance of his teaching? Why, Sunday Schools would close and Bible Classes would collapse because a ride in the country or ... a game of football would be much more beneficial to body, soul and spirit. It is unthinkable.

The whole article savours ... of piousness without sacrifice; this the schoolboy calls ... Cant, but I will not go quite so far ... The writer says that he has been led to think of higher things whilst "lying on the grass, gazing up into the blue sky" and this star gazing has compelled him to admit that "the wonders of Creation are beyond comprehension". So they are ... but, to discover it I did not have to travel to Reigate Hill on a Sunday morning ... and gaze up into the sky. I may also mention that should the preacher on a Sunday evening touch on the beauties of nature my imagination is not so limited as to render me blind to the full meaning of his words, unless I had spent the previous part of the day on the wheel.

... A ride into the country and a deep impression caused by the beauty ... of the surroundings may be merely Pantheism or Nature

[p. 12]

Worship, it is not ... the true worship of God ...

Looking at the question from the Christian standpoint we are forced to the conclusion that the Continental Sabbath is a ... danger to us nationally as well as religiously, and that Sunday Cycling is the thin end of the wedge, and ... not expedient.

We need to learn that the ideal Sabbath is not a day upon which pleasure ... must be sought, but rather one which should be spent in the ... best of all occupations, namely Christian Service.

"SABBATARIAN"

PARAGRAPH

A major is a person of high rank and is looked up to by his subordinates for an example. Now we have a major in our class but of course where you have a major you must have a minor.

In this case the major and minor are both the same person. No doubt you will think it strange but it is so.

Were this not the last issue we should heavily fine him, for, in our opinion, 15 days is rather a long time to keep the mag, even though the Major only regards it as a minor offence.

[p. 13]

THE FATE OF THE FOOTBALL FLATS
MORAL APPENDED

Eleven little footer boys, thinking they were men,
    One made a rotten kick, and then they were ten.

Ten little footer boys, getting near the line,
    One made a wretched foul, and then there were but nine.

Nine little footer boys, "swanking" round in state,
    Long haired class were lacking, and then there were but eight.

Eight little footer boys, bold as Drake of Devon,
    One showed his ignorance, and then there were but seven.
Seven little footer boys, missing all their kicks,
    One of these was winded, and then there were but six.
Six little footer boys, vainly did they strive,
    The enemy secured a goal, and then there were but five.

Five little footer boys, looking sad and sore,
  Their rivals scored another point, and then there were but
  four.

Four little footer boys, calling "Referee",
  He gave a goal against them, and then there were but three.

Three little footer boys, reckless chaps but who
  Couldn't get a single goal, and then there were but two.

Two little footer boys caused the crowd some fun,
  Half exploded with conceit, and then there was but one.

One little footer boy, last of all the race,
  Emitted then a feeble groan and vanished into space.

THE MORAL OF THESE VERSES IS, THAT WHEN YOUR
FOOTBALL'S "ROCKY"
  YOU SHOULD NOT SEEK TO COMPENSATE BY CRITICISING
HOCKEY.

<u>A long haired chum.</u>
Quite right! But can the efficiency of the two teams be compared. Only
a few weeks ago the T.H.C. was opposed to a club which had never
won a match in its existence. Our fair friends lost hopelessly and yet
they are capable of reproaching us with "rocky" football.

HAU LOJIKUL!

[p. 14]

A FOOTBALL CRITICISM
THE CAPTAIN

The question, "Has the play of Trinity Football Club improved
during the present season?" must be answered with an emphatic <u>NO</u>.
Our defence at the beginning of the season was very strong but lately
it has become woefully weak. The goal-keeper is not ... responsible
for this deplorable state of affairs; it is due to the weak tackling of the
halves and to the fact that the backs do not combine with the goal-
keeper, but "muck him up". Strong and clean clearances are quite an
exception and the backs have a very bad habit of dribbling with the
ball instead of giving it a good hearty kick.

The forwards are certainly not as good as last season. The absence
of an efficient outside left is largely responsible ... , whilst of the three

inside men, only the centre forward can shoot with any strength ...
True the first line has shown good form on ... occasions, but this is no
good. What is wanted is bad play to be the exception and not the rule.

But the question of improvement is not the most important. The
thing is have the men had some good games and thoroughly enjoyed
themselves. I think they have so I am sure they will not mind what
critics say. Any fool can criticise but probably can't shoot a goal for
toffee.

R.S.R.[3]

[p. 15]

[Drawing of a man and woman on roller skates – the man pulling the
woman who is smiling broadly.]

[p. 16]

HOCKEY

(The writer of this article has our deepest gratitude for so admirably
filling up space, but we have one great fault to find with his contribution.
He sent it to us on a long strip of TOILET ROLL. This was most
inconvenient and rather unpleasant for every time it was read in the
tram ... Well, you know what a sniggering, squeamish creature the
modern schoolgirl is.)

The Girls' Hockey Club has already been referred to in your magazine
but I do not like the way in which it was treated. I think it is ... worth
a little more respect ... than was accorded to it in the last issue.

One thing is very noticeable; they sadly need a "Ref." or might I say
someone who has a <u>little</u> knowledge of the game to officiate. It is quite
true he does not give his decisions at once ... but it is not necessary
to have a consultation with the players before giving the verdict. Then
again, ... there is a rule dealing with the "off-side" offence, which was
entirely neglected in a match witnessed recently.

They have a good set of players, but they need ... training, as every
Athletic Club does.

In Miss Lansdown they have an invincible back who cleared well on
several occasions yet not without removing half the Park. Miss Annie
Messent is another player who deserves to be

---

3   R. Stanley Rowe.

Roller Skating

[p. 17]

mentioned. She scored a couple of fine goals ... The play ... lacks combination and finish. One notices while watching the game, that the idea is there, but it needs cultivating, and this I must emphasise, for one has only to look back upon the persistent efforts of the Trainer of the Football Club, to realize ... what can be done.

Once taken in hand, I believe that this Club will be quite as good as the T.F.C. ... I can only look forward to the time when both clubs will be taking a prominent part in their respective branches of the Amateur Athletic Association.

"LINESMAN"

SINNERS v. SAINTS

In the March number of the "Angels Voice" we were favoured with an article ... devoted to ridiculing the hockey of our fair friends. In justice to the young ladies I thought it would be hardly fair to let this matter rest there, so last Saturday I strolled up to the Park to see a match in which the Trinity Girls were opposed by "All Saints" of Peckham.

On my arrival I found that the game had already commenced, at which I was rather surprised, considering the weather and the state of the ground. Owing to this it was painful ... to witness with what difficulty the players prevented their usually graceful movements from developing into a scramble. It reminded one uncommonly of the Cake Walk at the White City.[4]

[p. 18]

Two members of the visiting team failed to put in an appearance, but Trinity lined up at full strength, therefore having a slight advantage. The first person to catch the eye ... was the centre forward, who showed an unusual fondness for an off-side position. The remaining forwards must have improved ... since the match reported in last month's issue, unless the reporter was dozing during part of the game, and fully deserved the seven goals which were credited to them.

It is a tribute to the impregnable defence that the services of the goal-keeper were dispensed with, and she was able to give her aid wherever needed. Our footer eleven would benefit if they sent their halves to study the play of the hockey halves, who admirably divided their services between feeding the forwards and assisting the defence.

The scorers were as follows: –

Miss. Hill 3	Miss. B. Nobbs 1
Miss. A. Messent 2	Miss. B. Hayley 1

None of these goals however were the result of individual effort; on the contrary they were the reward of good combination. It was unfortunate that the Saints failed to score, but as usual the sinners prospered. It is to be regretted that our friend was denied the privilege of seeing a match, as we understand the game he saw was a practice in which Trinity's combination was utterly spoilt by the inclusion in the team of a number of outsiders whose idea of hockey was rather elementary.

"CHAFFER"[5]

---

[4] The cake walk was a mechanical promenade on which people walked accompanied by music. It was in operation at the White City in west London. *Oxford English Dictionary.*

[5] Presumably Harry Lansdown. See *AV* 3 (Jan. 1911), 31.

[p. 19]

[This is a handwritten Cash Account for 34 subscriptions at 3*d*. each + a Whisper enclosure = 8*s*. 6¼ *d*.]

[p. 20]

[This is the balance sheet for 1 November 1910 to 31 April 1911.]

[p. 21]

[This is the Profit and Loss Account.]

[p. 22]

A DAY IN THE COUNTRY.

Dear Friend, the Reader, have you ever spent a day in the country? The real country? Not traversing your stereotyped lanes and footpaths, but 'far from the madding crowd', ... shunning the frequented paths and penetrating to where you find Nature at her best, – Nature in her glorious, complex simplicity – and where Man, the de[s]poiler, the devastater, [sic] has not yet carried his depredations.

A twenty mile ramble in such virgin country constituted one of the most enjoyable excursions I have ever undertaken. The primary object ... was the discovery of bird's nests, but, in order to anticipate any accusations of cruelty, I must emphasise the fact that <u>my</u> motive was to ... investigate the domiciliary edifices erected by the ... feathered tribe, and not to molest or interfere with them in any way.

The first 'find' of note was that of a foreign egg in a thrush's nest, the culprit being that unworthy favourite, the cuckoo. Why! Oh why! is this detestable creature the subject of such laudatory panegyrics and heralding as the "harbinger of Spring'? It transfers all parental responsibility to unwitting foster-parents, who doubtless note with admiration the rapid development of their supposed progeny. But the intruder often

[p. 23]

[Painting of an ostrich bending down to a caterpillar. Astride the ostrich is an oriental figure with antennae holding a bag labelled:] IDEAS FOR VOL. II.
DID YOU SEND FOR US?
[Signed:] ETJ.[6]

---

[6]   Elizabeth Taylor Johnston.

[p. 24]

rewards their anxiety and attention by forcibly ejecting the rightful residents of the nest and monopolising their home. Surely such a bird must be branded as the black sheep of bird land!

After a cursory inspection of many nests of the commoner varieties, including those of blackbirds, thrushes, sparrows, linnets, robins, whitethroats etc., attention was arrested by a marvellous specimen of architecture, designed and executed by the namesake of the architect of St. Paul's, but whose craftsmanship dwindles into insignificance beside that of Mr. <u>or</u> Mrs. Wren. Covered with leaves and twigs to imitate the natural surroundings, and thus minimise the risk of discovery, this nest, unlike many other works of art, combines the often neglected attributes of utility and comfort.

A beautiful specimen, symbolic of purity, was next furnished by the egg of the snakebird (or wryneck), which save for a snow-white circle at one end, is wholly of a pale cream colour.

The butcher-bird with its well-stocked larder is justly named. Its nest is built amongst thorns, upon which are impaled numerous insects and small animals, to await consumption by this provident bird.

The strong parental instinct of protection to the young was well exemplified in the case of a missel-thrush, [sic] which refused to leave its nest although subjected to a fusillade of twigs, pebbles etc., and was only persuaded to desert her home by placing a hand within a few inches of the nest.

[p. 25]

If ever a bird expressed consternation ... , it must have ... on returning to her nest, which had previously contained four pretty blue eggs, a thrush discovered that some mischievous and heartless school-boys (my companions) had deposited ... twenty eggs, ... therein. One can imagine Mrs. Thrush's impassionately pleading "Not Guilty", when duly arraigned before Chief Justice Rook, and gravely charged with 'baby farming'.

If you wish to examine a dabchicks nest, you must ... wade into the middle of a dyke and remove ... the all-prevailing weed. When disturbed, this bird always carefully covers its nest, before taking flight, and thus renders discovery most difficult. This of course greatly enhances the value of the eggs to a collector.

A most noteworthy feature is that the majority of birds' nests are built in the vicinity of water, and the artist has yet to arise who will faithfully depict in its full beauty ... a loving nest, with its beautiful eggs, swaying over the rippling stream ...

Our days finds have amounted to more than 150 eggs, so we will now desist. Having thus wearied you ... , will you adjourn with me and take tea at this farm-house? Mine hostess, having survived the double shock of seeing strangers for they are almost as uncommon here as Halley's Comets – and further of being asked to prepare tea, serves us right royally ...

[p. 26]

After "toying" with real new-laid eggs, real and original farm house bread, home-churned dairy butter, home-made jam, made from home-grown fruit, and substantial cake, we are horrified to find that we have been swindled to the extent of sixpence each, for our sumptuous repast: such formed a fitting termination to a day spent in the heart of Nature, a day for which kings might well envy us.

Alas! Man with his devouring hand, creeps on unmercifully, and thus renders such excursions more and more impossible, to the intense regret of all those who love the natural beauty of our little forests.

H. R.[7]

Why not rambles such as these for Trinity? Easter and the Coronation will give the necessary time. Ed.

We should like to thank all those who have helped to make this volume such a success. None of the artists are ... in our own class, although several ... are well-known Trinitarians; there are still some whom few of us know. Amongst the advice given to our successors will be the addresses of these useful people ... Some of the most interesting articles were written by those who professed literary inability ...

[p. 27]

SPRING POETS

At this time of year there is one thing that's certain
    For Spring has arrived and it raises the curtain
On buds and young shoots and the flowers that show it;
    It's bound to bring forth what is called the "Spring Poet".

The Editors rise from their couches with fears
    From a knowledge of what must be poured in their ears;
And from morning to night do what they ponder and worry
    Saying things that make office boys scoot in a hurry.

But still do the poets their efforts combine
    To welcome the Spring and the gladsome sunshine;
And though they don't like it, they all seem to ask it,
    I mean what they get, that's the waste paper basket.

How sad must the hearts of poor poets be now?
    Their calling seems done for – I think I know how!
If only they'd leave it to just one or two,
    I'd tackle an Editor's job – wouldn't you?

But sure as it is there are birds on the wing
    So surely do some mortals harp on the Spring.
It's all very well, but we're always prepared
    To accept the first Season without being scared.

[7]   Harry Reeves was a science teacher.

Now how would you like to be – well, – very busy,
    Checking an essay that makes you feel dizzy;
And just as you're thinking the best place to stow it,
    Your sanctum's invaded by – Help! The Spring Poet!

He planks down his verses and asks you to read them.
    You've read them before, so you say you don't need 'em.
It's then he'll explain they're the best ever written,
    Until with a rush, he retires, badly smitten.

However one longs for and welcomes the Spring,
    The signs of fresh life, when the joyous birds sing;
There's one man whose presence we all ought to shun.
    If you see a Spring Poet – let fly with a gun!

A.P.A.

[p. 28]

OUR POLITICAL PAGE

(OUR READERS MUST PERUSE THIS ARTICLE WITH AN INDULGENT EYE, FOR SOCIALISTS FEEL RATHER KEENLY WITH REGARD TO JOHN BURNS[8] AND THEIR UTTERANCES RESPECTING HIM INVARIABLY ASSUME A WILDER FORM THAN USUAL. Ed.)

Are we downhearted? No! Even though Welshmen pull our articles to pieces, and literary societies pour forth their objections to Socialism, we still continue to write on behalf of democracy for we have never yet heard an objection to Socialism that would hold good.

But what is this I read? "Politician … seems very proud of the fact of two Labour gains (not Socialist). It will be remembered that I said the Liberal Labour Party had lost one or two seats, so therefore the Labour Party was more socialistic than ever. Welshman does not deny that, therefore the two gains are Socialist and not merely Labour as Welshman would have us believe.

I am also told that where there was a prospect of a three cornered fight, the Liberals withdrew their candidate rather than let both be defeated. I like this allusion

to the sacrificial spirit of the Liberal Party … Now it must be remembered that the Labour Party invariably vote for a Government measure; so, seeing that the Liberals had everything to gain and nothing to lose, I fail to see where the sacrifice comes in.

---

[8]   For Burns see *ODNB*.

[p. 29]

Welshman thinks that the Socialist candidatures at Kennington and Battersea were unsportsmanlike tricks. I don't. They openly admitted that they wanted to keep the Liberal out and had no chance of getting in themselves ... The ... Kennington candidature was a protest against the Liberal Government's insincerity; and until the Liberal Party ... commence business, we have a right to split the vote in ... every constituency in the Kingdom.

We are further charged with being jealous of John Burns. Let us see what there is to be jealous of? John Burns is paid £5,000 a year by the Liberals to betray the Socialist Party and the workers. John Burns voted against the right to work bill and against the payment of Trade Union rates of wages to government employees; and when offered a £3,000 rise last year he had the bare-faced audacity to accept it. It is not long since the Right Hon. John Burns was granted the sum of £100,000 by Parliament to provide work for the unemployed. But the people's John has granted only about £9,000 to the Central Body, wherewith to provide work for some 17,000 men and women. Some 500 men might have been usefully employed in coast erosion work at Herne Bay, but John withheld his sanction.

If he had been kept out of this Parliament ... we should have been spared the trouble of reading that disgraceful outburst made on the occasion of the

[p. 30]

Labour Party's amedment [sic] to His Majesty's "gracious" speech. It was ... shameless impudence for him to rave about palliatives; and it was all very well for him to talk about "making inroads into the manly independence of the poor" but inroads have been made already into their "manly independence" by futile journeys to useless Labour Exchanges.

He predicted disaster if the Government took up relief works; just as 25 years ago he predicted the same thing if the Government did not come to the rescue of himself and other unemployed and put them out of their misery.

This done he veritably choked himself with his final platitudes -- and for doing all this I suppose he will some day be relegated to the House of Lords. A fine figure he would cut with a coronet upon his plebian [sic] brow -- Baron Burns of Battersea.

I must ask to be forgiven for indulging in personalities, but when we are charged with being jealous of John Burns it reminds me of many things. I think I have written enough to show that we are not jealous but ashamed of him.

With regard to the Socialist Poll being encouraging; I qualified that with the remark, "taking into consideration what they had to contend with", which makes all the difference. To close I did not say the balance of power would rest with the Socialists in this Parliament. We can afford to wait for we are in true line with evolution, we are aligned with the Universe.

POLITICIAN.

[p. 31]

THE DANDY

F. A. B.[9] is a smart young lad.
But his green and red socks would drive you mad.
He has also a very peculiar taste,
For he likes his coat drawn at the waist
His shoes are so shiny, they're patents, it's clear,
But his hosiery staggers you when you get near.
I repeat once again, vivid green – vivid red,
Enough to drive anyone quite off his head.
But they seem to appeal to the girls alright,
For he's out with them nearly every night.
Wherever he travels there seems to go
With him, a beautiful coloured rainbow.
You hover around him but find with a shock
You're only admiring his beautiful socks.
But we mustn't blame him, for all have said
"It's a mania for colours he's got in his head."

One of the B's.[10]

Please note that the sub. editor must not be included in the B's. He objects to having his name connected … with a joke or humorous poem.

[p. 32]

FOOTBALL
SPECIAL REPORT.

Trinity v. Christchurch 2nd.XI.

A … well fought … and most interesting game. Such must be the unanimous verdict upon the return fixture with our oldest rivals. The

---

9   Frederick Albert Butcher.
10   Possibly either of the Butcher brothers or one of the three Bedwell brothers.

Christchurch team is a good one. The men are so even in size and ability. There are no slackers for all are keen and ... they play football and do not merely ... kick a big ball about the field. Trinity! Please note ... You cannot improve unless you make a study of your play, for Football is a science and needs to be taken seriously ...

Christchurch were assisted by two of their 1st.XI men. One played back and the other ... was at inside left. This of course strengthened the team considerably ... Special mention must be made of the "church's" wing men, especially the outside left ... , his centres were perfect and but for Trinity's halves ... would have been ... converted into goals.

Trinity notified their best team, W. Cramp, however, failed

[p. 33]

to turn up. This proved not to be all loss for a good substitute was obtained who took the centre half position and ... with the brothers Rowe on either side ... Trinity had a half back line that many a better club might envy.

Trinity suffered from their forwards ... their play ... lacked pace, cohesion, and dash. Several times they got near to scoring but ... the Christchurch defence was at its best. Individually, Barrett ... worked hard ... but it passed the comprehension of the spectators why he did not feed his outside right ... Poor little "Biggens" ... was absolutely uneffective. This was not his fault for ... he tried hard ... but obviously he should have been placed outside ... to have given the other four forwards a chance to play together. It would have been much better for Biggens to have been ... out on the touch line ... than L. H. Messent who ... would have been more ... able to cope with the opposing defence. Whenever he got the chance he rushed ... up fairly well, and ... he scored the only goal of his side.

[p. 34]

Harry Lansdown was mediocre ... and often had the ball taken away ... Arthur Jones tried hard but pace and smartness beat him.

Fred Handy in goal was good. One thing was very noticeable and that was his improved kicking. Once he should have been penalised for carrying but other than that he made no mistake. All three goals were unavoidable ... W. Fagan and Harry Jones and the centre half were each responsible for one ... when ... they should have passed back to the goal keeper ...

The match ended with a bombardment of the Trinity goal, but Mr Morgan had to give "time" ...

CHRISTCHURCH	3
TRINITY	1

122

TRINITY v. ST. GEORGES.
March 11th.

Playing at home, Trinity ... met with a crushing defeat. In the previous match at Raynes Park, Trinity won

[p. 35]

and it was generally anticipated that St. George's would seek to wipe off this defeat ... Trinity were represented by their best eleven with one exception ... , for Guy Barrett ... could not play, his place being taken by Harold Austin who ... can hardly compete ... with him in the central position.

The ground was very heavy, and ... the visitors were ... bigger and stronger men. Trinity's forward line was ... unable to make any progress against the St. George's halves ... throughout the whole game ...

St. George's won because they ... adapted their play to the condition of the turf.

ST. GEORGES.	4
TRINITY.	0

TRINITY v. WREN F.C.
March 19th.

The Wren Club failed to answer the secretary's communication.

[p. 36]

TRINITY v. LARCOM.
March 25th.1911

Playing at home but severely handicapped through the absence of W. Fagan, G. Barrett, H. Lansdown and H. Austin, Trinity lost what should have been an easily won game ... there was no excuse for the home side failing ... to ... draw ... The truth is that the forward line failed ... to take advantage of the hundred and one openings made for them.

During the ... first half Trinity kept the ball in their opponents territory ... the result of good work by the half backs, but ... the forwards could not score ... It must be admitted that the condition of the ground ... was very bad ... Biggins was much too slow in his passing, ... whilst L. H. Messent might have scored at least once ... C. Bedwell ... did remarkably well considering

[p. 37]

that he has only turned out twice this season. A quarter of an hour before time Trinity was two down, so R. S. Rowe decided to take the centre forward position, sending L. H. Messent to right back and W. Cramp outside right. This ... proved ... a good move for he tried to introduce a bit of dash into the attack. Unfortunately ... he had to work by himself and was well rewarded by scoring a brilliant goal absolutely unaided ... Larcom played no better football than at the first meeting at Beckenham Hill and had Trinity had their regular forward line out the result would have been very different.

LARCOM   2

TRINITY   1

WHY TIP THE KNIGHT OF THE SCISSORS?

During a talk amongst three subscribers to the "Angels' Voice" it was casually mentioned by two that they always give the barber an extra penny for a hair cut. For the income tax paying section of the community this habit is all very well but for "Voicites" to indulge in it is ridiculous.

The barber's wage is higher than that of an average young man so why make the gap wider? What is the reason for presenting a gratuity to the barber? – Because after he has chatted to a young fellow, brushed him down, helped him on with his coat and generally fussed around him, the budding Rockefeller has not the moral courage to walk out without slipping a penny into the waiting palm.

By refusing the tip one not only gains a penny, but what is more valuable still, one's stock of moral courage is added to.

ESAU[11]

[p. 38]

LIST

Time Limit:– Two days; for groups in brackets three days.

Mr. D. C. Messent
Mr. W. J. Messent
Lewis Messent

F. Rowe
H. Rowe
S. Rowe

---

[11]   Esau was a 'hairy man'. Genesis 27:11.

W. Crosley

F. York

C. Smith

H. Lansdown

W. Cramp
L. Snoswell

G. Harper

A. Holman
P. Shearer

G. Barrett

[p. 39]

F. Jones
A. Jones
H. Jones

F. Perkins

A. Carpenter

A. Austin
F. v. Rittershausen

C. Bedwell

Mr. C. Moxley

Mr. A. H. Evans

A. Marriott

H. Beagley

[added in pencil are]
H. J. Butcher
"F A B".

End of Volume I.

THE ANGELS VOICE

No. 7
ANNIVERSARY ISSUE
Editor: J. Godden
Sub-Editor: E. H. Bowler

[p. 1]

THE ANGELS VOICE.

Sat. Nov. 25.Number 7.
1911.
Anniversary Issue.

EDITORIAL.

Dear Readers,

It is just a year since for the first time we took up the Editorial pen, and it amuses us to remember with what trepidation the act was performed. We now wield it with the greatest pleasure and welcome it as an old friend. One reason for this change may be that our readers themselves have at last realised their responsibility in providing articles for publication, and have therefore made the Editor's task somewhat less laborious.

It has been our aim to make this a really good anniversary number, worthy of the bright periodical whose inception it recalls, and on looking over it for the last time, we do not feel that there is any need to apologise for it's quality, whilst so far it is certainly our largest issue.

We have been specially favoured in receiving an article from a former class member now in Switzerland, and our staff of artists (the cover artist in particular) have evidently been fully alive to the fact that they were working for a special number.

We thank all concerned for the help they have given and with a confident spirit we commit this our latest publication to your perusal, and, at some later date, when circumstances call for another special number, to your comment and criticism.

Ed.

[p. 2]

[Drawing of a puppy sitting on a woman's hat, with the hat box open behind him. He is happy. Signed:] E.T.J.
"ALWAYS MERRY AND BRIGHT"

[p. 3]

A JOURNALIST'S DAY.

It is bad form to talk shop and my only excuse for selecting a subject like this is that I know something about it and that my article will pass through the hands of a ruthless sub-editor. In Fleet Street you will find that the most widely accepted definition of a sub-editor is "a blue pencil wielding heathen who works inside a newspaper office and whose principle occupation is to get reporters by fair means or foul (mostly the latter) to do his work for him". I once asked a 'Daily Telegraph' man whether he was prepared to subscribe to a fund ... for the reclamation of sub-editor's. His reply was that that was an idiotic waste of money but if the scheme were altered to provide a crematorium for them, he would give generously.

Will you kindly imagine yourself taking a day's holiday from the daily task and spend a day with me in the City? We arrive shortly before 11 am., call in at a certain Lyon's depot, and take an accustomed seat beside one or two colleagues who have already got their "hot milk and a dash of coffee". In ten minutes we have discussed the list of financial company meetings for the day and possibly received an order ... to "cover" a meeting ... Then there is adjournment to the City branch office for final arrangements. They are just completed

[p. 4]

when ... a request comes from headquarters that instead of the dinner at Mansion House which we had been instructed to attend that night, we must join ... four others at a meeting ... addressed by Mr. Lloyd George at Holborn Town Hall.

It is now getting towards noon so we go to Winchester House, a large block of offices ... in Old Broad Street. A notice board ... bears the names of ... companies holding meetings there and selecting our 12 o'clock meeting – that of a rubber company – we sign our names on a list ... and take a seat ... facing the Chairman and directors. Sixty or seventy shareholders are present and we know ... that there is going to be trouble. The ... Chairman goes into a long apology and tries to explain how the board has been gulled, while the shareholders interject nasty remarks. As he tells them the property has been found to be miles from the place mentioned in the prospectus, that all the mahogany trees from which they were to get handsome profits were cut down ten years ago, and that the wild rubber ... cost more to collect than could be got for it in the London market, the atmosphere gets hotter. The Chairman plaintively states that the few rubber trees ... on the estate had been "tapped". "So have we" comes back ... from the other side of the table. And so the game goes on ... and then the meeting, being

[p. 5]

human and hungry, carries a motion for adjournment. We write up the thing carefully because the libel law is severe and juries are usually against newspapers.

We ourselves get ten minutes adjournment to "stoke up" with sandwiches and coffee and then turn up at our second meeting in the same building – that of a gold mine company – and soon we are revelling in a speech about levels, and drives and winzes[1] and ounces and dwts. to the ton with complaints about the demands of Australian labour, winding up with a complicated scheme for the re-arrangement of the various classes of capital. The dividend is 40% so there is not much trouble about adopting the directors report. Then we turn to a gas company meeting and hear a long discourse on the price of coal and residuals and the competition of electric light. By this time the afternoon is worn out and we adjourn to an A.B.C.[2] depot with a colleague or two for tea. The condensation of some of the meetings takes a lot of time but in the case of others ... it is better to call at a typewriting office and dictate it. Every proper name and every figure however, must be checked. We write up the reports ... wherever we happen to be, hand in the "copy", and so the first part of the days work is behind us.

It is now 6.45 pm. and a quiet half hour with a steak and chips and a Westminster Gazette[3] in Stewart's at Ludgate Circus

[p. 6]

arouses all the optimism within us.

At eight o'clock our "corps" of five sit together in front of the platform. The instructions are to give the Chancellor of the Exchequer "fully, first person and well trimmed." The last expression means leaving out all superfluous verbiage from which not one speaker in a thousand is exempt. It is decided that there shall be three minute turns first round, and five minute turns afterwards. When the roar of

---

[1] A winze is a shaft connecting two levels in a mine. *Oxford English Dictionary*.

[2] ABC or the Aerated Bread Company ran many cafés: <http://discovery.nationalarchives. gov.uk/details/rd/od27d92e-1eb8-4be5-9c54-20b5fca6bb1f>, accessed 23 Mar. 2015.

[3] *The Westminster Gazette* was a national newspaper, published 1893–1928: <http://www. bl.uk/reshelp/findhelprestype/news/diffnews/>, accessed 25 Mar. 2015.

cheers that greet Mr. Lloyd George have subsided and he commences his speech the first man begins to take his three minute turn. We take the watch on the table and see that he doesn't get more than his dose. Some time is lost while some interrupters are thrown out, but that is not counted in the "take". At the end of the three minutes there is a burst of cheering. We give the note-taker a nudge to stop. We then commence taking a shorthand note and the next man checks our three minutes. Meantime No.1. has commenced to write out his "take", in longhand, numbering the pages "A 1", "A 2", "A 3" etc. We number ours "B 1", "B 2", "B 3" etc, and so the thing goes on until the end of the speech. With only five in the corps the shorthand turns come again before we have finished writing out the first "take", but that does not matter so long as the numbering and lettering is properly carried out. In the second turn the speaker has warmed to his subject and has gathered speed. There must be no hesitation or mistakes now ... Excitement is fatal to good work and must be suppressed ...

[p. 7]

... The speaker suddenly drops into a colloquial style and it is difficult to hang on, but at last ... the five minutes turn is over. The writing up goes on ... and then the great speech closes. We leave a man behind to see whether anything happens during the latter part of the meeting and get back to the newspaper office. Each has to complete the writing up of his take and to draw up a summary of the principal points in the speech.

Soon after 11pm. We are crossing Blackfriars Bridge on a car[4] homeward bound, to find on arriving chez nous a letter of instruction to attend a public dinner on the following night. We have got back in good time because we were not dozing sufficiently hard to miss the Conductor's cry of "Water Lane!"[5]

Why not a morning ramble from Brixton to the White Horse.[6] I passed seven in one morning all making this pilgrimage to the goddess of economy.

...

[p. 8]

[Drawing of boy in bed heavily bandaged. Signed:] HR.
THE MORNING OF NOVEMBER 6TH.
"NEVER MIND! THE FIREWORKS WERE WORTH IT!"

---

4   Tramcar.
5   Brixton Water Lane is a turning off Brixton Hill, near Trinity.
6   The White Horse public house was situated a mile from Trinity on Brixton Road heading towards Kennington Oval.

[p. 9]

HAVE YOU?

Have you ever had a feeling
  That you've not a thing to say,
When the Editor comes stealing
  Down upon his helpless prey?

Have you ever felt exactly
  Like a rabbit 'fore a snake,
Whilst he tells you quite compactly
  How much copy you must make?

Have you ever been persuaded
  By his careless, easy laugh,
Hoping not to be degraded
  By a subtle paragraph?

Have you ever sat up thinking,
  Waiting for a bright idea,
Till you find your eyes are blinking
  And your head feels shocking queer?

Have you ever when despairing,
  Written off a page in haste
On some subject, hardly caring
  How much ink in blots you waste?

[p. 10]

Have you ever some time after
  Seen your writing scored with blue,
Whilst the Ed. with scornful laughter
  Says he cannot make it do?
                    I. Have.

(Not this time Mr. Contributor, Ed.)

                    T.L.H.C.

We are the "Angels" and our name we have carried with honour
from time immemorial, till now it has become famous. Our fair friends
on the other hand have always suffered under the reproach of being
nameless; they were nothing, they had no name. Now however, they
have seized upon the title given them in jest, and "Long Haired Chums"
they seem likely to remain for ever.

They intend to distinguish themselves and cover their communal appellation with glory by dint of toil and vigour at the noble game of hockey. They are enthusiastic and have even chosen them a sign to be embroidered on their shirts; – T.L.H.C.[7]

(TRINITY LONG HAIRED CHUMS)

A strange name for the club it is true, but if they refrain from naughty ways there is no reason why at some future age it should not become almost as respected as our own.

For report of their first business meeting see page [in pencil is added:] somewhere further on.

[p. 11]

[Drawing of train pulling out of station. Signed:] IM
Porter. (as train begins to move) "Here's your ticket Lady; four and tuppence it cost"
Flurried Passenger. There's Four shillings. Keep the tuppence for yourself.

[p. 12]

THE WORM TURNS.

An outburst from Master Snoswell.

Having promised to write my opinion of the Editor of "The Angels Voice", I will endeavour to put my opinions into words. First, I think the editor has forgotten that although an editor must have wit he <u>must</u> be a gentleman as well. It is <u>not</u> gentlemanly to write a paragraph on another's misfortune. I allude to Mr. M. In the Ed's opinion is it Mr. M's fault that when he speaks he cannot control himself, being very exciteable? [sic] Was it a great fault to get his papers mixed up? Again the hockey team being composed of girls, their hair is of course long. What right has the worthy Ed. to make remarks concerning their hair? Do they write articles about the Ed's curly hair or his face. I don't wish to be rude but ... I must say what I think. Then I should ... remind the Ed. about another article. In a witty article by J A G the Ed. with great condescension I was given a couplet in his (poem?) Not being a literary man I would call it a poem for want of a better name, although I think when the Ed. wrote it, he had been reading "Answers" and got the "Ditto" fever. What offended the Editor was me walking with a girl on a Sunday afternoon. Is it anything to do with him what I do? If I ... had to follow the Ed. example the only thing I should learn would be

---

[7]   Trinity Ladies Hockey Club must be the original spelling of the initials.

[p. 13]

"S W A N K". Everyone swanks and therefore I must have my share, but I think the Editor has more than his. If the Editor gave more attention to politeness and less to backbiting and mischievous sarcasm he would be more worthy of post.

THE TABLES TURNED.

Our little friend … is writing out of … annoyance and indignation and in consequence his utterances are childlike and quite at random. He starts well by proclaiming that he has kept a promise, … a sure indication of his disturbed state within. This is followed up by an indirect acknowledgement that we have the necessary wit, but then comes his first weak point. His words themselves are fairly true, an Editor should be a gentleman, and it would certainly be ungentlemanly to make sport of the misfortunes of others, but I defy him to point out a single instance of another's <u>misfortunes</u> being made the object of ridicule in this magazine. His pet grievance seems to be the treatment of Mr. Marriott's <u>mistakes</u>, and he wants to know if it were a great fault for him to get his papers mixed. Evidently he himself does not think so … To judge from appearances he never takes any interest in the afternoon's proceedings and doubtless the confusion pro-

[p. 14]

duced was to him a most welcome break in the monotony of an hour which must seem long and tiresome. From such a standpoint he regards comment upon a serious … error as ungentlemanly.

His protest on behalf of our good friends, the girls, is even more foolish … It is our right to do as we please so long as we do not wantonly hurt others and although some of the girls are very susceptible, … we do not think they greatly upset themselves when it was pointed out … that they had long hair. We now come to the crux of the whole matter. The publicity given to his own shortcomings has tinged his innocent young character … , hence this outburst. Doubtless it was very ungentlemanly … to call attention to the fact that he was making an absolute ass of himself, but he will see that we were right as the years add slightly to his present stock of wisdom …

But now for his last and most curious remark. If he were compelled to look to the Editor for instruction he could see a long course of studies in <u>SWANK</u>. As he is evidently a person of sound judgement, we will not dispute the point with him, but … the Editor could certainly show him to write better English, and … with … a quantity of carrots or other modish delicacies, might instil

[p. 15]

[Two photographs of boys, girls and teachers at an N.A.M. school in Shebin-El-Kom, Egypt, with Mr and Mrs Fairman.[8]]

[p. 16]

into him some of the rudiments of logic. But a good teacher should be willing to learn of his pupils, and accordingly I should be glad to know how ... to adopt a remarkable gait, half shuffle, half hop, and so to waddle ostentatiously to church, without SWANK. Again is it SWANK or poverty which prompts him to parade his coarse mop uncovered in all circumstances. Still again, will this unimpeachable youth inform us how ... to parade up and down the football field, sucking a pipe almost as big as his own empty head, without the action being stigmatised as SWANK.

NO Master Snoswell, this your first contribution to the mag. is only worthy of a small quibbling girl and we are afraid that too early and too constant intercourse with the softer sex has led you to adopt their most unlovely characteristic, a petty quarrelsome temper which it will take many years of steady company and the bottling up of much idiotic nonsense to eradicate ...

Ed.

On the preceding page are two pictures which show Mr. Fairman in ... his Missionary work ...

[p. 17]

[Drawing of a young man, in Elizabethan attire, holding a lute, and looking forlorn. Signed:] C.V.M. 5.11.1911.

[p. 18]

There are not many members of the class who remember the Nobles when they were a part of Trinity – it was before I came, for by that time they had already moved to Streatham ... Some time ago Alec Noble went out to Switzerland and the following article gives an idea of the political condition of the country he is living in.

J.G.

---

8   Walter Fairman and his wife served with the North Africa Mission.

[p. 19]

ZURICH AND THE SWISS.

I suppose most of my readers know where Zurich is, but for ... those who don't, it is ... in the north of Switzerland, not very far from ... the German State of Wurtemburg.[9] It is by far the most important town in Switzerland, although to a person coming from ... London it seems a town in minature [sic]. By this I mean that though the population is only 185,000 the town has its tramway service, electricity works and other corporations exactly like a big city. These points seem ... more remarkable when one compares the population of London, over seven millions, against 185,000.

Switzerland is noted ... for its beauty and Zurich has got its full share. Possessing a lake about 18 miles long by 1½ miles wide, with a background of the finest mountains in the world, it makes a beautiful picture. These Swiss lakes are very deep ... being the valleys of the mountains filled up with water.

Zurich has ... several large engineering firms and it is altogether a very business-like town. It is a great contrast to ... Lucerne, which must ... depend upon ... its beauty for its livelihood. Of course a great drawback to Zurich, and ... to all manufacturing towns in Switzerland, is the lack of seaports ... Switzerland has no sea-board, the

[p. 20]

nearest ports being Antwerp, Hamburg, and Genoa, and as the freight charges are heavy, owing to the high altitudes the railways [reach before they] can get to the coast, it makes entrance into business competition practically impossible. Add to this the lack of coal and then it is seen what a hard fight Switzerland has to become a manufacturing country. The only thing in the favour of the manufacturer is the lowness of wages.

Living in Zurich is not to be compared with living in London as owing to high Tariffs, several items of luxury are prohibitive. Here can be seen the other side of the question of Tariffs versus Free Trade. Nearly everything entering the country has a tax put on it, thereby making the use of Swiss goods absolutely necessary to the lower and middle classes, but at a high cost. Everything has to be judged by the Swiss standards of beauty. By this I mean that such articles as pictures, porcelain and everything which adds to the refinement of life are prohibited owing to their cost. One has ... a smaller outlook on life when in Switzerland. Everybody earning a salary of £100 or more has to pay a tax and when one considers that it is only possible to live

---

[9]   Now part of the state of Baden-Württemberg.

on 100fs. a month, it is rather severe to pay taxes. The cost of food is high, but that is counterbalanced to a great extent by the aptitude of the Swiss people in making use of such cheap articles of diet as rice and macaroni. Naturally, such foodstuffs are healthy enough, but ... cannot be said to be so sustaining as the English meal, or so it seems to me.

[p. 21]

After all ... until one has tried the living of differing countries one cannot say which is best. A Swiss would retaliate ... by saying the English meal is a heavy cumbersome affair and that the English ... eat too much. Clothes are very expensive, there being a heavy tax on cloth, and even corn has a small tax on it.

The Swiss life is rather ... monotonous ... Having to start work early in the morning and finishing late at night, there is not much time for improving oneself or pleasure. The general amusement seems to be sitting in the Cafes or Beer Houses and chatting. The number of beer houses in Zurich is amazing and would give the "reduction of licences" committee of England, much room for thought. In most small streets can be seen two or three beer houses, and some are practically next door to each other. However, credit must be given to the Swiss for their school system. The children have much longer hours than English children and seem to be taught very thoroughly. When the ordinary school curriculum is finished they are compelled to attend evening classes. The children generally learn two or three languages, but one must remember that it is absolutely necessary for a Swiss to speak at least French and German, as his country is divided into a French, a German, and an Italian portion.

The Englishman's life is much ... more comfortable than that of the Swiss, although it is true that he

[p. 22]

can have a wife and family on 100fs. (£4) a month. It is a very hard life. Even his English equal has a much better time for the simple reason that in England one can have, thanks to the so called "dumpling", many things which a Swiss who has lived all his life in Switzerland, has probably never seen, but which ... make life more cheerful. Swiss life ... seems ... mainly a question of work and sleep, and probably that is ... why so many ... get out ... into other lands where ... the outlook upon life is wider, and therefore contains more possibilities.

Conscription is in power here and that is ... bad .... It means taking a man away from his work at the age of 20 to learn militarism. With all the talk about the drill making a man more physically fit, there does not seem ... to be any great difference between the physical condition generally of Englishman and the Swiss. They are also keen gymnasts, but one can hardly agree with the Swiss who goes in for gymnastics and yet drinks enormous quantities of beer and smokes. It is hardly in accordance with our idea that to improve one's physical condition one must also look after the diet. Generally, the Swiss at 50 years of age, is, thanks to cheap beer, fat and lazy.

But … it is the Mountains … that tourists come to see …

A. Noble.

[p. 23]

[Two photographs – one badly fading of a young man and the other of 4 men sitting on the ground.]

[p. 24]

…

BUTCHER.
(See previous page)

We will confess that this photo puzzles me. What first caught my eye was the fob, and we at once looked for an evening suit to match, but could not find it. Possibly he is wearing the very latest thing in evening dress but even then we cannot account for the hat.

This hat is a remarkable article which occasionally brings him to church, but even though it does confer upon us this privilege we would willingly see it thrust into the dustbin. If only for the pain it inflicted when we first saw it we would take this revenge for our eyes still smart when we remember the optical shock we received on first acquaintance.

Time however must be left to do its work but we hope it will attack speedily … this hideous monstrosity.

[p. 25]

[Bright drawing of a man in a red jacket, with his back to the viewer, being questioned by an elderly woman who holds an envelope marked 'To The Editor, Angels Voice, London'.]

[Signed:] E.T.J.

Mistaken Identity.

Short-sighted Old Lady (to golfer lighting his pipe): "Lawks! you did make me jump young man. I thought you was the Pillar Box".

[p. 26]

LONDON'S OLDEST CHURCH.

No Cockney really knows London; he may know the situation of St. Paul's and might possibly recognise the Mansion House, but the quaint old-world corners he has never visited, and has often never heard of.

Such a spot is the church of St. Bartholomew the Great, and ignorance of it's position may be excusable, for it is remarkably well hidden. The fact that it cannot be seen from any thoroughfare is partly due to it's great age, for here ... the ground level gradually rises and leaves buried the remains of a former age. For instance, the successive destruction and re-building of houses, making up of roads and other works ... have covered Roman remains to a depth of about twenty feet. So it is with St. Bartholomew's, the ground round it has slowly risen ... so that now the church is standing in a pit at least six feet deep, and not having any high tower or high gabled roof, it is of course easy to miss.

The church itself is nothing from the outside ... but the little entrance court quite makes up for it. Here you have an exact type of the picturesque towns of the Continent. The quaint over-hanging houses leaning right against the church, and the trees rustling over the neglected tombstones, form a picture almost unique in London.

[p. 27]

[Two postcards of the interior of St Bartholomew's the Great.]

[p. 28]

Let us pass inside however, and ... we have one of the most beautiful pieces of Norman architecture still left in England. The colour is one of its great features. Everywhere is the mellow brown or grey of old stone, and that not always the same, for it seems to change with every passing cloud. First light and then dark, and then light gain, whilst on a fine evening it reflects with a sullen glow the fiery colour of the sunset.

As we wander round the aisles we shall be struck by the unusual shape of the church, the transepts being at the west instead of the east end of the nave. This is because we are in the choir only of what was ... a vast abbey. Originally the church covered the whole of the court we first passed along, and in those days the long rows of columns must have presented a beautiful vista.

It is only lately that the church has been restored to a regular plan. Not many years ago the Lady Chapel was a factory, whilst houses had been built right into the North Aisle, which at the same time sheltered a blacksmith's forge.

There are many monuments in the church but ... the most interesting is that of Rahere, the founder of the old abbey, and also of the hospital on the opposite side of the road. His tomb is a beautiful piece of Gothic work and though nothing now

[p. 29]

[Two more postcards of St Bart's – one of Rahere's tomb and the other an exterior view.]

[p. 30]

remains in it, the body of the old abbot once reposed there.

The building is a ... delight to those with some knowledge of the English styles, but none can fail to be impressed by the venerable calm of the place, whilst if you ... visit whilst a service is going on in the Lady Chapel, you can sit in the main church, listening to the drowsy murmur of the priest's voice, and then, if you have any imagination ... , the place will once again become peopled with devout old monks and you will be transported ... back to the middle ages. St. Bartholomew's is quite separated from the busy life around, and as you enter you ... feel the influence of the old world charm which still clings to it.

As a parting word I would remind my readers that from Holborn Viaduct up Giltspur Street, to this medieval treasure is only five minutes walk ...

J. Godden.

[p. 31]

[Drawing of a young woman's face and shoulders set to one side, with her eyes closed. Signed:] C.V.M. 5.11.1911.

[p. 32]

"ODE TO A CARBUNCLE"

I'm sure I never shall forget
　　The fateful day when first we met;
Your presence was the beastly cause
　　Of keeping me – you wretch! – indoors.

Though you were very shy at first
　　(I wished ten thousand times you'd burst)
You slowly swelled through five long days
　　And tried my poor old roof to raise.

My vision you in time impaired,
  I don't believe you ever cared;
For though I hoped you'd soon desist
  You brought your brother to my wrist.

A wretched day and sleepless night
  With agony my teeth shut tight;
Through a Sabbath day you never ceased
  To swell and pulsate – Oh! You beast!

But then a night of reckoning came,
  You'd played enough your little game,
And quickly did I end the strife
  Assisted by the surgeon's knife.

[p. 33]

Your like I trust I ne'er shall meet,
  No more my head you'll thund'rous beat;
And last of all I hope my trunk'll
  Always flout you – you CARBUNCLE ! ! !

A.P.A.

THE INVINCIBLE THREE

L et me tell you of three brothers,[10]
A ll three members of the team,
T hree who play as well as others
E ven though they lazy seem.

A ccidents can't be avoided.
L ittle man the sport of fate
W ill be ever made it's plaything.
A ccidents <u>may</u> make them late.
Y et if they don't come at all
 S hould we heed their careless drawl?

"L ook however it was" they say,
A nd true there was a little rain
T hough others thought it fit to play –
E nough! – Don't stay away again.

---

[10]   The Jones brothers. See *AV* 3 (Jan. 1911), 31.

[p. 34]

REPORT OF ANNUAL MEETING.

On Thursday, November 16th, was held the fourth Annual Meeting of the Trinity Bible Class. It was the most interesting that had so far been held and several important resolutions were passed. At 7.30pm, the members began to arrive and ... light refreshments were indulged in till 8.30, when all assembled in the larger room and the meeting commenced. Mr. Lansdown, our president was in the chair and 25 members were present. The proceedings opened with prayer and then the Secretary presented his report on the years work. There were several points that deserve mention, especially that our membership has dropped from 33 to 30. The report was so suggestive that on the recommendation of Mr. Messent it was unanimously agreed to hold an afternoon's conference on the many points it contained, especially on the failure of the attempt to draft the elder boys of the Sunday School up to the class.

The Treasurer's report followed and it was extremely satisfactory to note that despite our slightly decreased numbers our receipts had risen. The balance in hand up to date was over £1 and the prospective expenditure did not seem heavy. The Mission Treasurer's report was less satisfactory and he made the rather humiliating remark that even on the Sunday when Mr. Fairman took the class, the collection was no higher than 1/8d. He concluded with the extremely popular suggestion that a

[p. 35]

closer connection should be kept with Mr. Fairman and Mr. Rowe[11] by sending some portion of the weekly collections direct to them. This suggestion produced considerable discussion and Mr. J. Godden moved and Mr. F. York seconded that the Money still in the hands of the Treasurer and all future collections should be sent to Mr. Rowe and Mr. Fairman. Mr. D. C. Messent moved an amendment which was seconded by Mr. W. Cramp that as we had really been paying into a London Missionary Society box, the money still in hand should go to the Society and any fresh arrangements should only come into force with the new year. This was agreed to. It was then proposed that future collections should go entirely to Mr. Rowe and Mr. Fairman, but Mr. Messent again moved an amendment that some portion should still go to the L.M.S. This was carried although the actual proportions were left for settlement later on.

---

[11]   John Rowe.

These reports were all adopted unanimously and the meeting turned to an affair of a totally different nature. It is over a year since our dear companion, Fred Berry passed away, and ... we have obtained a fine enlargement of one of his photos. At this point the photograph was shown ... and whilst the class stood up, the secretary hung it against the wall, a most impressive silence being maintained.

After a short pause, Mr. D. C. Messent rose and in a few suitable remarks pointed that although the late Secretary had been with us for the past month or so, unfortunately it was not

[p. 36]

a permanent return and we were soon to lose him again. He then asked him on behalf of the class, to accept two volumes of Morley's Life of Gladstone[12] as a token of appreciation of the many services rendered to the class and of his untiring efforts to further it's success. Mr. J. Godden replied, thanking the class ... and assuring them that the two volumes would constitute his most valued possessions.

The election of officers was now dealt with. For some time the position of Prayer Meeting Secretary had been filled by the Class Secretary, but Mr. W. Cramp was now elected to act in that capacity. All the other officers were unanimously re-elected and the positions are now filled as follows: -

President.	Mr. M. Lansdown.	Mission. Tres. Mr. H. Rowe.
Leader.	Mr. D. C. Messent.	Prayer Meet. Sec. Mr. W. Cramp.
Secretary.	Mr. R. S. Rowe.	Auditors Messrs Crosley & Barrett
Treasurer.	Mr. L. Messent.	Organist. Mr. C. Moxley.[13]

All officers except the Organist and Auditors have seats on the Committee, EX OFFICIO, but these may be elected to that position. The Committee is composed of the officers and the additional members, and the following names were proposed:– Mr. C. F. Bedwell, Mr. E. H. Bowler, Mr. W. Crosley and Mr. G. Barrett.

Messrs W. Crosley and G. Barrett, the Auditors, were duly elected.

The meeting was here thrown open for suggestions and remarks and Mr. Godden took the opportunity of pointing out the dilapidated condition of the wall paper. He suggested that as a large

---

12   John Morley's *The Life of William Ewart Gladstone* first appeared in 1903 and was regularly re-issued.
13   Given the room's size, the 'organ' was probably a harmonium.

balance was in hand, we might invite the Literary Society to bear half the expense with us of re-papering the room. The chairman informed the meeting that a promise had been made to see to the decorations ... but possibly not for another year or more. Under these circumstances the Secretary was instructed to communicate with the Literary Society and to find their views on the matter.

Whilst the discussion on the state of the room was being held Mr. Godden rose to make a few remarks on the prints which disfigure our walls. He pointed out their very obvious unsightliness and ... that to the majority of the members present they meant nothing. Under the influence of the Chairman who in this case seemed somewhat biassed [sic], several members stated that they derived great inspiration from the prints in question and thought there could be no better way of filling the frames. Mr. Godden enquired whether ... a few good views of the spots we have rambled through would not be far more interesting and fill some purpose in giving another tie ... to the class unity. The uproar which one or two disorderly and hypocritical members now made caused the matter to be dropped.

The question which aroused the greatest interest during the evening was brought forward last of all and occupied some considerable time. Mr. Crosley wanted something definite to be settled with regard to the past and future copies of the magazine.

[p. 38]

He proposed that all future annual numbers should be produced absolutely as the class property and kept in the class locker for reference. The objections to this were brought forward and it was also pointed out that the enormous inducement offered would doubtless make the Editor extremely anxious to go on producing. Mr. Messent remarked that the members of the magazine fraternity had paid their threepences and in return had read the magazine and in the natural course of events they should return to the producer. He thought it would be the most convenient and practical plan if they were permanently left in charge of the Editor, who expressed his willingness to let the subscribers have any particular copies for a reasonable time.

Before any motions were brought forward it was pointed out that only about half of the magazine subscribers were present and that as the magazine was not strictly about business, due notice of a meeting should be given. Some members still agitated for an immediate decision but on the vote of the subscribers present the matter was referred back until a special meeting should have been called. It was settled however, that the Editor would supply to the class a copy of the report of the annual meeting as it appeared in the magazine as often as the annual number was produced.

There were no further matters brought forward for discussion and Mr. Lansdown closed the meeting with prayer.

[p. 39]

[Drawing of a man's stern face within a heart.]
[The artist's monogram appears to read:] HEC
    Jealousy

[p. 40]

MY HAT!!

To be chanted in a thin squeaky voice.

I wear a funny little thing
    Upon my foolish head;
But while in church I sweetly sing
    My heart is filled with dread.

For others do not seem to like
    My hat of gaudy green:
One even called me "swanky tike",
    I think it's very mean.

And why should I whose heart is gay,
    Dress up in sober black?
I'll wear my trilby, though it may
    Put some eyes on the rack.

Its shape is quite the proper style,
    The dent is simply fine,
And though you walk for many a mile,
    You'll see no hat like mine.

And so although you others rave
    About my lovely thatch,
I'll set to work the cash to save,
    To buy a suit to match.

                        "Harry"[14]

---

[14]   Probably Harry Butcher. See *AV* 7 (Nov. 1911), 24.

SOMETHING FOR THE FRENCH SECTION.

Je suis ce que je ne suis pas; je ne suis pas ce que je suis.
Employez suivee et être et remarquez les estranges choses que la
phrase pourrait dire.

[p. 41]

[Photograph of Trinity Ladies Hockey Club – 17 young ladies.]

[p. 42]

[Drawing of a mischievous young boy wearing a top hat sitting on
luggage with a basket labelled "Jones Minor". Signed:] M. Gladwin.
[Above the signature is a deleted alternative name – now unreadable.
Below the signature is a deleted date – 20.1.06]
THERE ARE MOMENTS WHEN ONE WANTS TO BE ALONE.

[p. 43]

[11 photographs of Bible Class members.]

THERE·ARE·MOMENTS·
WHEN·ONE·WANTS·TO·
BE·ALONE·

[p. 44]

STICKYBACK PORTRAIT GALLERY.

1   <u>Mr. D. C. Messent</u>, our leader is prominent in almost every undertaking at Trinity. He is the guiding spirit of the class; to him we owe the institution and organisation of our cricket and football clubs whilst in rambles or any other form of open air amusement something is wanting unless he is present. He is an enthusiastic and practical supporter of the magazine and our gallery is greatly honoured by the inclusion of his photograph.

2   <u>Mr. G. Barrett</u> was the first Secretary of the class. He has at times been captain of both cricket and football clubs whilst in his earlier days

D. C. Messent

he was a keen gymnast. An injury at the latter pastime has inflicted on him compulsory but we hope temporary rest.

3   Mr. J. G. Godden is the late Secretary and the Editor, and as he himself is writing these paragraphs he won't say anything more.

4   Mr. R. S. Rowe is the class secretary and the captain of the football club. He is a great walker, and if reminded often enough becomes a welcome contributor to these pages.

5   Mr. C. Bedwell has unfortunately for us left the class to take up work downstairs. He still however maintains a very close connection with us and has the honour of being one of the oldest original members of the class downstairs.

6   Mr. W. Crosley has a genius for making treasurers uncomfortable he also has the gift of making everybody who walks with him uncomfortable, except Mr. R. S. Rowe.

[p. 45]

[Nine photographs of Bible Class members.]

J. G. Godden

[p. 46]

7 Mr. H. Rowe is a crack bowler. He is fairly lazy as regards the magazine.

8 Mr. L. Messent has lately been perplexing the auditors with his accounts for he is the treasurer. Nevertheless he fulfils his post satisfactorily and is a keen member.

9 Mr. C. Moxley serves us every Sunday at the organ. His chief hobby is reffing for the girls. His nickname is "Major".

10 Mr. W. Cramp has long been connected with the class but has not long been a regular member. He is as enthusiastic on all class affairs as anyone could wish.

11 Mr. A. H. Evans turns up at class as often as possible and invariably turns up if there is anything resembling a ramble. He has a mania for cheap travelling and big railway stations.

12 Mr. E. H. Bowler acts as the sub. to the magazine editor and as you will probably guess from his puckered face is a punster.

13 Mr. H. Lansdown is now assisting Mr. Bedwell in arrangements for the senior boys as regards sports and club evenings.

14 Mr. F. Jones recalls very old memories. My first recollection of him is as a short haired little Frenchman straight from Paris, but before that, in his English childhood he was a regular attender and now he is a keen supporter of the class and magazine.

15 Mr. F. Perkins has long been connected with the class. In his early days he was a sweet songster but now he is a songster of another class. Known by "Uncle", "Irk" or "Tec".

[p. 47]

[Nine photographs of Bible Class members.]

[p. 48]

16 Mr. A. Austin although not a member of the class is very closely connected. He regularly fills a page of the mag.

17 Mr. F von Rittershausen we never see at class for some unearthly reason, although we hope to some day. He it was who made the boxes for the mag "Besten Dank".

18 Mr. F. Butcher has now been with us for some time but owing to his awkward hours is often prevented from attending.

19 Mr. H. Hayman is a dark horse as we found out in the mile race last summer.

20 Mr. F. York is one of our "lads", but all the same that need not stop him from patronising the class football team instead of an outside lot.

21 Mr. F. Morse is still to be found in his corner. If he's not careful he will wear that chair out with his constant sitting.

22 Mr. E. Munro has the welcome power of raking up drawings for the mag.

23 Mr. C. Cloak is another dark horse.

24 Mr. F. Biggins is a successful graft from the Sunday School. He is a useful footballer and seems likely to serve well in the future.

25 Mr. F. Rowe is another sweet songster or at any rate was recently.

26 Mr. L. Snoswell is a severe critic but nothing else.

27 Mr. L. Shearer we welcome for himself and on account of his brother.

28 Mr. C. Smith is coming on. We always promised that he would.

29 Mr. L. Jones will we think support the class as far as he is able.

[p. 49]

LOST.!
[Drawing of an armed crusader.]
   C.B's trumpeter!!!

149

It is feared that he may have died, of grief, as his late master refused his services.

R.I.P.

[p. 50]

OUR LONG HAIRED CHUMS AT BUSINESS.

The Ladies Hockey Club held on Thursday, 14th. September, their first business meeting of the 1911–1912 season. Matters of the gravest importance were to be discussed and all members … resolved to be present … in spite of any sacrifice punctuality might entail.

The meeting was fixed for 8pm. at "Maxton",[15] and by 8.25pm. three … enthusiastic members had arrived. As the evening wore on more members dropped in till the total reached eighteen. But long before this all trivial matters such as election of officers, subscription and rules had been settled and only matters of a more vital nature were left for discussion. The question … was What should they wear? The club colours are white and mauve, the predominating colour of course being the darker. (The colours … have been changed from the white and blue they borrowed from us last season; presumably these did not suit their complexions.) They all agreed to wear cream shirt blouses with a mauve badge (T.L.H.C.) and mauve ties, but the question of the skirt was far more difficult to decide. Some said they would not mind the bottoms being two feet from the ground whilst the opposite party pleaded (happily in vain) for a complete screen from masculine eyes. A middle course was adopted, and eight inches will be the amount of ankle visible.

[p. 51]

For a lengthy interval the meeting now gave itself over to that most enjoyable of occupations – buying the material for their dresses. A roll of cloth was produced and Miss Johnston was … cutter in chief. Here, however, an unforeseen difficulty arose. The meeting was being held in the drawing room which … does not boast a dressmakers bench, so … the cloth was rolled along the floor. Then the members who … are always so … dignified, gave way to their primeval instincts and wriggled ingloriously on the carpet, … pretending to assist. In these days of conflicting reports it is difficult to say who these squirmers were, but some likely names can be supplied on application to the Editorial office.

The members … insisted on a tape measure being used, hoping we supposed that it would get stretched in use. Vain hope! It was of the

---

15   The Messent family home, 16 King's Avenue.

toughest and Miss Johnston used it as to the manner born. Her cutting gained universal approval whilst her faultless judgement bordered on the miraculous. The lanky ones got long pieces according to their lankiness; for those admirably proportioned suitable lengths were cut, whilst the dumpy ones received proportionate pieces at proportionate prices. We learn that the middle class boasted an extremely limited membership, whilst "dumpy" was claimed by almost all present. Tennis apparently has failed to keep them even reasonably fit during the summer months.

[p. 52]

[Two faint photographs – Alfred P. Austin diving into a swimming pool and Trinity's harvest festival.]

[p. 53]

The style of headgear was not definitely settled, but Poke Bonnets[16] seemed to enjoy the greatest popularity. For the ... reader ... these look like inverted jelly bags, if this does not call them up ... , you must see them for they resemble nothing else on earth.

The meeting was speedily brought to a conclusion by shutting up the shop. We hear however that a committee meeting was held in the following week – a senseless proceeding it seems, for ... there could be no further business to discuss.

MR. A. AUSTIN.

Not many of us could recognise our friend in his scant attire and graceful attitude but some who have witnessed his diving would not have been mystified for an instant. The Photographer has succeeded in catching him in a really excellent "Swallow Dive". Several ... readers may recognise the swimming pond shown, the others ought to make its acquaintance as soon as the water is warm enough for their tender skins.

The ... Harvest Festival ... . the decorations were pronounced to be a greater success than in any previous year.

---

[16]   A bonnet with a projecting brim, traditionally worn by women of the Salvation Army.

[p. 54]

RARE METALS.
(AND RARE WORDS. Ed.)

The discovery of Radium in 1898 by Mme. Curie, attracted public attention to a series of substances, viz. the rare metals which had hitherto occupied the interest and attention of scientists only. The great price of Radium (£750,000 per ounce) and the remarkable properties of this substance cause it to be of popular interest. The enormous cost is easily accounted for ... a "rich" ore contains only about one ounce of the substance in 140 tons. The fact that it has been possible to separate this infinitesimal quantity is an eloquent testimonial to the care ... exercised by the discoverer.

This marvellous substance possesses properties which would seem fictitious, e.g. the rays of light emitted by Radium can penetrate three inches of lead, and the writer has, by means of this substance, seen a sixpence which was placed behind two copper coins. These rays have a very powerful effect on the skin, and cause burns ... most difficult to heal. The use of Radium in the treatment of Cancer appears to be in the experimental stage only, although ... it will destroy rodent ulcers. Sir Robert Ball ... stated that if he had only a pound of Radium in the room, it would be sufficient to kill every member of the audience ... [17]

[p. 55]

If it were possible to get a pound of this substance (one scientist has stated that he doubts whether there is a thimbleful in the world) and to suitably use the energy stored up, it would be possible to drive an Atlantic liner for a very long period.

There are several other rare metals which been brought before the public notice ... on account of their application in the Arts. Osmium, Ruthenium, Tantalum are now largely used in the manufacture of electric bulb lamps, displacing the older filaments which were made of paper and not platinum as is popularly supposed. Osmium is the heaviest known substance, being heavier than either platinum or gold, and about twice as heavy as lead; one cubic foot would weigh more than half a ton.

Gold, although not a rare metal from the scientific standpoint, would be classified in this category by the majority of our readers. An ounce of gold can be drawn into a wire fifty miles long, whilst gold leaf has been obtained of such fineness that 280,000 sheets would only be one inch in thickness. The textbooks state that gold is extracted by "washing" and ... purified by "parting". This may account for the

---

[17] Sir Robert Stawell Ball FRS. See *ODNB*.

scarcity of the substance among our readers, none of whom would ever try to purify it by "parting". Palladium, a metal allied to platinum, has the remarkable property of absorbing about 900 times its own volume of Hydrogen.

[p. 56]

The more popularly known "Palladium" absorbs Gold, silver or copper.

Platinum has been extensively used recently on account of its resistance and non-rusting properties. Its use in Jewellery will probably be restricted, as it will not take a very high polish and resembles dull silver. The price of this metal is now about three times that of gold. It is largely used in the manufacture of electric lamps and in dentistry. Alloyed with Iridium, … it forms a very hard substance and is used for the tips of fountain-pen nibs. On account if its unvarying nature and resistance to rust, weather etc., the standard weights and yard measure of this country are made of this alloy.

Coloured fires[18] have been rather in evidence recently and the names of the substances used in their production may prove of interest. Crimson is produced by Strontium, Green by copper or Thallium, Lilac by Potassium and Yellow by Sodium, in the form of common salt.

The fact that gases … such as Argon, Neon, Helium, Krypton and Xenon exist in the air, in addition to the well-known Oxygen and Nitrogen may be startling, but when it is remembered that the proportions vary from one per cent. for Argon, to one part in 170 million for Xenon, free breathing may again be indulged in.

[p. 57]

Since 1850, twenty two new elements have been discovered, some of which have been designated:– Dysprosium, Gadolinium, Gallium, Neodymium, Praseodymium, Rubidium, Samarium, Scandium, Lutecium, [sic] Thulium and Ytterbium, but these are of very rare occurrence, and are of little or no practical use, save for tormenting students in their examinations.[19]

H.R.[20]

---

[18] Chemists used a substance's colour in a flame to identify its constituents. *Oxford Dictionary of Chemistry*, ed. J. Daintith (6th edn, Oxford, 2008).

[19] These elements were identified before 1900 with the exception of Lutetium (as it is now spelt), discovered in 1907. *Oxford Dictionary of Chemistry*.

[20] Harry Reeves.

EJACULATORY CYRIL.

When he goes to fight the Tory
　With his hands all red and gory
And his napper crowned with glory
　From the strife on battle field.

Or persuading the elector;
　Then his words are far corrector.
Better chosen and selector
　Than those of the Grecian schools.

But in peace when life is easy
　And trousers have a crease, he
Learns a set of soft and greasy
　Phrases for the Football Field.

"Now then Sonny!" "Buck up Laddie!"
　Shouts this hoary bearded daddy,
Making everyone feel mad e-
　Nough to throw him to the Bulls.

(Pardon Cyril! We mean wild buffalos. Ahem!)

[p. 58]

F O O T B A L L.

An article by our serious and sober captain

The prospects for the present season a month ago were like those of the younger son of the younger son of a costermonger's donkey – distinctly gloomy. But now everything is changed. The old dog has ... a new lease of life. His blood is up ... proudly he sniffs the air. With bristling hairs, ears cocked, stubby tail erect, and teeth bared he plunges into the fray and victory is his.

Bow-wow! Let 'em all come !!

Since last season Trinity has lost three of its best players, G. Barrett, W. Fagan and F. Handy, and at the beginning of the present season it seemed ... it would be difficult ... to raise a team. However, R. Chippindale and P. Coomber ... have turned out to be very useful centre forward and half back respectively, and with Mr. Reeves coming to our aid ... when our new goal-keeper, A. P. Austin was injured, the team has done much better than anticipated. Of the six matches played four have been won and two lost. The first match v. Clapham Crusaders was lost 2–0 and three men did not turn up because it was raining. Think of it! ... Salute the three wise men and then expire. Our forwards,

[p. 59]

... assisted by one of the backs, are playing quite as good, if not better football than last season, although the two partners of the wing men are still apt to pass when they should shoot. The halves have improved somewhat and as the backs have not been fully extended yet, an accurate opinion of their ability to keep out the opposing forwards cannot be given, but I should say there is likely to be a weakness in this department. The team has been served by three men in goal but ... Trinity should always be able to rely on ... a good goal keeper.

On the whole the prospects of the team are good ...

R. S. Rowe.

I tell a tale of maidens three,
Kathleen Avis and Girlee
Who each in turn successively
Captured the heart of A.H.E.
The first he met upon the sea,
The second he dandled on his knee,
The third we really didn't see.
We're quite surprised at A.H.E.

Copy supplied my Miss. M.V.[21]

[p. 60]

SIGN PLEASE!

You are allowed two days each for reading the magazine, whilst the groups in brackets must not exceed three days together. Please try to get it round by Christmas.

Mr. D. C. Messent
" L. Messent
" W. Messent
Mr. A. H. Evans

R. S. Rowe
H. Rowe
F. Rowe

---

[21] Madge Vale.

W. Crosley

F. York

C. Smith

W. Cramp
L. Snoswell

A. Austin
F. V. Rittershausen
E. H. Bowler

F. Jones
H. Jones
A. Jones

A. Carpenter

G. Barrett
A. Holman
F. Perkins
F. Butcher
H. Butcher
C. Bedwell
Mr. C. Moxley

[Silhouette of a hook-nosed old woman.]
[The artist's monogram appears to read:] HEC
The Landlady

No. 8

ANGELS VOICE

SUMMER NUMBER
EDITOR: J. GODDEN

[p. 1]

[p. 2]

THE ANGELS' VOICE

No. 8.July. 1912.Special Summer Number.
Five Copies.

EDITORIAL

Dear Readers,
The Trinity reading public (us) much prefers the Editor's articles to all others and to this end it invariably refrains from sending in any of its own.

This issue is almost full of his work, and however good that may be for the mag, it is very bad for the editorial. He gets writer's cramp so badly, that on this page, ... always written last, it is a wonder that you can read the scribble.

With our last jerky strokes we implore that this issue may be read quickly and the pages turned carefully, for you all see a copy twice, and the binding is somewhat experimental.

Ed.

[p. 3]

LEADER'S LETTER.

"MAXTON"
July 3rd. 1912.

Dear Fellow-members,
Since the last issue ... , we as a Class have much to be thankful for, because in every branch of our work, progress must be reported.

It is pleasing to note how ... those who have recently joined us are entering into our fellowship, and we are anxious that they should share to the full the friendship that exists amongst us.

It is ... vital ... that we ... have no misconceptions concerning ideal friendship; we must be on our guard lest we mistake for friends those who in reality are our enemies.

"The friendships of the world are oft
Confederacies in vice, or leagues of pleasure:
Ours has severest virtue for its basis,
And such a friendship ends not but with life."[1]

---

[1] From Joseph Addison, *Cato, A Tragedy* (1713), Act III Scene i.

True friendship is, therefore, not a thin, superficial thing ... that leads into useless frivolities and utter waste of precious time, but rather it is the knitting together of hearts in a fine sympathy and affectionate regard for one another's welfare.

[p. 4]

True friendship signifies service; it really requires it. Affectionate regard must not be limited to mere sentiment but must be seen in actions. As friends we demand of one another not kind looks nor mere professions but rather deeds and oftentimes deeds of real sacrifice.

"He loved me well; so well he could but die
To show he loved me better than his life;
He lost it for me –"

Again the best friends are those who stimulate each other to do good, those who are as our Brotherhood[2] Hymn puts it:–

"Leagued for service and salvation
Lover for each and all!"[3]

Let us be very thankful that ... that this type of friendship is not unknown amongst us; but let us also be frank and ask ourselves if there is as much of it as there should be? Is there not a real danger that the other sort may make its appearance to our detriment? Of course real friendship is a slow grower and it may ... take a long time before it can develope [sic] into a strong and helpful bond, but are we on the right road to these things?

The cloak of friendship is oftentimes of such poor stuff that you can easily see through it, and underneath

[p. 5]

... is hindrance and a bias in the wrong direction.

There is nothing more dangerous than a friend selected without discretion, for a ruined life is an almost certain consequence. Our aim should be to find a fellow of real worth, ... in whose company we find true companionship and health enjoyment, and then stick to him, never letting go unless those virtues which at first attracted us should cease.

---

[2]   The Brotherhood Movement began in the late nineteenth century in the English Midlands. It appealed especially to Congregationalists but was interdenominational, with the Baptists John Clifford and F. B. Meyer and the Clapham-based Labour MP Arthur Henderson among its supporters. In 1913 Silvester Horne was president of the National Brotherhood Council. Its social gospel was revealed as shallow by the First World War. W. B. Selbie (ed.), *The Life of Charles Silvester Horne* (1920), 299; J. C. G. Binfield, *So Down to Prayers: Studies in English Nonconformity 1780–1920* (1977), 211–12.

[3]   Messent appears to have misquoted the hymn 'Hail our Brotherhood foundation!'. The last two lines of the refrain are: 'League of service and salvation, Lover for each and all!' *The Fellowship Hymn-Book* (4th edn., n.d.), hymn 30.

With these ideas just briefly enumerated shall we … test our own experience and see how far short we are of this high aim. We all desire that the Y.M.B.C. shall continue to be … noted for its fine comradeship, – then let us studiously set ourselves to check any alien spirit which might spoil this feature.

By the time that this issue has completed its circuit, the winter session will be fast approaching: May I appeal to all to do their best to make this the finest session we have ever had. We want still further developement [sic] … and if all will set to work with a will, then indeed, we are assured of a great time.

Very sincerely yours,
D. C. Messent.

[p. 6]

THE RAMBLE.

Mr. D. C. Messent.	E. H. Bowler.	C. Smith.
R. S. Rowe	F. York.	H. Rowe.
J. Godden	L. Fouracre.	H. Lansdown.
Mr. A. H. Evans.	C. Bedwell	L. Bedwell.
Mr. C. Moxley.	W. Cramp.	P. Coomber.
G. Harper.	N. Bedwell.	N. Yates.
	L. Jones.	J. Habergrutz.

A crowd is something more than the sum of its units.

This is a fairly recent … philosophical discovery, and its truth is amply demonstrated by ourselves. Taken individually we are not such a bad lot; in fact, we are a most charming, engaging, respectable, and entirely desirable group of beings. But on Bank Holiday, May 27th. it was … evident that we were all enthused with some spirit other than that in which we go about our everyday affairs. Whit Monday was a day of music, song and dance, and such strenuous, exercise, that a continental friend was led to exclaim on the following day, "Z'ey not walk, z'ey runs".

On a ramble in which 20 hearties participate you will expect a striking collection of sticks, and must not be surprised if amongst them there is at least one incongruity. As we write these words, the form of the

[p. 7]

great nabob, Rajah Lansdown, rises up before us. His was a stick so shiny, so slender and refined that you were quite certain that its daintily mounted handle, adorned with Eastern tracery, would never mix in such rough sports as golf with stones for balls, or hockey, in which the chief aim was to smash the cokernut [sic][4] doing service.

Once at Boxhill it did not take long to strike up, and before five minutes had passed the venerable old reproach of "lagging on behind" was hurled at a gaudy figure some distance in the rear. This figure we shall all remember. Pure art and unalloyed does not often go stalking over the countryside. The hat was a cast off "Evan's [sic] Ordinary" raked out for the occasion. The tie was the badge of a hated political creed. The suit itself was fairly respectable, except that we never saw the jacket or waistcoat buttoned up. His mackintosh was rolled up and slung across his back, whilst last and most striking of all, his P U T T E E S, of which more anon.

Our direction was taking us over Ranmore Common, and the post office with its minerals was the objective. Just outside is a pleasant grassy space, the scene of a memorable performance by Messrs. York and Bowler.

[p. 8]

The strains of distant music came floating through the trees and these two irrepressible spirits began to kick their heels up into the air just the same as all other lambkins always have done and we suppose always will.

Down the hill in front of the Post Office, across the Railway, over two fields, and then, in some mysterious manner, the "lagger on behind" found himself the centre of a ring of "Angels". It was his P U T T E E S. We wanted to know why he wore them? ... What was the matter with his dainty calves? But not a ... word of explanation could we obtain. It was apparently no use prolonging the fun and so we resumed our way, disturbing many a spooning couple with groans of execration.

We called a halt for dinner just near a little cottage where drinks might be procured. As usual, a mutton chop was smelt in the vicinity. During the time allotted to stoking up we were serenaded by E.H.B. and the Major. No one ... will ever forget their expressive rendering of "One man went to mow". Unfortunately they were disturbed by a report from the drink shop that milk and sodas had failed.[5]

"What" said the Major, "No more sodas?"

---

[4] One of a number of alternative spellings for coconut cited in the *Oxford English Dictionary*.
[5] This could mean soda water but more likely, given the context, fruit-flavoured drinks. *Oxford English Dictionary*.

[p. 9]

"We must investigate" said E.H.B., and so they went.

We waited ten minutes and at last they re-appeared. But what a change! If there were no more sodas there was evidently something liquid left, and the two stalwarts came struggling up the road filled to bursting point, whilst the Major seemed unnaturally gay. A voice from the feeders cruelly remarked that if the Major once got the taste for drink he would surely come home "tight" every morning.

Our route lay through a park, which being private ... we behaved. From the Park we tramped to Friday Street,[6] and although it was but two o'clock, some old women were already clamouring for tea. After a rest, however, we pushed on and blindly trusted to our guide to bring us to the delectable place where drinks and food might be procured. He said he would take us over Leith Hill, but thank goodness we took the matter into our own hands or we should still be wandering aimlessly ... in the vicinity of Dorking. Every three minutes we raised the cheerful sound of "One, two, three". At last we reached the Hill and after a short halt for more drinks, we made our way down the

[p. 10]

precipitous slopes to Coldharbour.[7] It was there that the Mad Hatter of the party, the Gentleman of the Yay! Yay! Yay! ... who would rush on in front of everybody else, showed to the assembled crowd how cheaply cokernuts [sic] could be obtained ... Wonderful!! Marvellous!!! this subtle mind gloried in the fact that he had actually become the possessor of three for 9d.

Tea at the Village Inn at 4 o'clock was simply scrumptious. That place we shall always remember as owned by the prince of Caterers. In the Inn Yard we found everything prepared for us, and Messrs. Messent, Lansdown and Cramp who respectively acted at the pot, were kept busy. During tea time some ducklings came to investigate the uproar, and it was R.S.R. who brilliantly suggested that the fluffy little ball on the off side had a waddle just like Wally.[8]

Four of our number asked our permission to leave us here, to catch an early train from Holmwood; for you must remember that the girls ... arrive at the Skating Rink soon after 7 o'clock. The rest of us continued our walk through some of the prettiest scenery on the whole days walk, but at such a pace that ...

6   Friday Street is 2 miles WNW of Leith Hill.
7   Coldharbour is ¾ mile NE of Leith Hill.
8   Presumably Walter Cramp.

[p. 11]

... the Major came near to being crocked.

Single file was adopted after about three miles and with Mr. Cramp as leader we were led ... down to Dorking, frequently interrupting our killing pace with a little fancy marching.

Once through Dorking we again joined up our ranks and the fun lasted right up to the last field outside the station; a field covered with long grass and providing innumerable occasions for the use of our musical Oh!!

At Boxhill there was another split, some desiring to stay on ... in the country air, but eventually each one arrived home with everything necessary for stiff legs, aching thighs and pleasant recollections on the morrow.

J.G.

It is rumoured that during the absence of the chosen one in Canada, Miss Hayley has engaged a Locum Tenens to perform his duties.[9] Of course this is a temporary arrangement, and as such should work satisfactorily.

Dan Hymen-Cupid.[10]

[p. 12]

BELGIUM AND THE ARDENNES.

Although the headline might seem to separate them, the Ardennes are an integral part of Belgium. There is however, in the minds of most people some distinction between the two. Belgium we think of as the country containing Brussels, Antwerp, Bruges, and Ghent; whilst the Ardennes mean hardly anything until we have visited them. As a whole, Belgium is admirably suited to shallow purses, and we found it possible to spend nine days there ... for a little under £4.

The route we chose was via Dover and Ostend, nominally a three hours sea passage, although it took us some time over. From Ostend we went straight to Bruges, arriving at half past nine in the evening, and for the first time in our lives we set out to find a lodging for the night. Of course we made a bad job of it, and paid nearly five francs for our bed, breakfast and dinner. The room was in a hotel near the Belfry, and we were both kept awake ... by the chimes, which play a fairly long tune every quarter of an hour. Next morning we awoke to a dismal splashing of rain, – which came down straight and heavy, and as we dressed, we almost

---

9   She married a Canadian sapper.
10   Probably Dan C. Messent.

[p. 13]

[A postcard of le Trône (throne), a stalagmite in the Nouvelle Grotte de Rend-peine.]

[p. 14]

regretted our departure from England. But after breakfast the clouds cleared a little and between the showers we managed to see the town fairly well. The canals are ... the most picturesque features and we often stopped to admire a pretty vista of quaint houses and green trees bordering a strip of quiet water.

That afternoon ... we went on to Antwerp. At the station we were beseiged [sic] by an army of hotel porters and we allowed ourselves to be marched off by one of them to a large establishment where everything was 'comme il faut'. Our quarters were comfortable and the extravagant one did not ... mind paying seven francs a day for them. We have both gained experience since then, however, and would now contrive to live just as comfortably but at a lower rate.

The great tower of the Cathedral is the show feature of the town and may be ascended for half a franc. Accordingly we both climbed it next morning and in the afternoon paid a franc to be let into the Cathedral during sight-seeing time.

On Tuesday our season tickets came into force so we had breakfast early and caught a fast train to Liege. The ride was rather monotonous: flat country stretches away for miles on either side, and every inch is covered

[p. 15]

with some profitable crop. Liege, however, was a change for the better. True! It had not so many large buildings and notable pictures, but it is surrounded by hills, and in the evening dusk the lights of the town were reflected with charming effect in its two rivers. Liege is a student centre, and in Belgium students are generally poor, accordingly a university town is a cheap one. So we found Liege; a good room, quite near the station, only costing us 2¼ francs.

I will next mention Brussels so that I may reserve the last part of this article exclusively to the Ardennes. The largest, and ... the best building in Belgium, is at Brussels. The Palais de Justice, a great classical pile, almost ... Egyptian, is extremely impressive. Its size can hardly be realized until a few human figures are seen walking through its courts and porches, dwarfed by their giant surroundings ... Belgium is not very fortunate as far as Gothic architecture is concerned, but the best ... is the Cathedral at Brussels, which ... serves as a framework to some of the most beautiful stained-glass windows in existence.

Another feature of Brussels of which intending

[p. 16]

visiters [sic] would do well to take a note is the Wiertz Museum. This is a collection of the works of a most talented, but extremely eccentric artist. It contains ... every class of subject; great triumphal religious scenes, figure studies, still life, and scenes of intense emotion ... These latter are often of a nightmare character, including such thing as "Visions of a Cut-Off Head" and "Napoleon in Hell".

All the while we were in Brussels, however, we had a feeling of regret at having had to leave Dinant. Liege we had left on Wednesday morning, arriving in good time at Namur. From Namur we intended to go by steamer to Dinant, catching the boat at 2–30. We went for a stroll round the town for a while, and then after lunch, went down to the pier. But there we found that this service would not start for another month so we had to look up a convenient train for Dinant, and ... we made our way back to the station.

If the scenery along the river is better than the views obtained from the train, it is indeed a trip well worth undertaking. Great cliffs of rock rise sheer up from the water's edge, and in the occasional breaks, you get glimpses of fertile valleys with trees on either

[p. 17]

[Postcard of Dinant with bridge and river.]

[p. 18]

side and small open spaces thick with poppies and cornflowers. After an hour's ride we got out at Dinant and were beseiged [sic] ... by a gang of hotel porters whom we had ... learnt to ignore. We only stopped to deposit our baggage and then went out to amuse ourselves.

The Ardennes being a lime-stone district it is simply honey-combed with caves and our first care was to visit one. The afternoon was hot and breathless but as soon as we got down from the few steps leading to the cave the icy coldness of the place made us shiver. This visit was ... a little exciting, for everywhere the water was trickling down the sides of the caves and slips were frequent on the wet rocks.

When we got back to the town we took the advice of our guide book and climbed up to the fort. This great collection of thick walls was ... strengthened under the superintendence of the Duke of Wellington and it is easy to see what a strong position it must have been before the invention of guns which could knock it to pieces from the opposite hill-tops. The view from the top is magnificent. The best hill-country of Kent and Surrey cannot beat the surroundings of this little town, and there is an added charm through the many old castles whose ruins

[p. 19]

[Postcards of Dinant. One of Rue Adolphe Sax and another of the church.]

[p. 20]

emphasize the prettiest features. It was evening-time, and the sun, low down in the sky, sent his slanting beams against the sides of the houses and still further twisted their distorted roofs, whilst further down the river it tinged the bare rocks with a red glow. For a long time we lay at full length across the top of one of the thick walls, either gazing at the general beauty of the country, or observing the evening movement of the little town 300 feet below us. At last we came down under the necessity of finding something to eat and a lodging for the night. In the picture of the Rue Adolphe Sax you can see well down on the right hand side of the road an advertisement for the Singer Sewing Machine Company. The place we stopped at was the house immediately to this side of it, and for 4¾ francs a day we lived most comfortably.

That evening we went for a stroll along the river side, and so peaceful was the whole place that we decided to visit no more lowland towns, but to spend the rest of our available time here. The next morning was bright ... after a storm ... during the night, so we set out along the river to Anseremme[11] and sat down for an hour's reading just near the great rock with the tunnel through it, shown in the illustration. It was a hot morning and we felt rather lazy, so when we saw a

[p. 21]

[Two postcards of rock faces beside the river. Le Rocher Bayard at Dinant and Le Tunnel at Anseremme.]

[p. 22]

little passenger steamer stop quite near us to go into the lock, we went on board and made the return journey by boat. From the boat one gets a totally different view of the town, and it looked more charming than ever when it could be seen standing over its reflection in the smooth water.

That afternoon we took the opposite direction, marching along the road which follows the river towards Namur. Often we found ourselves softly humming that someone was "lagging on behind" or else shouting

[11]   Anseremme is 1¼ miles S of Dinant.

out the tale of the man who went to mow. It made us both wish that instead of two there were twenty "Angels" swinging along the sunny road. At one point where the cliffs towered above our heads, we were warned to stop by the toot-toot of a horn, an instrument which replaces the bell or whistle in Belgium. We soon saw the reason. At the top of the cliff there was a slight movement and the next instant down came a great lump of rock weighing about half a ton. It crashed from point to point, smashing off a shower of stones at each impact, and presently bounded down the final slope and on to the road with a terrific thud. That, we found, was their way of collecting material for road-making.

The following day we went for two extremely fine

[p. 23]

[A postcard of Château de Walzin, Dinant.]

[p. 24]

walks, and one of these took us past the Chateau Walzin, of which a picture is given. Such a rambling district we have never had the good fortune to visit as a class. Long paths wind up the hill-sides, but so covered in with trees as to resemble tunnels, and when at last the top is reached, straight ahead there seems to be a wide plain, covered with crops. As we advance, however, we find that the level surface is but a mask for many extensive valleys; and so, up and down, over streams and through quaint villages, until the setting sun reminds that dinner time is near and we have good appetites.

In this manner did our three remaining days all too quickly pass and we left this beautiful district feeling that we had only just commenced to discover how fine a rambling ground it really was. After the peacefulness of the evenings spent by the river at Dinant, Brussels with its gay life did not attract, and when at last we found ourselves on the boat, with wind and waves doing their best to drown our past happiness in present misery, we determined that next year we would return again, but accompanied by a dozen of Trinity's keenest ramblers.

J.G.

[p. 25]

HULLO!

The fellows marked with an asterisk do not want to be rung up unless you really have something to say ... Mr. H. Rowe, would be obliged if callers would first ascertain if he is in with the "boss", and if so to ring up later.

Mr. A. Austin.	Central 3168
G. Barrett.	Gerrard 4011
E. Bowler.	Gerrard 4011
C. Bedwell.	Lond. Wall 4900
L. Bedwell.	Battersea 4
N. Bedwell.	Holborn 2055
F. Biggins.	Central 924
P. Coomber.	Central 8281
A. Carpenter.*	STRAND 1247
W. Cramp.*	CENTRAL 5648
L. Fouracre.	Central 10448
J. Godden.	New Cross 36
A. Jones.	Brixton 379
T. Lynch.	Hop 1431
Mr. D. Messent.	Holborn 606
Mr. W. Messent.	Holborn 606
L. Messent.	Holborn 606
Mr. C. Moxley.*	Holborn 5330
S. Rowe.	Head Office 108
H. Rowe.*	Holborn 3036

RING OFF!

It is proposed to hold a meeting ... to discuss the ways and means for removing the "excrement of valour" affected by Messrs. Bedwell and Perkins on their upper lips.

[p. 26]

TRINITY JUNIOR FOOTBALL CLUB
Season 1911–12

This our first season was not a bright one in the light of success or conditions of the weather. We arranged for about 25 matches, and ... only played eight, a rather disappointing proportion. Yet the games we did play, we enjoyed. We commenced well, winning our first match although, unfortunately, the only one during the season. Our second was lost to a decidedly better team. We also went under in our third, but we were unlucky ...

The next match ... was against ... St. Paul's Church, Herne Hill ... The visitors scored first; a really good goal ... out of the reach of our goalie. They scored again, but were then surprised by a ... spirited attack ... and we scored just as the whistle blew for lemons.

In the second half, the visitors ... shot well

[p. 27]

over the tape, and a sigh of relief was heard all over the ground. The kick was taken and play remained very slow until another unexpected effort. The ball was swung out to the left winger in the best Chelsea style, and he shot. It ... resulted in a goal of the first order. Thus we were only one down. We had another five minutes to go and ... our Captain ... dashed straight through, beating five men ... This run ended in a goal which ended the game at three all. It is my good fortune to act as skipper during the coming season, I have no desire to see them play better.

I should ... mention ... the team ... F. Eagle, with our Vice. E. T. Lynch, played excellently at back. Our goalies varied, but G. Davies[12] did well ... It was not until nearly the end of the season that we found a "certified" keeper ... and we hope that we shall not lose H. Randall. Our Captain, Montague Davies ... has it in him to become a good footballer, provided he becomes a little faster. ...

Ref.

[p. 28]

The class has now a cricket team,
A group of youngsters, it would seem,
Who love the dainty cigarette
Although they aren't quite sixteen yet.
Unhappily, these little chaps
Are often verging on collapse.
They run a stylish hit for four,
But if they knock a couple more,
Then their faces show the pain
That it gives to run again.
Four times up and down the pitch,
Then they're writhing with the stitch.
At times like these they must regret
Their fondness for the Cigarette.

[12]   Gwilym Davies, brother of Montague.

[p. 29]

A REPORTER AT HOME

"Let us come into the dining room, we shall get the breeze from the garden." So we are settled down beside the opened windows and chatted comfortably for a while. But then – the cat. I suddenly noticed it in the middle of the lawn. An enormous cat ... deserving of the greatest respect. It had a great flattened head and its ears were torn into unnatural shapes by the teeth of past opponents. In fact, it ... would easily have passed for a young tiger cub.

Up jumped the Reporter and with a whistle like an engine blowing off steam he tried to attract the cat's attention, but in vain. He then raised his voice – "Hi! Barabbas! Come here you wicked old robber. Come here!" But Barabbas squinted out of the corners of his cunning eyes and slowly edged away.

The Reporter lost patience and with a jump was down the stairs, out into the garden, and well after the unlucky cat. "Ah! You old offender, come here to your lawful master. Let's see how you've been feeding at other people's expense". But with a mad rush the cat ... took shelter behind a flower bed. Bold as the Reporter was, he dare not

[p. 30]

trample on his sister's handiwork, and whilst he looked around for a stick, Barabbas ... cleared the bed, dashed across the grass, scrambled up the wall and commenced a mad rush for home.

The Reporter ... hurled himself at ... the bushes ... and with his outstretched hand just stopped the enormous cat with his Scriptural name. Barabbas ... allowed himself to be ... stroked and generally examined, ... maintaining a passive, dreamy look in his grey eyes. But then the Reporter made a mistake. He overestimated the extent of feline endurance; and when he got out a pocket knife ... and began to trim the creatures claws, I was not surprised that the animal struggled. At last, with a mighty effort, it seemed to bounce out of his arms, ... out into the garden.

"There he goes, the old robber", said the Reporter, "gone visiting in the neighbour's pantries. No wonder the beast can't eat any supper when he comes home at night".

As I took my departure I noticed one or two spots of blood on his cheek. The cat must have got one home en route for liberty.

[p. 31]

Next morning ... outside the church, someone asked him if razor-cuts hurt much, and ... I smiled and thought of cats.

X.Lea.

Y.P.M.

These meetings have been held on alternate Tuesdays and have been ... very enjoyable and profitable. We commenced at 8 o'clock and finished at 9 <u>sharp</u>. We conducted it ourselves, so it was really a Young People's Meeting. It is a regrettable fact, as well as an unnecessary one that we are always far out-numbered by our "Long-Haired Chums". It is a pity that we cannot command a bigger attendance of the fellows, seeing what a large number gather Sunday by Sunday ... We discuss all kinds of topics but do not ... pretend to be a Theological Class; we simply try to explain ... things of real importance in trying to live a Christian life.

We had many good papers during the session, and one on "Influence" was particularly good. We came ... to see that there are two distinct kinds, for which we are equally responsible; that is

[p. 32]

conscious and unconscious influence, – an eye-opener to some of us. Others were "The Crosses we put upon each other", "Why I am a Protestant", and "The Christian and his Newspaper".

We are looking forward to the coming session and trust that many more will ... turn in and spend an evening which they will afterwards feel to have been profitably utilised.

C.F.B.[13]

We hear that our friend A.P.A. has completely recovered from the effects of his prolonged side-car run last Easter. Congratulations!

We also hear that the car in which he was a passenger, failed by six minutes. Commiseration!

The run was from London to Edinburgh and was a reliability test. Many people have an idea that in these runs the first man wins, but ... every competitor completing the four hundred miles in 23 hours receives a gold medal.[14]

[p. 33]

[Drawing of a man playing a penny whistle with a mosquito hovering near his nose.]

THE DUET.

[13] Cyril Francis Bedwell.
[14] The Motor Cycle Club organised annual trials from the early 1900s, with two-, three-, and four-wheeled vehicles competing together. <http://www.themotorcyclingclub.org.uk/events/edinburgh.htm>, accessed 27 Mar. 2015.

[p. 34]

FAITES ATTENTION!

Fares	£1	10	0
Lodging	1	5	0
Sundries		5	0
	£3	0	0

August to May
Inclusive

TEN MONTHS

You have only to put by six shillings a month and your next year's trip to the Continent is assured.

It is intended to organise a party to go on a rambling holiday in the Ardennes, making Dinant the centre. The early part of the year would be ... best for such a trip, as the towns would be freer from tourists and lodgings therefore cheaper. The majority of our members get a fortnight's holiday, and there should be no special difficulty in their taking it a little before the regular holiday season. As shown above, the comparatively small weekly contribution of 1/6 a week would clear all expenses comfortably, and it will be easy to appoint someone to receive these payments if such a system is thought desirable.

[p. 35]

You will easily understand that ... as in all other movements we have undertaken as a class, the larger the number participating, the greater the success of the effort. To this end we wish for a large attendance at a meeting to be held ... on July 30th. You may not have any intention of joining the party, but all the same, we should like you to come and hear our propositions.

Further notice of this meeting will be given outside these pages and it is hoped that the class will ... back up a project ... originated in its midst.

J. Godden.

It is hard to understand why the Pastor and Deacons continue to retain the choral Amen at the end of the prayers. Everyone in the church can notice how the "blower" is feeling round Mr. Lansdown's words and pumping in a quantity of wind whenever they seem to be leading to a termination.[15] The spoken Amen may not be quite so gorgeous, but ... the solemn silence would not be rudely disturbed by the clattering of the pedals and the wheezing of the bellows. We understand that Mr. D.C.M. has ... tried to secure its abolition for the past twelve months.

[p. 36]

OUR LONG HAIRED CHUMS.

Miss Messent	Miss Johnston	Miss Maynard	Miss Armston
Miss H. Snoswell	Miss W. Jolly	Miss K. Osland	Miss N. Osland

MISTER EVANS
Trissie Hayley   Stella Hill

Saturday, July 6th. was the occasion of the first ramble of the T.L.H.C. They recognised ... that they were not very sure of themselves and discreetly refrained from doing anything ... original. The Path chosen was, with one or two minor exceptions, identical with that of the last ramble of THE CLASS. They have, therefore, literally ... followed in our footsteps. Throughout the proceedings the interest was sustained although it would appear that the attendance was not. This is ... the most puzzling part of the whole of this strange afternoon. Where did two of the party get to after crossing the first field? You will see that this little report is headed by the names of those who took part, accordingly, two names have had to be kept separate as being absent at the finish. We of course absolutely refuse to tell you which are the two, or how they are separated.

[p. 37]

Mr. Evans was borrowed ... without our permission, and their sin in this instance found them out. He indicated every place our feet had hallowed, and proclaimed aloud that here THE CLASS sat down to eat, or here THE CLASS quaffed ginger beer. We can't understand why they ... objected to hearing so much about THE CLASS but still they did, and serve them right.

Nothing else happened apparently with the exception of the incident we now relate. They rolled poor Mr. Evans in the grass. Mr. E! Why did you allow it? We feel pretty certain that ... there was no combination of forces strong enough to overturn a sturdy masculine carcase. It might have been that he was showing them how to play kiss-in-the-ring and got overwhelmed in the rush, but even then --.

---

[15]   The "blower" is the person pumping air into the organ. An electric blower was installed later.

They all came back early with the exception of the lost sheep, who ... were escorted home by some very dear, if not very old friends, at the early hour of 12.5 am. "Esprit de corps" is a foreign phrase, but it would pay these two to learn a dozen languages if ... it helped them to a clearer conception of its meaning.

'Long Ear.'

Say! Where did you pick it up Freddie?

[p. 38]

CRICKET

In April ... , when we had quite finished with football, and got over the excitement of seeing Chelsea return to its proper sphere, we ... faced ... whether we should be able to run a cricket team this season. It was a struggle ... last year to raise a full team, and when a cricket meeting was held in March it was seen that three or four of last season's players could not turn out; the remainder ... felt that they would like to play on a private ground, so it was found impossible to run a senior team in the park.

A senior team being impossible, the question was raised as to a junior team. There were plenty of younger members in the class who were very keen ... , and the remaining members of the senior team passed a resolution, handing over all the possessions of the senior team, excepting the balance in hand, to the junior team.

When one remembers the good games we used to have ... , it seems a pity that the old team has passed, but every club has to take a new lease of life, and it is better that an entirely new team has been formed, because when younger members come into an old team they must at first be put in at the tail, and if

[p. 39]

they play a week or two without getting a whack, they are apt to ... throw it up.

We all hope the team will have a good season, but there is one thing to be remembered, and that is, there is no necessity for the slips, point and wicket to hold a mothers' meeting. It is more than annoying when you bowl a ball on the off, see it go up, and then find that slips and point are excitedly arguing, the catch, of course, – – – – ! !

Hobbet.

The Literary Society deserves more support from the Y.M.B.C. Those who complain that the programmes are not to their taste have no ground ... to excuse their absence. They have but to suggest subjects, and ... the Committee will welcome them ... even as the Editor ... welcomes good 'copy'. Mr D. C. Messent and Mr. A.H.E. are both on the Committee, and you can make known your requirements ... without the slightest fear that they will fail to reach the proper quarter.

It is a sign of degeneration when the Class can send no more than three representatives to a society of which a former member was the Assistant Secretary.

[p. 40, p. 41 and p. 42 consist of small photographs of the Long Haired Chums – 25 in all. Often they wear hats, with their hair pushed high on their heads. They do not smile.]

[p. 43]

OUR PORTRAIT GALLERY

This is a most delicate situation. The photos have been sent in for publication with a stern condition attached, – we may make no adverse comments. This might not mean much to the majority of Editors especially if spoken by similar persons, but in ... the "A.V.", one must walk circumspectly. The poor harassed editor hardly dares to say a word which might bring the T.L.H.C. into public notice; if he does, ... his action is publicly proclaimed as a piece of slanderous libel. Of course ... we are ever striving to fulfil their well-known wishes, and to bestow upon them the publicity which of themselves they cannot obtain. You now, of course, see the whole situation. We are expected to say something: they would complain if we did not; but with such a condition what can we do? Their words themselves seem to admit that there is something which might appear unfavourably: but as to that we say nothing, meantime cherishing in our hearts that wise old saw, "Silence gives consent". We must apologise for having kept you so long on such a subject, but it really was a delicate situation and we found it really hard to say our say and yet not break the contract.

Flapdoodle.

[p. 44]

A GLORIOUS ANNIVERSARY

This year the Church Anniversary was a unique success. Especially may this be said of the mid-week meeting which took the form of a "Roll-Call", with a special address by the Rev. H. Carlisle, M.A. of Balham.[16]

---

[16]   H. H. Carlisle (1863–1945) was minister of Balham Congregational Church 1908–19. *CYB*

The sections represented were The Ladies Working Party, The Girls Guild and Classes, The Womens Meeting, The Sunday School workers, the Men of the Church and Congregation, and the Y.M.B.C.

There was a splendid attendance in all these sections but we are especially delighted to record the fine muster of our Class, for in spite of several prominent members being unavoidably absent, ... thirty stalwarts arose and sang our Brotherhood Hymn with heartiness and zest.

D.C.M.

ARDENNES TRIP

The meeting on Tuesday, July 30th depends for its success on everyone having read the magazine ... See, therefore, that you pass it on with no delay and in no case after the limit.

Ed.

[p. 45]

A TALE OF TWO CITIES.

The City! That little parcel of land with St. Paul's at its centre, and an area hardly large enough for a modest farm; we know it by heart. The Bank at the centre of London's traffic and just within a stone's throw, Gracechurch Street with its continuations. In the other directions, Cheapside, Ludgate Hill, Ludgate Circus and then, although we are not yet outside the actual City boundary, we stop. The City proper does not seem to pass beyond these limits.

As we cross one of the bridges every morning we see St. Paul's, – or at least we might see it if we would but look – towering over the dens of the money makers; harmonious in its proportions, majestic in its size, softly glowing in the sunlight or stern and gloomy in the shadows of the clouds. Most of us soon forget the domed Cathedral ... We have to get to work, and so rush along with the other workers in this great hive, knowing that we have ten minutes walk before us and only five minutes to do it in ... the City means roar, and rush, and hurry, right up to the welcome hour when in the last final rush we strive to reach in record time the quietude

(1946), 406.

of home.

Now the other City! A City in which all is hushed. The sunlight gleams between towering warehouses and streaks with yellow light the grimy office walls. Occasionally a motor bus is heard swishing along over the smooth roads. It is Sunday, the only day that London will reveal its fullest beauty. Buildings ... associated with ... business life, have closed their doors and drawn their shutters, and everything lies in perfect rest. Yes! Sunday is the day for a walk through the City if you would catch its chiefest charm.

Then too the bells! Every day they are ringing but the Babel of sound rising from the thronged streets drowns their tones, and those who pass their week-day lives in hearing of this charming music, have no time to listen. For a while we tread in perfect silence the familiar haunts, now strangely unfamiliar, but then our echoing foot-steps are lost in the sudden tumult of sound, as the Cathedral Bells commence to fill the air with throbbing melody.

And so we leave this novel, unfamiliar City, waiting for Monday to convince us that we only dreamed so great and impossible a change.

"Topper".

[p. 47]

OWR FONETIK PAJ

It is mutch mawr difikult than u wuld thingk too rit a fareli sensibul shtikul strate owt in fonetil spalin withowt ferst triing too doo it in the awdinri manur. But nevrthles it eksursizes a most saluteri inflooens on wunz sikolojikul kondishun if induljd in regulerlt and with kare and rezun. Meni pepul wuld thingk it mutch esier too rit the wurdz as the sownds naturili sudjest, but in praktis it wil be fownd distingktli contewzing, hens its sootibiliti as a mentul eksersis.

Dowtless if tawt in skoowlz from the childz erliest infensi, the nekst jenerayshun wuld be entirli fre from awthografikul ererz, but unfawrtunatli the Edukashun Awthoritiz doo not sem inklind too adopt eni such sensibul mezhur. Nevertheles it wuld sem rather unkani too have a child ov onli fiv yurz spelin even the longest wurdz with infalibul korektnes.

Stil, too the unpraktist awr uninisheayted redur it iz ekstremli weerisum and so it is too the ritur, watevur praktis he ma hav had in this inuzhuel aht. Therfawr I tak advantej ov the opawrtunati thus givn too mak a grasful eksit from an ekzawsting paj.

C.Ra. N.K.

[p. 48]

[Drawing of a bald man with a magnifying glass examining cheese.]
"SEEING LIFE."

[p. 49]

SOUTHWARK CATHEDRAL

The Boro' with its market and tall, dingy warehouses, and Southwark with its grimy factories, constitute ... as unfavourable a setting as it is possible to conceive of for a Cathedral Church. The steadily rising ground level, which was referred to in an article in the last issue, is here again demonstrated. The Building must be approached down several steps from every entrance, and although it would be imposing enough on a hill, in its present position, the tower alone saves it from being swallowed up by the surrounding walls.

Let us enter by the west door and we then get a view of the whole building at a glance. The nave is quite bewildering in the multitude of its lines, and although they give at first a rich effect, the eye soon tires of gazing, and searches for some individual character on each pillar and each arch. In almost all other Cathedrals these would be found, but not here; the nave is a modern product, the last of many that have stood on this spot. Everything in this latest erection is ... exactly fitted, and all follows on with such machine-like regularity that we are glad to go on to the older transepts and choir.

[p. 50]

The choir is beautiful ... and the lightness of its arches and their beautiful curves cause many ... to place it even before Westminster Abbey. It is in the choir, too, that we find the Cathedral's most famous feature. Southwark, together with Winchester and St. Alban's contain the only three altar screens of their kind in England. It is covered with niches for statues, which are gradually being supplied by generous donors. Behind the screen we pass to the Lady chapel, and its gloominess fits well with ... its history. In this place, in the time of Mary, a court was held, and some of her many victims were here condemned to death and hauled away to the stake.

In our walk ... we shall notice in the North Transept a stack of great wooden bosses, all that is left of a former timber roofed nave. They are all quaintly carved, and in the middle ... is a flaming face with the body of a man hanging from its mouth. What this is meant to tell is not quite certain, but ... guesses say that it is Satan swallowing up Judas. There is another interesting collection at the end of the nave; this time the remains of a long-time destroyed stone roof.

[p. 51]

It is interesting to compare the fragments of capitals here, adorned with fighting monsters, church symbols, and well cut foliage, with the apparently machine-turned blocks of stone which leave us so unmoved in the present building.

At five o'clock evensong commences and it is worth while stopping for it. Prayer Books are placed on every chair, and (... particularly pleasing to the average Nonconformist) a slip is pasted inside the cover, giving the order of the service and the pages on which the correct prayers will be found. By its help we go through the service without feeling particularly conspicuous, and after listening to the dreamy tones of the reader, and the rich singing of the choir, we stand up as the procession winds round the shadowy aisles, whilst ... the setting sun streaks the high vaults with the hues of the painted windows.

J.G.

Mr. A. H. Evans is going to ... Normandy towards the end of September. Anyone who has a week or fortnight free ... might like to know that a weeks visit to one of the old historic towns of France can easily be made for £4. Communicate with Mr. E. ... to come to some arrangement.

[p. 52]

A SENIOR GYMNASIUM AT TRINITY

There is no senior gym. ... but one is going to be formed next September, provided ... permission be obtained from the Deacons. In order that this may be gained it is essential that the application should come from a fair number of Class members.

Mr. A. P. Austin is keen as mustard (D.S.F.) ... and is longing ... to put some muscles on our spidery limbs, and some chests on the vacant sites. He thoroughly understands his business, and being in touch with some of the foremost exponents of physical culture ... , he is quite up to date.

Do you ever come home from business feeling fed up ... ? If not, you will deteriorate into a millionaire or a convict. If so, one of the best remedies is a dose of gymnastics, after which you will sleep like a top and dance up to the office next morning feeling on good terms with everybody, and as happy as Little Peter, the famous beer salesman. In these days of hustle, physical fitness is an extremely valuable asset and the weakling goes to the wall. Just think how much more profitable it is to spend an hour or two in the gym. than, for

[p. 53]

instance to say "Good evening Miss!" and the waste of time consequent on the success of this daring deed.

A meeting will be called during September … and if you wish to join the proposed gym. class, you must come … , because if there is only a small attendance we shall not get one. So roll up you lazy beggars, roll up!

R. S. Rowe.

The angriest member of the class is Crosley.
The most painful of our officers is Cramp.
Fishier than all others is Rowe
Whilst the dottiest of the lot is Morse.

A monthly number of this mag. need but be very small. Editorial, Athletic News, Personal Pars and two short Articles would amply suffice.

A small Committee should find it possible to run the whole thing at the cost of two hours work a month to each.

The Y.M.C.A. do a great deal by co-operation, especially in holidays. Next year's trip to the Ardennes should interest you as being our first attempt in a similar direction.

[p. 54]

[A photograph of six young men, all suited with waistcoats and ties, sitting in a garden and laughing heartily.]

[p. 55]

STRAY REMARKS ON THE GARDEN PARTY.

As is invariably the case, the Garden Party was a great success, and the weather, although somewhat chilly, was still fine enough to make the garden pleasant. We feel especially thankful for this, seeing how disconcerting the weather reports were during the early part of the day.

The attendance was large … and the competitions were hardly sufficient to occupy everybody, but the cake was certainly well "weighed" and Mr. Austin's "Band" proved extremely amusing. With dusk came the illuminations and the concert, and simultaneously no more people were allowed to admire the flower garden (except Mr. Lansdown and a friend or two).

Strangely enough the conversation on the following day was not upon the Garden Party but someone who attended it. Her lovely parasol with the big handle, the way she did her hair ... gave a chance for criticism such as the T.L.H.C. with all their eccentricities have never done.

Turning from those present we deal with the notable absentees. Of course there was much small fry that failed in its duty, but no one expected to find

[p. 55]

Mr. F. Perkins taking his stand with them. We try to think that he was called away to lend a hand in the Yarmouth mystery,[17] but being Saturday we are rather inclined to believe that he was enjoying his customary Turkish Bath. Failing this we can only think that ... he failed to obtain a suitable shine on his boots and had to stay at home.

It is too soon to write at length on the ordinary, inevitable, features that attend all Garden Parties, although we shall ... remind each other of the experience gained when the time again arrives to put it into practice. But before closing I have to convey to you the Major's thanks. It was very kind of you to chair him up to the platform and he was very pleased. He ... is eagerly looking forward to next year's Garden Party.

We have had the following articles promised for the next issue:–
The Selection of Half-Hose.   F. York.
The Permanent Crease.   E. Bowler.
Rock Cakes and Toffee Drops.   H. Lansdown.

[p. 56]

COPY NO. 1.

Time limit two days. Bracketed groups may take three days.
As each reader will see both the illustrated number and a carbon copy, there is no excuse for taking more than the allotted time.

Mr. D. C. Messent.	The magazine must be passed on	
Mr. W. Messent.	by the evening of ...	
L. Messent.		July 27
R. S. Rowe.		
H. Rowe.		
F. Rowe.		July 30
W. Crosley.		
F. York.		Aug 2

---

[17]   *The Times* 16 July 1912 reported the discovery of a murder victim on a Great Yarmouth beach.

C. Smith.	Aug 4
F. Biggin.	Aug 6
A. Austin.	
F. von Rittershausen.	Aug 9
W. Cramp.	
P. Coomber.	Aug 12
C. Bedwell.	
N. Bedwell.	
L. Bedwell.	Aug 15
A. Munro.	Aug 17
G. Barrett.	Aug 19
E. Bowler.	Aug 21
L. Fouracre.	Aug 23
F. Jones.	
A. Jones.	
H. Jones.	Aug 26
A. Carpenter.	Aug 28
H. Lansdown.	Aug 30
Mr. C. Moxley.	Sep 1
Mr. A. H. Evans.	Sep 3
C. Morse.	Sep 5
T. Lynch.	Sep 7
F. Squires.	Sep 9
C. Cloak.	Sep 11
Mr. D. C. Messent. FINIS.	

THE ANGELS' VOICE XMAS NUMBER 1912

Editor Jas. Godden

[p. 1]

[Drawing of a sleek cat, white with black spots and apparently smiling, wearing a bow-tie.]

[p. 2]

THE ANGELS' VOICE

CHRISTMAS NUMBER
December 1912

EDITORIAL

Dear Readers,

The journalistic song of "Copy-lack" has ceased to echo through the palatial offices of the "Angels' Voice", and for the past week articles have littered the Editor's desk, and subsequently, his waste paper basket. The blue pencil spared a fair percentage, however, and for the first time ... has the Editor really known the exhilaration of editing.

If contributors would promise that their support should be regular and copi – ous (Pun. Ed.), a monthly issue could be re-commenced ...

The only hindrance ... is the fact that our readers need six months to circulate one issue. We have adopted a new and more rigorous plan ... and if it has the same success as our appeal for "copy" – - Pass along please!

Ed.

[p. 3]

TO THE EDITOR

Welshmen declare when first old Adam's choice
Whispered love to Eve, t'was in their tongue.
But greater marvel yet, the Angel's voice
Is modern French, no matter "said or sung".

185

They may not trust thee in the modern choir
In this degenerate age, where Bedwell stands
With Barrett, Messent, Moxley, who aspire
To emulate the song of angel bands
At Bethlehem; but these are voices thin and weak,
Save when the minister his lungs expands,
Then from some foreign tongue relief we seek:
To ancient fogies it may seem a wrench,
But sing O Jimmy in thy modern French.

Read the next page quick, before your mind is prejudiced.

[p. 4]

TO THE UNKNOWN SONGSTER

O wicked man, with Pipes of Pan
To sing at first so sweetly,
But then to change your subject's range
And tick me off so neatly.

But what a shame to put no name!
The enemy is hidden.
Methinks the knave will not be brave
Enough to rise when bidden.

His rhyming bluff and all such stuff
Reveal humiliation,
And all his breed most surely need
A wordy flagellation.

His spoken French I guess would quench
Le gai esprit de Paris.
But off you go, you're far too slow.
The Angels may not tarry.

It is not necessary for our younger members to talk so much nor so loud during service. Their tongues are as great a nuisance as their predecessor of "IT" fame.
Please remember this and oblige.

[p. 5]

THE ANNUAL MEETING.
Full Report

Our Annual Meeting is to us the most interesting gathering of the Trinity year. It is class news that everyone understands ... , it is copy "par excellence". The temptation is to treat it merely as such but it was decided last year that this article should be also the sole official record of the meeting, and that must give it several characteristics apart from the ... aim ... to amuse.

The Annual Meeting of <u>The Class</u> is quite distinct ... inasmuch as that although refreshments are provided, not a single member, self included, turns up for the sake of them. That naturally brands the social function which precedes the business meeting as of minor importance and we therefore turn immediately to those proceedings which were ... to secure the record attendance of fourty [sic] four ...

The President, Mr. Lansdown, was in the chair, supported by Mr. Snoswell and our Leader. Mr. Lansdown rose at 8.30 to briefly introduce the meeting and afford an opportunity for late-comers to be present from the beginning. He then opened ... with prayer and ... thereafter called on the Secretary for his report.

[p. 6]

Mr. Rowe gave us a clear statement of the year's doings, intermingled with ... suggestions and frank criticisms that it was evidently hopeless to deal with it satisfactorily in the short time that we had before us. I think that the whole of those present would like to feel that in following committee meetings this report was more fully considered, for it is not our secretary's habit to dwell on matters of trifling importance.

He commenced by a brief review of ... our membership, referring especially to the loss of W. Crosley who ... "has gone to warmer climes". The changes in attendance, as has always been the case, were favourable. The number of enrolled members had risen from 33 to 37 and the average attendance from 21.5 to 23.6.

In view of our increased strength he thought it was desirable that we should associate ourselves with some branch of church work. The best way ... was first, to increase the church membership from our class. During the past year only one of our fellows had sought membership, whilst in his opinion, the time was come for several ... to take a similar step. Whether this were done or not, the need for our engaging in some work still remained and he suggested that the coming Bazaar would afford us the needful opening.

He then turned to the consideration of the musical side of our service. First, of course, came the thanks of all to the organist,

[p. 7]

Mr. Moxley, his work left nothing to be desired. It was otherwise, however, with our choice of Psalmody. We started out with the intention of learning a dozen new tunes during the year, but after all we have only added two or three to our stock. He suggested future openers might be a little bolder in their choice and the desired end would then be attained.

Our monthly Prayer Meeting had all through met regularly and obtained a constant attendance, there was, however, no reason why more members should not join in this helpful exercise.

He touched lightly on our continued connection with the Mission Field, leaving a more detailed account for the Mission Secretary. He also stated that the Young People's Meeting had been dropped, adding that it was not a very serious matter for us as the support from members of our class was extremely small. He greatly regretted the lack of support we afforded the Literary Society, which deserved considerably more attention from those whose Tuesdays are free.

In his conclusion he once more advocated a serious attempt on our part to join in some phase of church work.

The report was carried after an objection from Mr. Barrett had been withdrawn. He did not like to see that the Secretary remembered sundry dark forebodings he had indulged in as to the future of the class, nearly a year ago. On the show of hands there was not a single dissentient from its adoption.

[p. 8]

The Treasurer's report followed, and here again an improvement was reported. The total collections during the past financial year had amounted to £2. 13. 6 as against £1. 14. 2 in 1911. This enabled him to report an increase of 19s. 4d. instead of 3s. 4d. as at our last meeting. The renovation of our class room which was resolved upon a year ago had since been carried out, and the cost which amounted to £3. 8. 4 shared equally with the Literary Society. A special collection was taken for this purpose to avoid suddenly depleting the class funds, and one guinea was obtained.

After meeting the various class expenses there was a balance of 7s. 7½d to carry forward, and the Treasurer pointed out the necessity of continued liberal contributions as the heavy expense of providing some poor familys [sic] Christmas dinner would have to be met shortly.

The report was carried unanimously.

The Mission Secretary's report followed and he also was able to report satisfactory increases. In 1911 the total collections amounted to £3. 10. 1, whilst for the current year they had risen to £5. 2. 3. The average afternoon collection was 2s. 8d. but on one occasion this had risen to as high as 4s. 2½d. there was enough money in hand to send about 30/= to Mr. Rowe, Mr. Fairman and the London Missionary Society, and unless the meeting decided to the contrary he proposed sending the money without further delay.

[p. 9]

The report was adopted unanimously although it was evident that there were several points that would call forth remark.

The question of leaving the London Missionary Society out of the distribution of the money collected was again broached the same as last year. Mr. Godden moved and Mr. C. Bedwell seconded that in future the money should be divided equally between the two missionaries in whom we had a personal interest.

Mr. D. C. Messent moved as an amendment, that however the money was divided, the London Missionary Society should be treated at least equally with any other recipients. Mr. R. S. Rowe seconded the amendment. After a few words from Mr. Evans in support of the original motion, the matter was put to the vote and the amendment carried by 28 to 4 votes.

The President next called on Mr. Cramp for a statement as regards our Athletic Institutions.

He gave a clear outline of all that had happened in this direction during the year. We had dropped cricket but had become considerably stronger in football, and he suggested that we should play stronger teams if that were <u>possible</u>. We had entered a Cup League and when after several changes and postponements the match was at last played, we had the misfortune to lose. He also mentioned that the Senior Gymnasium was now once more in full swing after a somewhat protracted period of inactivity.

Owing to the growth of the class, there are now two sections in our

[p. 10]

athletics, which touch at certain points such as the Gymnasium and the rambles, but which are rather more distinct in football.

Accordingly Mr. C. Bedwell was called upon to give us some account of the doings of the 2nd. XI. He had not much to say for he had written at length in the last issue of the "Angels' Voice" but he made several interesting remarks, amongst which he advocated a match between the 1st. and 2nd. XIs. and also the sharing, if possible, of a private ground.

Mr. F. Rowe, one of the members of the 2nd. XI, followed Mr. Bedwell and in a few words thanked him for the interest and pains he took in their organisation. He also endorsed the suggestion that the two teams should meet and that shortly, although to quote his own words, "We will wait till we have finished the season before we start".

Mr. D. C. Messent as Secretary and Treasurer of the 1st. XI, briefly stated that he was pleased at the close connexion between the two teams, a fact which would make the 2nd. XI, of real use in Trinity Athletic life. As they developed more, the 1st. would inevitably draw on them for supplies, and that possibly before long, but until the 2nd. XI. was able to command greatly increased funds, the scheme of a joint ground could not possibly take on any further financial burden.

After a few words of appreciation and advice from Mr. Snoswell, the election of officers was proceeded with.

[p. 11]

The Secretary was unanimously re-elected, and similarly the Treasurer, the Mission Secretary, Prayer Meeting Secretary and Organist.

Messrs. C. Smith and G. Barrett were proposed as auditors and unanimously voted to that position.

The following five nominations were received for the vacant places on the Committee :- R. Chippindale, P. Coomber, F. Jones, E. Bowler and C. Bedwell. The three whose names appear in the list of officers below were elected by ballot.

LIST OF OFFICERS

SECRETARY. – R. S. Rowe.
Treasurer. L. Messent.   Mission Secretary. H. Rowe.
Prayer meeting Secretary – W. Cramp.
COMMITTEE – R. Chippendale, F. Jones, C. Bedwell.
Organist – Mr. C. Moxley.

Mr. D. C. Messent announced that he had received apologies for absence from Messrs. Perkins, Carpenter, and Holman. He also urged the necessity of an even larger attendance at our monthly prayer meetings, as therein lay the whole secret of our strength as a class.

At the conclusion of the meeting it was decided that a message of affectionate gratitude should be sent to our friend, Will Crosley.

Mr. Lansdown then closed a most successful gathering with prayer.

[p. 12]

THE SENIOR GYMNASIUM

Mr. Lansdown makes a mistake every Sunday when he says that the Young Men's Gymnasium will be held on Thursday evening. He should say that the "Physical Culture Class etc. etc." Still if he called everything by its proper name, some of the other notices would sound rather funny. For instance, the phrase, "The Ladies Working Party" would have to be altered. This reminds me that while ladies can work hard and talk hard at the same time, mere man, if he is to be successful, must concentrate all his efforts upon one thing at a time. Therefore, fellow squadites, remember that full benefit cannot be derived from a course of physical culture if some members indulge in little chatty conversations now and again. Anyway, if A.P.A. drops on one of the guilty ones and makes him feel like an incompressible worm, he has not gone without a warning.

The squad has smartened up considerably since the commencement of the session; but there is still a very noticeable lack of finish even in the simple movements, such as marching etc.

The physical culture exercises are new to the large majority and if the gain in health is proportional to the amount of noise made while doing "Breathers" no one will worry about the fact that Lloyd George has not come to terms with the Doctors.

[p. 13]

Why! one "Breather" causes more noise than the Girl's Club three squeals for Miss Eve rolled into one. If we don't look out they will be wanting to borrow A.P.A. so that he can teach them to get wind enough to give three decent cheers. (Alf, my boy, If you should see two or three ladies bearing down on you, with a business like gleam in their eyes, do what I do when I see the Hon. Sec. of the Literary Society with his weather eye on me. Do a bunk!!)

There have been plenty of amusing incidents on Thursday evenings. The dismay on the face of our heaviest member as he tried to struggle into his brother's nether garments was very comical. On a subsequent occasion the latter gentleman wore his brother's duds and looked like a Dutchman. Another member, hearing coarse and ribald laughter burst from all the hooligans present, enquired the cause and learnt for the first time, that when doing a certain exercise, he resembles a Gibson Girl.

All thoroughly enjoy the evening's arduous work and after a wordy warfare among the units in the dressing room, the members depart home feeling top-hole, both physically and mentally. In conclusion, I should just like to say that all members are very grateful to the Church Officials who have made it possible for the senior Gymnasium to be re-opened, and we feel equally grateful to our excellent instructor, A.P.A.

R.S.R.

[p. 14]

LEADER'S LETTER

"MAXTON"
King's Avenue,
Clapham Park.

My dear Fellows,

Again it is my privilege to record a continuance of prosperity in the affairs of our Class. I am delighted that several new faces are to be seen with us on Sunday afternoons and especially do I hope that both Mr. Edward Cotsworth and Mr. Leonard Miller will make themselves quite at home in our midst. We welcome them most heartily.

Lately I have noticed what must be considered as a very healthy aspiration amongst our members. I refer to the desire frequently showing itself that our Class should "do something". It was voiced by our Secretary in his Annual Report at our General Meeting held last month, and its rumblings are often heard amongst our general affairs.

It is felt that all we do is for ourselves. Our Garden Party, our Magazine, our Football and Cricket Clubs, our Gymnasium, our Rambles etc. etc. etc. all of which are in themselves huge successes but are obviously centred in No. 1.

As I understand the current spirit, it would deprecate and rightly so, the abandonment of any of the foregoing, but what it does desire is that some of the enthusiasm and wholeheartedness which

[p. 15]

characterise these agencies might, and should be carried into something which shall

have for its direct aim the helping and benefiting of the Church and immediate neighbourhood. That is the position, briefly stated, as I read it.

Now, of late there has been some outlet for our energies in this direction and it was good to see a number of our fellows spending their evenings assisting in the cleaning of the Church. Our Secretary, Messrs. Cyril and Leslie Bedwell, Mr. W. Cramp, and Mr. E. H. Bowler, not to mention many others, entered into the undertaking with such enthusiasm and did their work so well that they gained the respect of their experienced foreman, Mr. Stanley and deserve the thanks of all. But it was not everyone, for various reasons, who could assist in this piece of practical work. But it is felt that something is wanted to which the whole Class can put its hands and make a great success. I am glad that just the very thing has presented itself. It is in connection with our forthcoming "Livingstone Bazaar" which is to be held at the end of February next.

At the average Bazaar, little or nothing is provided (barring refreshments and buttonholes) that the menfolk can buy. The Deacons, therefore, have invited us to do something to obviate this, and in response, as all are aware, we have decided to run a Y.M.B.C. Hosiery Stall.

Now as this enterprise is to be made a great success, every member

[p. 16]

is bound to have a hand in it, so a subscription list has been opened to raise a sum of at least £15 so that when the time comes a Committee may be appointed to purchase at wholesale prices, attractive and saleable articles. The minimum subscription has been put at 2s. 6d. and Mr. C. F. Bedwell has been appointed collector.

I am pleased to hear that gifts are beginning to roll in, and as the minimum is within everybody's reach, there is no doubt whatever that our stall will represent the sacrifice of all.

There is another thing that we might put our hands to. The outside of the Church very badly needs doing up. There are Doric Columns, window frames, doors, stack pipes, coping, railings etc. etc. all simply crying out for a coat of paint. Supposing we could get a plan of the exterior of our Church and against the various dilapidated parts, mark the approximate cost of repainting, could not our class volunteer to canvas the members of the Church and Congregation and possibly other friends with the object of getting some to pay for a window, others some railings, another a Doric Pillar, others so many feet of coping and so on. In this way we could do a most valuable piece of work and I think it is worth our consideration.

All our endeavours must of course be animated by the right Spirit. We must think of what the Church, and all that it stands for, has been to

[p. 17]

us. I am conscious that this Spirit prevails else there would not be that general desire to "do something" in return for the blessings received that gives one so much encouragement and augurs so well for the future.

Trusting for the united support and best endeavour of all our members in whatever we put our hands to, and the continued splendid attendance at all our meetings,

Believe me to be,
Yours very sincerely,

D. C. Messent.

Quite recently a certain Miss Elizabeth Johnston of Brixton was arrested and subsequently convicted for telling fortunes. Quite a long time ago we seem to remember a similar fate befalling a Miss G. Evans in connection with some Suffragette outrages at Dublin. The relatives of the Brixton Miss Evans inserted an emphatic denial of any connexion with the disorderly one in one of the daily papers and proved an alibi for the innocent Brixtonian. What then is the meaning of the prolonged silence in this case, for even the A.V. has received no communication. The inference is obvious and I shall save up 2s. 6d. for home industries must be supported, whatever their nature.

Ed.

[p. 18]

[Drawing of woman sewing.]

[p. 19]

ANCIENT HISTORY

History repeats itself, and with the restarting of the Senior Gym. come recollections of a similar institution which existed some 10 years ago and to which some of us belonged.

The annals of that society, had they been written, would have made most exciting reading for it had a chequered career and there were some rare characters belonging to it.

There was W. Johnson, the celebrated sub. collector and who, although secretary, skilfully avoided any writing and saved paper and ink by presenting to the members his communications regarding any approaching event verbally, so that if there were any absentees through not having been notified, they were considered personally responsible for not having knocked across him.

His method of collecting the subscription, which was 1s. 0d., being also very startling, for in the most peaceful moments one would feel the warning slap on the shoulder, with the "Now then!! What about that bob? When are you going to dole out?" With perhaps a few more sympathetic remarks admonishing speedy settlement. But he was a good sort, and there were no arrears when he had charge, and as he had control for a considerable time, the finances were usually pretty up-to-date, and his regular attendance to his duties was an example.

[p. 20]

Then there were the three brothers Swan who were great on muscular development, twisting and writhing about on the floor, and were certainly good examples of what may be done with "free" exercises. They never by any chance assisted in putting away any of the apparatus after use so they were the objects of a considerable amount of sarcasm, indeed at one banquet we held, we presented large cardboard medals to each one of them, and the chairman pinned them on in recognition of their services in the matter of putting the apparatus away. Alan Swan was for sometime the treasurer and was generally known as the "oof-bird".

Then there was A. H. Evans of immortal fame, and G. Goodwin who used to circle the bar with the assistance of the whole class, and who generally landed on all fours on the other side, to the great amusement of all the onlookers, who, although it was oft repeated, never seemed to tire of this little item in the evening's programme.

We had one or two banquets at which all the celebrities were present and to which a great many more who were unable to be there, including Julius Caesar and William the Conqueror, sent suitable excuses, which were always read amid great merriment by the secretary.

The magazine was a frightfully personal organ and the "Court News" column included remarks on the way Mr. A. H. Evans should wear his "top hat" with several retorts from his practised pen. There were

[p. 21]

also other items reflecting on the peculiarities of the members, in this publication we styled as the "Gymnasium Gazette".

These things have now passed away, but we had some jolly times and although the members of that time are distributed all over the world, they have no doubt very happy recollections of the old gym. The new Society has come and everyone hopes that it may have a long life and fulfil the purposes of its formation much more successfully than its predecessor.

W.J.M.[1]

> Here's Evans, who tramps thro' the rain,
> Will spend a week in Belgian train.
> He'll do the Continent again,
> A Brussels sprout for ever.

This verse was written by two colleagues of Mr. Evan's [sic] and read out at a Press dinner. Similarly the verse on Mr. Probart whom we know.

> To PROBART we must give a place
> His Shakespeare quotes are sometimes terse
> At other times quite the reverse
> But he loves work without pleasure.
> He is a spearman of that ilk

[1]   William J. Messent.

Who thrives on buns and pints of milk,
And moans of babies socks of silk
Which will not last for ever.

Though these writers are accurate enough in their observation of peculiarities, their versification is far below A.V. standard, a striking tribute to the rare quality of the journalistic staff of that periodical.

[p. 22]

THE GIRLS' CONCERT

The work of washing and polishing the church had been progressing for over a week when we were asked to lay down our tools for an "Evening Concert" by the Girls' Club to be exquisitely rendered on the evening of Thursday, November 19th. First of all Mr. Editor, they were not punctual in commencing, but one overlooked that as it was given by the ladies. However, when the first item on the programme was to be given by Our Mr. Redman, we wondered how long he had been a long haired chum. True, he is till studying music, but we believe he will always continue to do his duty by the hairdresser. Can we forgive them for this bold burglary? I suppose we must go to even that length for the sake of encouraging them. Having passed over this awful misdemeanour they had the impudence to state that the next item was to be given by THE CHOIR!! You agree with me, sir, when I say that there is only one CHOIR at Trinity, and that it certainly did not grace the platform on this disgraceful evening.

Alas! This was not all. We were simply speechless when they had the effrontery to sing OUR Brotherhood Song. This is one too many and they deserve all that mere man can possibly think about them.

They secured the services of a lady who sang "Come sing to me", a beautiful song with the word "sunshoine" so exquisitely rendered

[p. 23]

that we were all profoundly touched. Having been promised a good time "In Arcady" we kept our seats. The soloists were not so bad, but the chorus was noticeably free from any feeling or articulation, and it was very fortunate that the book of words was on sale.

Contrast them with the, THE CHOIR, particularly in similar special efforts, and then be thankful that it is not of the cock and hen variety.
LUCEM DEMONSTRAT UMBRA.

Evidently, there are at least four members of the Bible Class who contribute unwillingly to the L.M.S.[2] This could be obviated, and for

---

[2] London Missionary Society.

liberty's sake should be. An envelope system could be introduced by which the sums enclosed in them would go exclusively to those funds favoured by the contributor. Loose money collected in the box could still be shared out equally according to past custom.

The Editor has received a letter from the invariably punctual Mr. Cramp, embossed with the strange device "EARLIER". This is only his firm's telegraphic address, and was no impress on private paper, as a graceful mark of somewhat tardy contribution.

[p. 24]

PHYSICAL CULTURE SONG

Tune:– "There is a happy Land".

I

There is if you so seek
A Gym. select for men,
Where on one night a week
Angels' tasks are given.
Oh! how those Angels sigh
When their drilling time draws nigh,
And how many of them cry
That they are ill!

2

Then in a certain place
All stand in files.
Seldom upon a face
Are there seen smiles.
Now all their chests they arch,
Then with backs as stiff as starch,
All round the room they march,
Seemingly miles.

3

Next on the floor they lay
Eiderdowns soft,
So that the Angels may
Look up aloft.
Upwards their limbs they fling,
Making the stitches sing,
Then to the ground them bring,
Gently and soft.

4
All have a tired air
When drill is o'er,
And with one voice declare
They'll drill no more.
But should you chance to light
There on a Thursday night
You'll see the self same sight
For evermore.

A Spectator.

[p. 25]

A UNIQUE EVENT

A Cup-tie and Trinity F.C. one of the teams concerned – Marvellous! And what preparations! Weekly runs, after which there was the rubbing into tired muscles of a copious supply of embrocation. Then there were periodical examinations by our medical expert of the doubtful players who had received injury during training or in some previous fixture, to say nothing of the general rubbing down and scientific massaging. And what was all this for? An event! a great event! the likes of which no living member of Trinity can recall. Trinity F.C. had entered for the Surrey Junior A.F.A. Cup and were drawn against Townley Park reserves on the Townley Ground.

The Tie should have been played on October 12th. but owing to various causes it was postponed until the 26th. when on an awfully wet day and a fearfully heavy pitch, our men lost by two clear goals.

The Townley side was no mean one. In weight they were much heavier than our men and as one looked at our little forwards lined up for the start, one wondered how they would fare against such hefty opponents. The Townley defence was very sound, but in spite of this our quintule on many occasions had terribly hard luck in not scoring, especially during the first half and it is claimed by some that the ball did roll over the goal line once, but of this we must not make too much.

[p. 26]

What we do know is this, that shoot as our forwards would, they were baffled either by the cross-bar or the posts or the really exceptional play of the Townley Custodian who brought off several truly remarkable saves.

Trinity were handicapped by the absence of E. F. Harris, their left back who had to undergo an operation during the previous week, this necessitated the captain, R. S. Rowe, taking his place and F. Jones filling the vacant half-back position. The team was therefore as follows:–

H. Reeves.
(Goal)

R. S. Rowe.   H. Jones.
(Backs)

F. Jones.   T. MacCormick.   E. M. Collins.
(Half-backs)

R. J. Chippendale. L. H. Messent. D. Rutter. L. Fouracre. H. Lansdown.
(Forwards)

To single out any players for special mention would be impossible for in the opinion of all who watched the match, our men, one and all, never played a better game. The combination of the forwards, the tackling of the halves and the splendid clearing of the backs all merited the highest praise, whilst our goal-keeper distinguished himself by saving several high and dangerous shots.

The two goals scored against us both came from the Townley right

[p. 27]

wing and bothwould undoubtedly have been avoided had our left wing dropped back a little, to assist in the "throw in", from which movement the two goals originated, a common failing among junior footballers.

Owing to it being a pouring wet afternoon, only a few spectators were present but all came away feeling that, although beaten, Trinity was far from disgraced. The Townley men testified to the fact that it was one of the best games that they had ever played in, and that up to well into the second half, the issue was in doubt, the general opinion being that the team that managed to score first would win. This proved to be the case.

D.C.M.

Those who only study ancient history will have learnt that the culturists of former years indulged in suppers. The good old custom survived for many years in the hands of the Literary Society, but now, unfortunately, seems quite dead. But so also did the Senior Gymnasium, whereas we now see it in all the pride of a renewed glory. It members, we suppose, are trying to beat every similar institution that has gone before, but their forerunners had suppers, and until the hopeful aspirants have conducted a similar and successful function, they are still far below the mark that has already been reached.

Remember this when you wonder how to suitably wind up the season successfully.

[p. 28]

FRIENDLY CRITICISM.	COMMENT THEREON.

There was an able Editor,
His name was Angel Jim;   A cheerful smile would not suffice
Who had a little fondness for
A patronising grin.   To melt contributorial ice.

Another weakness, I narrate,
A secret it must be.   That's all very well from one whose pa
He counts the Plum-stones
on his plate
His future fate to see.   For all we know is père Le Ddra.

He prowls around for
something good
His magazine to fill.   The facts this time have proved you
His "Angel" pals, such lumps   wrong
of wood,
Are unproductive still.   The girls sent nothing but this song.

The latest thing his friends
propose
To put next year on view,   Yet you show off, and daily too,
Will be a show of "Angel"
hose,
Bright green, and red,   Your hosiery of dainty hue.
and blue.

For want of time this verse
I cease,
But scarce can let it pass   Alas! Alas! Alas! Alas!
Without one word –
No prejudice –
Great Wonders! –   'Tis but an envious female donkey.
What a Class!

        ANON.   ED.

For the first time since "Angels' Voice" has been in existance [sic] have we had to hold over several articles owing to want of space.

The "five senses" collection we must also leave to our next issue, when we hope those ladies who promised to contribute, but as usual broke their word, will strive to make amends.

[p. 29]

A.P.A.

AN APPRECIATION

As a humble member of the Trinity Young Men's Physical Culture and Gymnastic Class perhaps I may be allowed brief expression through the medium of your most valuable magazine.

From what I know of Mr. Austin I should say that the T.Y.M.B.C.[3] has in him a unique member. His uniqueness is not to be found in his great enthusiasm for the highest welfare of all its members, for many share that spirit with him; but rather is to be found in the fact that a Bible Class can seldom count among its members, or better still, amongst its most earnest members, one who is so eminently qualified by years of experience and study to conduct upon the latest and most up-to-date lines, Classes which have for their object the developement [sic] of the physical frame.

Mr. Austin is not merely a setter of certain exercises which according to experts are calculated to benefit those who indulge in them. He <u>is</u> an expert ... In cases of ... the minor calamities that befall us when engaged in the more robust sports, like Football, he has been ever ready to examine and advise ...

[p. 30]

He realises that man's highest aim should not be the developement [sic] of muscle, but of character, but he holds that we have a duty to our bodies, namely to see that they are kept healthy and fit. It is this conviction that has prompted him to devote his Thursday evenings to the Service of our Class.

In conclusion may I say a hearty thank you to our esteemed instructor ...

"Telephone"

!!! CALF !.!.! LOVE !!!

There has been of late a vague movement in the hearts of the sentimental small fry at Trinity, with a result now to be seen any Sunday at the evening service.

It is a craving for sympathy (nothing more I assure you) and the little sisterly sympathisers sit tight next to the little brotherly cravers, and the sight is enough to effect strong men to tears – of laughter.

---

3   Trinity Young Men's Bible Class.

The last issue took six months to get round. Quicker please!

[p. 31]

LIVINGSTONE BAZAAR
February 26th. & 27th.
and March 1st.
1913.

On Tuesday December 3rd. the class was called to a seating to decide what part we should take in the above endeavour to wipe off some of our renovation debt. After discussing several ideas, we came to the conclusion that a Gentlemens' [sic] Hosiery Stall would be something which we might indulge in. Tidies and tea-cosies are not much good to bachelors, but collars, cuffs and ties we could make some use of. Mr. Coomber is going to make some ferules to sell at about 2d. each. We also decided that we should open a subscription list, and the minimum should be 2s. 6d. to members of our Brotherhood. The names of several other gentlemen were mentioned, who might be approached with idea of soliciting a small sum. Of course when 2s. 6d. is mentioned, 5s. 0d., or even £1 will not be refused I assure you.

Collecting money at any time is not a nice occupation, but will gentlemen kindly help me by not having to be asked, but see that I am kept busy with my pocket book and pencil. I do not mind if it comes in on the instalment system, because you might give a little more that way, than if you gave everything in a lump sum.

[p. 32]

There is also a Bank to be opened, and that will be another way of saving for this notable event.

Gentlemen! [sic] Book it now! Feb. 26 & 27 and Mar. 1st. 1913.

C. F. Bedwell.

Collector.

The list of readers in this issue will be found to have the names opposite the Sunday dates underlined. The magazine must be brought or sent to the class every Sunday afternoon, and any readers failing in this, will be excluded from any further lists until a fine of 6d. has been paid. Any readers who have been passed over during any week must fix a written protest on the notice board, and special arrangements will be made for them. The magazine must be passed on to the reader whose name is down against that date every Sunday, and in the event of his absence or of a representative, to the next one on the list. This it is hoped will ensure the original time-table being rigidly adhered to.

...

Certainly.

Number 9, December 1912

[p. 33]

T.L.H.C.
Stray thoughts on – Brotherhood.

We were not really at the Girls' Concert but we have heard all that was apparently <u>worth hearing</u> from those who had been persuaded to attend. We also gained much illumination from the article sent in by that distinguished Roman, Lucem Demonstrat Umbra. He seems to be of the opinion that they were trying to claim our Mr. Redman as a <u>Long Haired Chum</u>. Had he studied the proceedings from a distance as it was the Editor's good fortune to do, he would have been able to observe the general trend of affairs and form a more accurate opinion in this particular instance.

The entire evening was nothing more than a thin attempt to raise themselves to the dignity of the status of our <u>BROTHERS</u>. Of course the great feature was our Brotherhood Song which they rendered. It is easy to see that their plan was such as I have named or we should not have had them appropriating a <u>Brother</u>hood song as their own. Such they undoubtedly did, for a normal band of girls, allowing themselves the treat of singing one of our songs, would have certainly inserted, as these should have done, "By kind permission of the Young Men's Bible Class."

Their pretentions finally broke down at the close of the per-

[p. 34]

formance. They tried to attain the true grunting quality of a masculine cheer, but their feminine piping has bound them down to sisterhood for ever.

Flapdoodle.

OUR SPIDER HUNTING.

As you know, the church has lately been thoroughly cleaned. I say thoroughly because the majority was done by the "Angels" and they certainly worked very hard. All the walls and paint were cleaned by the rather mystical process of two well rubbed in coats of "Pickle", and a wash down in clear water. This was very hard work, but the sturdy "Cymites" soon showed some good results. The organ was an object of Great interest to those who were small enough to get inside. The dust was quite ½" thick. The walls around it also caused some excitement, for as soon as anyone touched them with their hands, they received a rather unexpected shock of electricity. During the working hours several dirty rags were unintentionally dropped on people's heads and

203

faces. But I must not put all the good work down to the "Angels", as one or two of our long haired chums came in and pickled the pews.

The fresh and clean aspect of the church we now sit in is an ample reward and justification of all the trouble taken to clean it.

L.B.[4]

[p. 35]

[Scrap of paper with initials: C.F.B.]

[p. 36]

C.B. – His "Scratch".

The Editor, as you know, occasionally receives an article; sometimes on the best cream-laid note paper, and sometimes on the backs of hand-bills. The "scratch" you see on the opposite page has been cut out of the contribution of a subscriber who uses far and away the nastiest stationery we have ever seen. We should think he works in a factory where they make the stuff, and tears off long strips for his articles before the material has been through the perforating machine.

We notice that this and all such disreputable scribblers never care to give their names, but prefer a nom-de-plume or an indecipherable "scratch". In this case we can distinctly trace the letters C.F.B. but these of course give us no hint as to the writer's identity. We are therefore compelled to trust to our skill in reading any clues he gives as to his character and then compare our finding with the characters of all who might possibly have written us an article. No better indications than handwriting could possibly be desired, accordingly let us delineate his leading traits and then if they seem to fit any of our readers, we shall be in a position to blackmail him for an unlimited number of articles.

First, there is noticeable throughout the whole, a prodigality of curves and a certain uncontrolled luxuriance which speaks of a voluble

[p. 37]

expansive individual, one who is ready to fill the air with his effusive speech.

We would then have you notice the comprehensiveness of the "B". It stands there shrieking out, "I AM B", and completely swallows up all else pertaining to the "scratch". May we not from this, conclude that C.B. considers himself no ordinary person, but as possessing those qualities which command attention and leave a profound impression?

---

4   Leslie Bedwell.

As for the three dots, what do they signify? You hardly perceive them at first, but there they are sure enough: which shows that the one who put them there has some sense of what is fit and proper. But when we see in what a perfunctory manner they have been inserted, we are sure that he must be a somewhat careless being, not greatly upsetting himself if he is precise or not. This may extend to speech, and although his sense of fitness would keep him from telling fibs, he might certainly be given to exaggeration.

Lastly, we would call attention to the underlining stroke. This is a finish which points to some considerable firmness, but without further examples we cannot decide whether this is any indication of a leaning towards obstinacy.

There you have what a few strokes reveal. If any reader thinks he has now discovered the owner of the "scratch", please let him communicate with the Editor and by return of post he will receive a putty medal.

Ed.

[p. 38]

A RAMBLE SONG
Tune:– La Marseillaise.

The Surrey hills and lanes of smiling Kent
To-day shall know our heavy tread.
Through them the earlier "Angels" went
To where they eat their chops and bread,
To where they eat their chops and bread.
Like them we walk through dust or mire,
Like them we pass the time in song
Or howl at pairs that pass along,
And quip the girls with mild satire.
   Chorus:–
        Loudly; Trinity!
        To the vicinity,
        Proclaim your name
        Of gallant fame,
        With rousing melody.

The class wants a ramble song and the Marseillaise has often been suggested as the tune. Above you see one verse and the chorus which time will doubtlessly add to if they seem anything along the right line. Readers may like to supply the two additional verses requisite to complete the balance. Why not try?

CIRCULATING LIST.

As has always been the case, the time limit for single members is two days and for groups, three days.

Some single members have been allotted three days in order to facilitate the carrying out of the new plan.

Dec. 23	Mr. D. C. Messent.	In this space any further names
	Mr. W. Messent.	will be entered by the Class
	Mr. L. H. Messent.	Secretary.
26	Mr. R. S. Rowe.	
	Mr. H. Rowe.	[written in pencil are]
	Mr. F. Rowe.	S. Gosling
29	Mr. C. Smith.	T. Eagle
31	Mr. C. Bedwell.	M. Davies
	Mr. L. Bedwell.	H. Messent
	Mr. N. Bedwell.	
Jan. 3	Mr. F. Biggin.	
5	Mr. A. Austin.	
	Mr. F. v. Rittershausen.	
8	Mr. G. Barrett.	
10	Mr. F. Perkins.	
12	Mr. W. Cramp.	
	Mr. P. Coomber.	
15	Mr. E. Munro.	
17	Mr. E. Bowler.	
19	Mr. L. Fouracre.	
21	Mr. F. Jones.	
	Mr. H. Jones.	
	Mr. A. Jones.	
24	Mr. A. Carpenter.	
26	Mr. H. Lansdown.	
28	Mr. A. Morse.	
	Mr. T. Lynch.	
31	Mr. A. H. Evans.	
Feb 2	Mr. C. Cloak.	
4	Mr. C. Moxley.	

[On the reverse of this page appears a verse from 'Lines written on Westminster Bridge']

Earth has not anything to show more fair
Dull would he be of soul who could pass by

A sight so touching in its majesty;
    This city now doth like a garment wear
    The beauty of the evening.

Wordsworth.

THE ANGELS' VOICE

July   1913

No. 10

EDITOR. J. GODDEN

[p. 1]

[Drawing of two young ladies – one sitting on the floor, the other tying up her long hair.]

[Signed:] C.V.M. 1913.

[p. 2]

THE ANGELS' VOICE.

No. 10.
JULY–1913.

EDITORIAL

Dear Readers,
When the regular publication of the magazine was interrupted in 1911, we promised that within four years, it should once more appear month by month. We did not expect, however, to take up the work so soon; with the help of our half yearly numbers, it is easy to think of the series as practically unbroken.
The August Number may be somewhat late, but readers must remember that if they get holidays, so do Editors and Printers. Still, if you insist on having the magazine in good time, send in the necessary articles and rest assured that it will appear.

Ed.

The Editor's address is now:–
31, Branksome Road,
Brixton, S.W.

[p. 3]

"MAXTON",

June. 1913.

My dear Fellow Members,

In thinking over the general affairs of the Class, one feels that there is much that one might call attention to, but of course, the limited space at one's disposal prevents anything like a full survey.

I should like to remind our members, that of late, T.Y.M.B.C. has developed; not so much in numbers as in that attitude towards Church life which is the sure sign of true progress and growth.

In these days, when favourable statistics seem to be popular signs of success, it is encouraging to be able to look into our affairs and note the splendid developments in our midst, developments which cannot be tabulated.

Of course, these developments have their outward signs. For instance, take the attitude of our members towards the general affairs of our Church, and one sees a unanimous desire to do all that lies in their power to assist. A Bazaar is in prospect, they must do something to help towards its success; the result is a Hosiery Stall the net result of which was as near to £20 as makes no matter. Again, the Church and Manse premises call for immediate external renovation, and without a

[p. 4]

dissentient voice; in a memorable meeting with the Deacons, our fellows pledge themselves to do their utmost to raise the necessary funds, and the result will be that before next Christmas, £30 will have been raised.

These are only two illustrations of what I mean. The straws, large ones in this case, certainly show which way the wind is blowing, and I am convinced that we are travelling along a road that, by God's Grace, will lead us all into an even closer and more vital relationship with His People, constituting the Church at Trinity.

Now whilst being very thankful for the real progress referred to above, we must just turn our minds to one or two things that are not quite so cheering.

The first thing is, that we have not grown in numbers as we ought to have done. Truly we meet Sunday by Sunday, about 24 strong, but that number ought to be increased. There must be a host of fellows in Brixton whom we could help to get more out of this life than they do at present. Surely most of us come into contact with such from time to time, and it should be our privilege to do a little recruiting amongst them. If, during the next six months, each of our men could induce one other to come along and join us – well –

[p. 5]

by Christmas our room would be too small.

The second thing that I feel is, that although our contact with God's Word, Sunday by Sunday, is becoming increasingly helpful, I am bound to say that much more progress might be made in this direction if we would indulge in a little more preparation. To attend our Study Circle without having given the subject for the afternoon at least a few moments thought, is a sure way to miss the helpfulness that should be derived; and besides the negligent one suffering, the whole Class must often be deprived of some amount of help which might have been contributed as the result of private reading and consideration. Attention to this matter would have immediate results, for a quickened interest means a vitalising of our Topics such as hitherto we have but partially known.

It is good to hear from time to time from our members who are abroad. We have nothing but good news from Australia, Las Palmas and India, and I am sure that we all feel thankful that these who have had to leave us are all getting along so well. "Commit thy way into the Lord and He shall direct thy path".

Believe me to be, Ever yours sincerely,

D. C. Messent.

[p. 6]

[Two postcard views of Las Palmas, Grand Canary.]

[p. 7]

LAS PALMAS – GRAND CANARY

You all know by now, where the Canary Islands are situated, so I need not describe their position, but many of you may have no idea of what the place is like.

It is almost impossible to give a pen picture of the country, but the photographs give one an idea of how pretty it is. The views show patches of cultivated land in the hills, but from the town, one only sees brown slopes rising one upon the other.

The richer Spaniards live in practically the same manner as the English, except that owing to the climate, they eat more fruit. The usual fare of the poorer Spaniards consists in bread, onions and "gofu". The bread, which is made of maize-flour and water, is very poor eating, but the "gofu" which is very similar to porridge and got from maize, is rare tack, and almost every Englishman has it for breakfast. Then there is also fruit which is consumed in large quantities. One need not mention bananas, but unfortunately, since the writer has been here, it has been the "off-season" for fruit. He has, however, had some grand oranges, and the only objection to them is that you usually smother yourself with juice. Mizprahs, which resemble a plum, and also

[p. 8]

[Postcard of women and children washing clothes.]

[p. 9]

mellon pears, tasting like a cross between an English pear and a scarlet runner seed, have been available. In June we get superb grapes at ½d. or 1d. a pound, cherries, raspberries, and plums.

The usual drink is wine, and every labourer you see has a quart bottle in his basket. It is very cheap, costing about 4d. a quart, and there are two kinds – red and white. Red wine is chiefly consumed owing to its being cheaper and stronger. It is easy to understand why the people drink wine, for the water here is not good, and has to be brought to the Port and Town, from the hills, by means of gutters running by the side of the roads. Of course, it must be boiled before it is drinkable.

In passing, a word on washing would not be out of place. Most of the poor people, who have no convenience in their homes, wash in the gutters. They are allowed to wash there until 4 o'clock in the afternoon, when everyone, under penalty of death, is required to stop, so that the water can be used for drinking purposes. The photograph gives some women washing, and it is a matter of contention as to whether it is better to be one of the first washers, thus getting clean water, or to wash lower down and then get good soapy water, but necessarily

[p. 10]

[Two postcards – one of a team of oxen pulling a plough and the other of a town and harbour.]

[p. 11]

a little dirt as well. Some of the T.L.H.C. might be able to settle this knotty point, but personally I am in favour of the lower washers, because the women dry the clothes by laying them about anywhere on stones, small trees and bushes, and they are therefore bound to pick up a certain amount of dirt.

Tobacco is fairly cheap and one can get a good cigar for ½d. If this price ruled in England, I wonder how many would be found swanking outside Trinity Church on Sunday evening.

The whole population is directly or indirectly connected with shipping or fruit growing. Owing to the large number of vessels which come into the Port, Sunday is more or less an ordinary day, except that most Spaniards make a point of going to Mass. The only days which are kept as holidays are Feast Days, and they average about one a month. They are usually held to celebrate the birth of some saint. The Fruit-growing Industry is important, and the farmers are beginning to use machinery, but the photograph of the ploughing shows they are still not quite up-to-date.

The Spaniards, on the whole, are very small men, their average height not being over 5 ft., although in

[p. 12]

[Two postcards of countryside and scattered houses.]

[p. 13]

the country the men are much bigger. I have not yet seen a fair Spaniard, and am told that you only come across the beautiful fair Spaniards in the Peninsula. The girls are very good looking for about five years, but after that they become rather fat. I put it down to lack of work, as it is infra dig for Spanish girls to do any house work, except among the lowest classes. The women are regarded as much inferior to the men, and one always sees the man riding on the donkey, whilst his wife walks at the side. The people are very hospitable, which is remarkable seeing how cruel they are to animals. On one of my walks, a farmer stopped his carriage and offered to give me a lift, and the poor people will never accept anything for water, and give you flowers for nothing.

Prices of various commodities are usually about 25% above those in England – the extra 25% being the charge for freight from England, and Port Dues. In the case of small articles, the price is very often 50% to 70% higher, and it would be an immeasurable boon to these Islands if a parcel post were established.

H.R.[1]

Information re Mr. C.

He has joined the class for young hubbies, and reports will be forwarded for publication month by month.

[p. 14]

THE WHITSUN RAMBLE

Mr. D. C. Messent.	Mr. A. H. Evans.	Mr. C. Moxley.
Mr. R. S. Rowe.	Mr. J. G. Godden.	Mr. C. Bedwell.
Mr. F. Rowe.	Mr. W. Cramp.	Mr. L. Bedwell.

[1]   Henry S. Rowe.

Mr. A. P. Austin.	Mr. R. Chippendale	Mr. N. Bedwell.
Mr. E. H. Bowler.	Mr. H. Lansdown.	Mr. A. Carpenter.
Mr. E. Munro.	Mr. P. Coomber.	Mr. M. Davis.
Mr. F. Lynch.	Mr. A. Snoswell.	Mr. L. Jones.
Mr. H. Eagle	Mr. F. Yates.	Mr. E. Oake.

Never in our rambling history, has a Bank Holiday been so eagerly anticipated, as our Wet Whitsun. But as time separates us from the actual day, we are able to forget some of the rain, and remember with keen appreciation, the wild fun and unconventional behaviour we indulged in.

Weeks beforehand, we knew that the attendance would be a record one, and there was an excited fluttering amongst the "Angels", which did not quite cease, even when their wings were drenched by the unseasonable rain.

On the actual morning, several enthusiastic early birds, turned out to catch the proverbial worm, and after making themselves an intolerable nuisance at many a temple of slumber, finally received the worm at the hands of a young lady in Arlingford Road.

The day really started, however, at Waterloo Station.

[p. 15]

The train was empty, and we had the rare privilege of picking our carriages. The rowdiest naturally tumbled into the same compartment, but they seemed to have a suspicion that a bird of similar feather was still missing. Of course there was! The major with his sweet voice, inflammatory appearance and geniality withal, had not recognised his true environment, and it took five "Angels" tugging at each leg, to convince him that he really had made a mistake.

Once the train had started, the noisy ones, suddenly ceased their tumult and became tuneful. Song succeeded song, and chorus followed chorus, until strained threats could no longer maintain the effort. At this point, our universally handy man produces a flageolette, and with the help of horrible splutters from Mr. Cramp, on the flute, treated the carriage to windy music, until their victims let down the windows and sang an appropriate and suggestive chorus.

It is a recognised fact that rambling produces a fine appetite, but some of the ramblers seemed to have anticipated sharing their food all round, and their parcels were of an extraordinary size. We had, of course, passed no remarks, being naturally considerate of each others feelings, but we did open our eyes a bit when these

[p. 16]

packages were produced at about 10 o'clock, and their owners began to cut strings with feverish haste. But – instead of sandwiches – in each parcel a lovely, shiny topper was softly reposing in its brown paper nest. The rush at a sale of ladies hats could not compare with what ensued, and proudly did the conquering "Angels" wear their sable haloes.

Before the end of the journey, several raids were made on neighbouring carriages, and the noisy crowd was increased by the captured quiet ones. So largely increased, indeed, that several bulky individuals were thrust into the luggage racks, to reduce the congestion.

We got out at Horsley, and marched fast and without any particular incident till we reached our old grazing ground above Shere. The weather was still supportable, and we settled down with satisfaction to a congenial task, amid congenial surroundings. Our next move was down to Shere for drinks, and after a short halt we pushed on once more towards St. Martha's. We had hardly done a mile, before the clouds, which had, for some time, been threatening to "drop fatness", began to splash us with something which did not in the least feel like grease. A.H.E. called a halt, and after a brief consultation, we decided to make for Chilworth Railway

[p. 17]

Station, two miles distant. We first grouped ourselves on a gate, with the top hats in honourable positions, and Mr. Leslie Bedwell took our photographs. We then fell in, four deep, and our six ranks made quite an imposing body. Messrs. Austin & Cramp constituted the band, but Mr. Cramp, I am afraid, paid more attention to his waddle, than to his instrument and the notes coming out of it.

Just a quarter of a mile before Chilworth, we came upon a stretch of road which was kept dry by some overhanging trees, and whilst the lazy ones reposed their well-nurtured carcases, the others formed sides and played hockey, first with a rubber ball, but when that broke with top hats. It was here that Mr. C. Bedwell sustained damage to his ankle. Some lusty club-wielder happened to catch a tender spot, which necessitated the services of A.P.A. A satisfactory job was made of the case, and the injured member was despatched to Chilworth per mineral water cart, seated in triumph on a crate of ginger beer.

Soon after, we all reached the station, and before the train came in, the place rang with such melody, as I warrant has seldom disturbed its quietude. The

[p. 18]

sorrowful history of Cock Robin was slowly chanted in harmony, and closed with such a solemn and impressive Amen, that there was hardly a dry eye on the whole platform.

Once in Guildford, the all-important consideration was – tea. Mr. Evans did not seem to know just the right place here, or else it was our unusual number which upset his calculations. However, eventually we broke up into two parties, the noisier ones drifting together as they always do, and with Major at their head, entered the shop of the pretty waitresses. The tea was quite a good one, and for our part, we were all well-behaved with the exception of the Major. He was badly smitten with the damsel who attended to our wants, and his eager glances made her blush. I rather think he imagined he was making good progress, but she accepted at his hands, the tip he had made us club up for, and I know that if I were a girl, and fell in love with a chap like the Major, I should not allow him to give me money under any circumstances. Of course, he may have tried to give her something else, but I was not looking at the time, and so cannot say.

After tea we all met again and signed two post-cards,

[p. 19]

one for Las Palmas and the other for India. Then we separated into two parties for the return journey. Those who had not brought macintoshes took the train from Guildford, and had "real" music all the way to London. The remaining ten walked on to Clandon, going through Lord Onslow's park on the way.[2] These last five miles proved as good as any during the outing, and everyone thought them well worth the extra exertion. We were fortunate enough to secure a carriage to ourselves, but could not strain our throats to the extent of a sing-song. The conversation flagged for a while, but soon Mr. Carpenter threw down the gauntlet on the subject of women's suffrage, and for the rest of an exceptionally slow journey, we had the pleasure of listening to his views, and the excitement of immediately squashing them.

The ramble really did have a considerable measure of success, even though it was disappointing, but with equal numbers, fine weather and similar enthusiasm, our next trip to the Surrey hills will be noteworthy indeed.

J.G.

---

[2] Clandon Park, West Clandon, Guildford, is now a National Trust property. It was the family seat of the Onslow family and the present mansion was commissioned by Thomas, 2nd Lord Onslow (1754–1827). The house was a military hospital during the First World War. *National Trust Handbook* (2015); *ODNB*.

Readers will be pleased to know that copies of this number have been dispatched to Will and Henry, in their respective quarters of the earth.

[p. 20]

CONGRATULATORY

Mr. G. Barrett.

Mr. E. H. Bowler.

Mr. F. Butcher.

Mr. R. Chippindale.

Mr. L. H. Messent.

Mr. F. Perkins.

A man's birthdays are probably as unimportant as any other days of the year, both to him and those who know him. But the day of his birth was most important, and his 21st. celebration of it, is a day which, contrary to the usual run of birthdays, is fraught with great significance and import, to himself and his fellows. He is no longer a child but a man; his voice counts as one in the assembly of those who take counsel together; the responsibility for the effects of his actions is transferred from his parents shoulders to his own. A man's coming of age, is, indeed, more than mere sentiment. An ordinary birthday, unless there be celebration, brings nothing with it, but the day on which his infancy is legally terminated, adds to his dignity and importance, though he have no friends with whom to commemorate it.

In recent months, several of our members have come of age, and it would be a poor class magazine which failed to take note of such events. We do most heartily congratulate our six friends, and hope that they may be

[p. 21]

given increased wisdom with their added responsibility, and that they may remain long amongst us, pillars of the class, and friends to all who need them.

Ed.

LOOK-OUT COMMITTEE.

True, we do not get many young men who are casual visitors at Trinity, but there are such, and we have not secured one for our class for a long time. Would it not be as well to form a Look-Out Committee, whose duty it would be to look after this branch of work. It may be objected that the whole class should form this committee, and that is true enough, but when the responsibility is shared out thus, each member, if he does not feel inclined to take an opportunity, can console himself with the thought that somebody else will undoubtedly step in where he has been found wanting. A committee that accepted this responsibility would be more decisive in its action, and time might prove it of immeasurable value to our class.

Did anyone notice that one of the choir boys was rather groggy a few Sundays back?

Anyway, he was, and got mal-de-mer rather severely. Curiously enough, he had just been to tea chez A.H.E.

[p. 22]

OUR WORK.

During the past month the Pastor and Deacons paid us the exceptional honour of inviting us to meet with them, on Tuesday the 17th. June. This invitation was accepted through the medium of our leader, and at 8.30 on the evening, every member who could call his time his own was present.

Mr. Lansdown opened with a few well-chosen words, and explained that the Deacons sought our help in a matter connected with the preservation of our premises. The whole of the exterior woodwork of Church and Manse was in urgent need of thorough painting. For the most part, these exterior portions had received no attention for nearly ten years, and would inevitably rot unless immediate steps were taken. The Deacons had had the matter under consideration for some time, but had felt that so many appeals had been sent out in the name of the Pastor and Deacons, and especially in connection with the renovation of our premises, that it would be far better if this time it could originate from a different quarter. They had been very near starting a scheme some time ago, but had delayed it for the above reason.

[p. 23]

However, in asking us to take the matter over, they felt they would like to make known to us what plan they had been able to arrive at. Mr. Lansdown now called upon Mr. Messent, who briefly outlined the scheme.

The exterior of the church had been divided into a number of portions, such as windows, doors and railings. The approximate cost of painting these separate items had been obtained, and these particulars had been printed on cards, with an invitation to friends to provide the funds for painting such portions as they felt within their ability.

A general discussion now took place, and it was pointed out that the coming anniversary services would offer a fine opportunity for putting the matter very insistently before the Church, and so prepare the way for our individual attack. The general feeling, however, was against openly commencing the campaign whilst so many other funds were already being collected for. The Autumn Rally Day seemed a more satisfactory point from which to commence operations.

Mr. Guy Barrett was of the opinion that this appeal to members who had already given liberally quite recently, was not advisable. He could not help noticing that the Church was often nearer empty than full, and that if our

[p. 24]

energy were directed into a channel with the aim of filling empty places, by the time the need for the money became urgent, it would be possible to collect the whole sum from new adherents.

After a few more remarks, Mr. Godden proposed that the responsibility should be accepted. The motion was seconded by Mr. Austin and carried unanimously. The Deacons now retired and our leader took the chair.

Mr. Godden urged the necessity of having a committee to direct our movements in this matter, and also of keeping a careful account of all the cards, so that we might see at a glance what ground had been covered, and what ground was left untouched.

Mr. D. C. Messent suggested that the class committee should nominate the members of this new committee and submit them for the approval of the class on the following Sunday. This course was not pursued and after a ballot, the following very satisfactory committee was elected:–   Mr. R. S. Rowe.   Mr. A. Austin.
                    Mr. C. Bedwell.   Mr. J. Godden
                              Mr. W. Cramp.

The meeting now adjourned, and private effort will have a free hand till the Committee embark us on a definite and vigorous course of action.

[p. 25]

IMPRESSIONS OF GHENT.
Our Organist rivals A.H.E.

Leaving Victoria by the 9.50 p.m. train on Friday night, we arrived at Ghent (via Dover and Ostend) at about 5.30 on Saturday morning in pouring rain, but cheerful.

The Ghent International Exhibition is, in one respect at least, like all others, in being opened months before it is finished. In fact most Exhibitions are not worth seeing until they are just on the point of closing. The time we had at our disposal was wholly inadequate for seeing the entire Exhibition, as we had our rehearsals and concerts to attend, and the Exhibition covers in all some nine and a half square miles.

The hall called the Palais des Fetes, in which our concerts were held (and, by the way, the boxing match as well) covers an area of 3½ acres. The flower show had previously been held there, and when lit up with long lines of electric lights, the effect is very fine.

One of the chief halls of exhibits that I got into, was the "Section Francaise", with the latest fashions in ladies dresses. Here there were some fine costumes and beautiful Brussels lace. There were also many wax-work

[p. 26]

[Two postcards of Ghent – view of the park and 'Panorama of the Exposition'.]

[p. 27]

figures, very true to life, wearing the various costumes, besides others shown engaged upon work connected with the materials used in the trade.

The buildings round the principal entrance are very fine. After traversing the path for some distance, a number of huge bulls are seen. Then, ascending the steps, there is a fine domed hall called "Vestibule d'honneur". This also, when lit up is very effective. All the buildings are painted white as in the majority of exhibitions. Passing on through this hall, a courtyard called "Cour d'honneur" is reached. Here there is a fine cascade of water flowing down from a huge piece of statuary, into a basin surrounded at intervals by other smaller statues, all continental in form. (Surely our Contributor means classical. Ed.)

Little trains, each consisting of two tram-like conveyances, open at the sides and drawn by an almost toy engine go all round the Exhibition grounds. The evening time is of course the best to look round. Things have hardly begun to go before, and the illuminations are then in full play. The cafes are very full and noisy especially on Sunday evenings.

On Sunday afternoon, in pouring rain, we made our way by tram to the part of Ghent where lie the Cathedral

[p. 28]

[Two postcards – St Nicholas's church and the Belfry.]

[p. 29]

and the other churches of interest. It is strange to visitors to find that on these trams they have 1st. and 2nd. Class. On some cars there is a division, but on others there is no such thing, but only a notice saying

"The first three benches are 2nd. class, and the back three 1st. class". There is no difference between them.

The Cathedral of St. Bavon is a fine old building, somewhat crumbling in parts, as in most Continental Churches, the adornments of the interior are very ornate, and the singing of the choir boys is execrable. One of the special features of the Cathedral is the picture, painted in 1420 to 1432, by the brothers Van Eyck, called "The Adoration of the Mystic Lamb". The colours are as fresh now as when first painted. The neighbouring churches of St. Nicholas and St. Michael are interesting in their way, being finely decorated within.

There are some very quaint old houses about this part of Ghent, and the Chateau des Comtes, a medieval fortress, is well worth a visit. I was, however much more pleased with Bruges, to which I went on the Monday, than with Ghent itself. However, the weather was so dreadful during our short stay, that it precluded us from making any very great investigation of the town in general.

[p. 30]

T.Y.M.B.C. TELEPHONE DIRECTORY.

We publish this list with the usual declaration of non-liability for inconvenience arising from mistakes.

Readers would do well to copy this list out, for since the last directory appeared, the Editor has been pestered for the telephone numbers of class members.

Asterisks must be noticed and respected. They mark men of business who may not be troubled with casual chats. Leave their numbers alone unless you have something important to say.

Barrett. Mr. G.	Gerrard 4011	Rowe. Mr. F.	North 3200
*Bedwell. Mr. C.	Bank 5034	(Accountants Dept.)	
Bedwell. Mr. N	City 1781	*Rowe. Mr. S.	Official
Bowler. Mr. E.	Holborn 2808		Switch 488
Butcher. Mr. F.	L. Wall 3857	Seymour. Mr. S.	Brix. 1800
*Carpenter. Mr. A.	Streathm 1247	(Costumes)	
Chippindale Mr. R.	City 2880	Smith. Mr. C.	Vic. 4954
*Coomber. Mr. P.	City 8281		
Cramp. Mr. W.	L. Wall 3768		
Davis. Mr. M.	Holborn 2370		
(Ludgate Hill Branch)			
Eagle. Mr. H.	Avenue 4032		
*Evans. Mr. A. H.	Bank 82	The notes in brackets show	
(If not in, leave a message)		what department should be	
	asked for.		
Godden. Mr. J. G.	New Cross 36		
Gosling. Mr. S.	City 6681		

*Jones. Mr. F.　　　City 3176
(FACTORY)
Lynch. Mr. E.　　　Victoria 4896
Messent. Mr. D. C.　Holborn 606
Messent. Mr. L. H.　Holborn 606
*Moxley. Mr. C.　　Holborn 5330

[p. 31]

OUR PEWS

IIo　　　　oIo　　　　oIIo　　　　oI

I can remember the first time I came to Trinity Church and how I sat in the gallery opposite our original class pew, and also what a crowd of young fellows seemed to be squeezed into that pew. I suppose it was the general emptiness of their side of the gallery which threw this little group into such prominence, for it was the morning service and the average attendance in those days was not better than it is now.

By that same evening I had already been admitted into the mystic circle of "Mr. Messent's Class" and proudly took my seat in our usual pew.

Our class always seems to have been pretty intimately connected with the choir, and at that time some of our regular members were the leading boys, whilst some of our more recent members, were new boys in the side pews. At the present time the whole of the men are members of the T.Y.M.B.C. – But what has this to do with our class pew? If you will look back just under our title you will see a most curious dividing line. It is just a rough plan of our pews, and the circles mark the seats that are usually occupied. If you will count them

[p. 32]

up you will find that they amount in all to a grand total of six. Judging from this you at once jump to the conclusion that the class is of exactly the same size as when five and sometimes six, sat squeezed together in former days, and that the only change is that its members like more room. This is absolutely wrong, our class in this time has nearly trebled its numbers, and the choir does not affect our church muster in the least, because what we lost by drainage into the back seat of the choir, we have had made up to us by an influx of younger members from the front seat. The fact remains, then, that as we grow bigger, we grow less inclined to come to Church. What a glorious result to show for five years class development. Buck up Trinity! Apply your football cry to your church life, and by the end of this month let there be no difference between our morning and evening attendance, and let that evening attendance exceed the plan which brings this growl to a conclusion.

A petition is being signed and will later be forwarded to the Home Secretary, begging that our erring member may not be dealt with too severely on this, the occasion of his first offence. His nightmare of clear roads, policemen and stop watches have been sufficient punishment.

[p. 33]

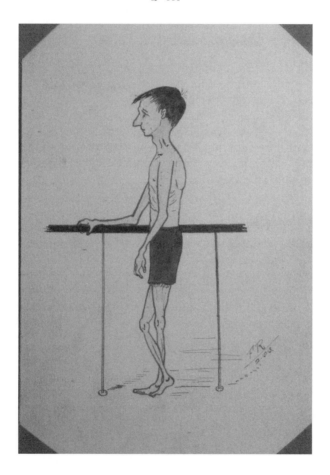

[Drawing of weedy looking young man in trunks.]
[Signed:] FR[3] – 2.1913.

---

3   Presumably Frank (Leonard) Rowe. See also *AV* 12 (Sept. 1913), 23.

[p. 34]

BEFORE AND AFTER

BEFORE   If I were you, Algy,[4] I should find out who borrowed your features for the preceding sketch. Once done, just slip in and prove that the rest of the portrait is a libel.
AFTER   O Trinity, what a picture! Muscles like under-done steaks, and a back like a 10" pile for stiffness. Somebody wants to make you like that for next winter.

Fashion has decreed that all well-dressed men shall wear brown. It rejoices us exceedingly to note that Mr. L. Jones has responded to that call. We also feel satisfied as to the good taste of our class as a whole, when we observe that Messrs. Rowe, Bowler, Bedwell and Messent, have clad their shapely figures in various shades of the correct colour.

We have it on inside information that the ARCHANGEL will also don a brown suit, although rumour whispers that it may be a near approach to mustard colour.

We regret to report that Miss. M. Vale has left Trinity. She is now living in Bexhill, and we can only hope to be favoured with occasional visits when she is in town.

[p. 35]

[Drawing of a strong athletic type in blue trunks. See opposite.]
[Signed:] F.R. – 2. 1913.

[p. 36]

PERKINS RING

Detective Irkins has at any time an imposing appearance, but never has he looked more sublime than when I saw him marching down Church Road with summer lightning flashing round him. I was awed … But as he came nearer, the electric sparks dwindled in size, and seemed to confine themselves to one hand. When we finally met, the nature-fireworks turned out to be nothing more than the bright sun playing round his new ring.

I duly admired the bauble, and even praised it, but suddenly I was stricken bashful and awkward – the ring was on the engagement finger. Was the great detective waiting for my congratulations and best wishes? Had he placed some fair damsel under life-long obligation

---

4   Presumably Algernon Carpenter.

during the unravelling of his latest case, and had she bestowed her hand upon him in return?

It was a mystery; it is still a mystery; it shall remain a mystery.

These Open Air Meetings are worth supporting. Our class can help immensely, and those few who have not yet attended one, will be sure to find a little gang of our fellows singing lustily, but needing your help.

[p. 37]

AUGUST BANK HOLIDAY

The South Eastern and Chatham Railway is still running its Bank Holiday Excursions to Boulogne, at the tempting fare of 10/- return. The train leaves London at 10 a.m. and is due back at 10.30 p.m., and the excursionists get five and a half hours ashore at Boulogne. It may be seen from this that quite a respectable glimpse at France may be obtained at a fairly reasonable rate. Several members have already visited this interesting town, and they are thinking seriously of getting up a small party to make this trip next month. There is no reason why even a good number should not go, for the expense would only be about double of that incurred on a Surrey tramp.

The last issue of the magazine was received back in a most woefully tattered envelope which evidently was not strong enough to bear the strains imposed upon it. The ideal cover, of course, should be made of wood, and one of our readers presented you with two such cases last year. Some persons have seen fit, however, to return the magazines and retain the cases. Will they kindly let the Editor have them back for the protection of future issues?

[p. 38]

WHERE MAJOR SCORES.

Ah! That's the question! Where does he score? Detective Irkins has made enquiries at Raines Park [sic], Brockwell Park, Clapham Common, and even at Trent Road, but nowhere has he succeeded in gaining the slightest authentic information. Even the urchins of Trent Road dolefully shake their heads and maintain that he never yet made a single run in their pavement matches.

It cannot be said that Mr. Irkins is on a false scent, for rumour attributes mighty feats to the Major's bat, and his average from all accounts, has reached an almost incomprehensible figure. We also hear from our Las Palmas correspondent that the local papers are full of vivid reports of his prowess, which they have good reason to believe do not exaggerate in the slightest. Numerous attempts have been made to secure confirmation of these reports from the Major himself, but with his customary modesty, he will not utter a single word on the subject. It is comforting that he does not deny them, but still allows us to assume that he does score somewhere. Can it be that he scores over us by his mocking silence? I say! That's not cricket!

[p. 39]

[A blank green sheet – a postcard is clearly missing.]

[p. 40]

"Sir" Daniel Messent.

We wonder whether the worthy gentleman who wrote this postcard had been reading the latest birthday honours list. If so, his character for sobriety will not stand much investigation.

Or is the simple foreigner having a sly hit at the lordly style of the English tourist?

It may be that there is an idea at the back of his head that every Englishman is raised to the nobility on attaining his majority, or more probable still – he simply does not know our usual form of address, and just fills up a gap with the politest word he can think of.

LAS PALMAS

Dear Ernie,

Cigars only cost a halfpenny out here. Why don't you come over and then you could swank about with them as much as you liked, and you would not need to pretend they were only smoked to deaden the smell of Lewis' motor bike? Of course, there is the risk that there would be no fun in smoking them out here, for it is not looked upon as swank, cigars being far too common.

Yours ever,

Enery.

[p. 41]

CIRCULATING LIST

Every reader whose name is underlined <u>must</u> return the magazine to the class room on that date

Name	Date magazine to be passed on.
Mr. D. C. Messent.	
Mr. W. Messent.	
<u>Mr. L. H. Messent.</u>	<u>July 6th.</u>
Mr. R. S. Rowe.	
Mr. F. Rowe.	July 9th.
Mr. C. Smith.	July 11th.
<u>Mr. C. Moxley.</u>	<u>July 13th.</u>
Mr. C. Bedwell.	
Mr. L. Bedwell.	
Mr. N. Bedwell.	July 16th.
Mr. E. H. Bowler.	July 18th.
<u>Mr. H. Lansdown.</u>	<u>July 20th.</u>

Mr. F. Jones.
Mr. H. Jones.
Mr. A. Jones.   July 23rd.
Mr. F. Perkins.   July 25th.
<u>Mr. G. Barrett.</u>   <u>July 27th.</u>

Mr. W. Cramp.
Mr. P. Coomber.   July 30th.
Mr. R. Chippindale.   Aug. 1st.
<u>Mr. A. Carpenter.</u>   <u>Aug. 3rd.</u>

Mr. A. Austin.
Mr. F. V. Rittershausen   Aug. 6th.
Mr. E. Munro.   Aug. 8th.
<u>Mr. A. H. Evans.</u>   <u>Aug. 10th.</u>

Mr. M. Davis.   Aug. 11th.
Mr. H. Eagle.   Aug. 13th.
Mr. T. Lynch.   Aug. 15th.
<u>Mr. S. Gosling.</u>   <u>Aug. 17th.</u>

Mr. E. Yates.   Aug. 18th.
Mr. F. Butcher.   Aug. 20th.

THE

ANGELS' VOICE

NO. 11

Editor: J. Godden

[p.1]

THE ANGELS' VOICE.
No. 11.   August. 1913.

EDITORIAL

Dear Readers,

What a predicament! The Editor returns from his holidays and would willingly find a sheaf of articles awaiting his approval. Instead, he finds nothing but his own bare writing-pad with its mute invitation to labour.

At the last moment, however, we received a contribution which will surely put the controversially inclined upon their mettle. Do you wish for compulsory military service, or do you favour peace at all costs? Read the article on conscription and see if it stirs you to indignation or approval.

There will be plenty of room in the next number for the ventilation of your opinion.

Ed.

[p. 2]

"Maxton",
Kings Avenue, S.W.

My dear Fellow Members,

By the time this issue is in your hands, the holiday season will be at its height. Already quite a number have been for their "Annual", but there are many who are still looking forward to a change of scene and recreation. During the early days of September, a party hope to be visiting the Channel Islands, and I am sure that we sincerely wish for them a good time. Their absence on Sunday afternoons will create a gap which can, in some measure, be atoned for by the extra faithfulness and enthusiasm of those who remain at home.

For four Sundays during August, it has been arranged that our Meetings shall be presided over by some of our own members. On

August 10th., 17th., 24th., and 31st., Messrs. Godden, Cramp, Austin and Bedwell respectively will be in charge. This is somewhat of an experiment and I would ask each member to "get aboard" something of what it means. It means that hearty support must be given; that the Subject must, more than usually, be a matter for thought and prayer during the week, so that when the time comes, each one may be ready to add his contribution to the proceedings. It also means that at the meetings, the

[p. 3]

authority of the Chair must be loyally respected, and that the opening and closing exercises be entered into by all in a reverential and sympathetic spirit. Above all, may a consciousness of the presence of God in the midst be felt by all, so that His word may be studied with profit.

It has been very encouraging to note the support that our members have been giving to the Open Air Work this season. Usually, ten to fourteen bare their silent testimony as the Word is being preached, and quite a number are always ready to take some part in the proceedings. The suggestion of Mr. Martin that we, as a class, should be responsible for one of these gatherings during Mr. Lansdown's holiday, fell through owing to a misunderstanding. Otherwise I am confident that we could have found the men necessary for the undertaking.

We have before us a good winter's work, and I hope that we are looking forward to it. Let none forget our undertaking re the exterior repairs to the Church and Manse.

It has been decided to devote Sunday afternoon, September 21st., to the consideration of our Syllabus. One or two other matters may crop up, and I would commend this meeting to your especial notice.

[p. 4]

Relying on the continued hearty support of all,
  Believe me to be,
      Yours very sincerely,
        D. C. Messent.

Our Garden Party was a great success; there was not a dull minute during the whole evening. We made one miscalculation as to time, however, and our excellent programme had to be somewhat curtailed.

Our guests arrived for the most part, a little later than was expected. By six o'clock, nevertheless, a good crowd had collected, and were busily engaged in the Advertisement Competition. At the same time, Major was charging them a penny for the privilege of guessing his weight. A little later, Mr. John Rowe very kindly exhibited a number of his Chinese Curios. The Conjuror, Refreshments, Concert and Marionettes, amply filled the rest of the evening.

Mr. Howard Evans[1] will organise a party to visit the Church of the Ascension, Hyde Park, within the next month. This is an opportunity not to be missed.

[p. 5]

THE MODERN MISS

I quite fail to see what the reason can be
    For the charm of the present-day girl.
But I feel it is there, and I frankly declare,
    In her presence I'm all in a whirl.

So please pass it by, if in this you descry
    That my thoughts are arranged without order.
In great trepidation I turn observation
    On what a proud pa must afford her.

"I have nothing to wear." (But she doesn't go bare.)
    Perhaps it's a hat that she's after.
For Fashion's stern law says, "A Panama straw,
    With black velvet streamers abaft her."

As summers get duller she goes in for colour
    That mocks at the lead-laden skies.
Cerise, mauve and blue, but of such brilliant hue,
    That her jackets are spoiling her eyes.

Her skirt's a creation of that naughty nation
    Whose women are noted for daring.
It opens quite wide since it's slit up the side,
    And shows off the hose she is wearing.

[p. 6]

In spite of her passion for each passing fashion,
    Her charm does not lie in her dresses.
It still is her face and her feminine grace,
    Which gain her a lover's caresses.

                                    Q. Pid.

---

[1]   May be either Albert Howard Evans or his father Thomas Howard Evans.

OVERHEARD!

One of our choristers was chatting about the church attendance and remarked that the reason for his keen interest in the choir work, was that he felt that in this way he was doing the best he could to increase the number of regularly occupied seats.

A useful man! – that Chorister!

The matter of the seat carpet for our pews was considered at the last committee meeting. We should require about nine yards, and the cost would be nearly 30/-.

It was felt that the advantage was not of sufficient moment to justify the outlay.

Where have we spent our holidays?

We shall publish a list next month, showing the places we could tell each other about if we chose.

[p. 7]

THE FIVE SENSES.

What combination of circumstances would satisfy all five senses at the same time?

Readers of the "Angels' Voice" will perhaps remember that the answers to the above question were to have appeared in a former issue, but at the time, space was rather scanty and they had to be left over. The replies we will give now; they are quite dissimilar and rather interesting:

1. There is no such combination of circumstances. The nearest I can suggest is; Lying full length in the bottom of a punt in some shady up-river spot on a warm afternoon, and looking after a nice pretty girl.

2. Legend tells us that the Chinese made much of their pigs, giving them the shelter of their palaces in lieu of sties. A certain Chinaman, shutting his pigs in his palace, set out on business. Returning, he finds his palace burning, and hastens to the rescue of his pigs. As he enters he stumbles over the carcase of his choicest porker. Putting out his hands for protection, they grasp the roasting hot carcase, so he places his burning fingers

232

[p. 8]

in his mouth. At that moment all his senses were satisfied. He <u>smells</u> the savoury smell, <u>hears</u> the carcase sizzling in its fat, <u>feels</u> the burning skin on his fingers, <u>sees</u> the roasted carcase, and <u>tastes</u>, for the first time, roast pork.

3. Observing the neat formation of her pedal extremities, listening to the mellifluent ripple of her voice, helping to eat the chocolates I have just given her, smelling the scent sprinkled on her snowy garments, and thrilling at the touch of her slender hand, is as much as I ever wish my five senses to experience coincidentally.

4. In my opinion one might often find oneself under circumstances in which all the five senses are brought into play.

I was spending my holidays at a charming little seaside resort some 200 miles from London and surrounded by a rugged and precipitous coast. One day I took a delightful trip. Seated comfortably on the deck of a steamer, I was conscious of the vibration of the engines (touch). I was sitting with my friends right up in the bow of the vessel, so we were just above the musical ripple made by the water splashing up against the prow (hearing).

[p. 9]

Passing along the coast, we could not help being impressed by the grandeur of the scenery (sight), and the ozone was so pure and strong, that its peculiar, exhilarating odour was noticeable to all (smell). As the trip was a rather long one, and the accommodation on board somewhat scanty, sandwiches and other portable provender had been provided, which were very acceptable by way of lunch (taste).

You will thus see that at a given time – lunch time – all five senses were in full swing.

It will be noticed that none of these answers would suit everybody. The man who could satisfy every sense with the help of a maid and her appurtenances, quite possibly might fail to find the vibration of a steamer satisfying to any sense. When the pleasurable exercise of any of the faculties is dependent upon something artificial or manufactured, there is a practical certainty that this set of circumstances would find little favour with some other mortal. If we turn to nature, a universally satisfying environment may easily be found. Take a warm summer's day, and after a walk in the sun, you stretch yourself full length in a shady corner such as the hill over Shere, and look over the surrounding country. The soothing rustle and the smell of the fresh

[p. 10]

clean country satisfy two of the senses; the view and the cool breeze satisfy two more, and some juicy fruit will serve admirably to settle the fifth.

In spite of the possibility of all these favourable environments, each one, after all, only affords a mere negative enjoyment, in which the most marked sensation is one of ease and absolute tranquillity. Even the youth who plumps for a lady love must inevitably forget what chocolates taste like, under the influence of her thrilling touch. So it is with every sense; if one is given any noticeable prominence, the others fade into insignificance. I noticed of myself, that a slightly uncomfortable seat was far and away better than an easy one, whilst listening to an organ recital. This was, of course, if I wished to get the most out of the music, and not strive to humour my other senses at the same time, which, if I did, usually resulted in the complete comfort of sleep.

Just before we leave this matter, it is interesting to note that throughout, we have all omitted one essential qualification – a quiet mind. With mental trouble, music becomes jangling discord; a fair vision, mockery; and each other sense, a source of trouble and aggravation.

Ed.

[p. 11]

THE LITERARY SOCIETY.

No one who has ever heard a fairly general expression of opinion at any of our class meetings, can have failed to notice that we do as a rule, lack the ability to make our meaning clear in a few words. Quite frequently, the majority of members receive a different idea from that which was intended for them, and the fault is not theirs.

Of course, insufficient practice is at the root of it all, and only more practice can provide a remedy. The ability to speak well and effectively before ones fellows is an accomplishment, and not a gift. Eloquence is the gift, and as such, does not belong to everybody. But the accomplishment is what the word signifies – an end achieved after effort. Clear and effective speaking is a thing we wish for in our class life, and still more, possibly, in business life. As in the practice of every other accomplishment, our early efforts may not meet with much appreciation, but a little boldness and not overmuch effort will be amply repaid, and where can you find a more sympathetic meeting for your first attempts, than our church Literary Society?

[p. 12]

OUR AGE.

A few interesting figures.

It is easily possible to notice in our class, three distinct groups, although in actual association there is no visible division. Our leader, Mr. D. C. Messent, our organist, Mr. C. Moxley, and Messrs. Austin and Evans, are very evidently a remnant of a former generation. Then comes the main body of the class, those who partook in its formation or its development. Lastly comes that welcome influx of younger blood, repairing an unavoidable wastage.

In dealing with the average ages of the respective groups we must be careful to keep the four "Patriarchs" distinct, or the resulting figures would be misleading. But in casually looking over a class list, it is interesting to note, that including these, 14 of our members have attained their majority, whilst 17 find themselves within the range of 15 to 20.

Our main body has an average age of 22, whilst our newer members average 17 years old. These two groups have a combined average age of 20. When the four "elders" are included, it will be seen that we may easily call ourselves an adult class, as far as average figures go.

[p. 13]

CONSCRIPTION.

With the absolute failure of the Territorial Force, the country is faced with the old question of how to secure a reserve force for the protection of our commerce and property should an enemy ever effect a landing in this island of ours.

Of course, to the majority of Englishmen, the idea of compulsory service is repugnant to say the least of it, but let me in the small space at my disposal, give you the reasons why every able-bodied man, if he has any grit in him at all, should be compelled by law to set aside a portion of the year to be trained in military discipline. It is erroneous to think that our fleet is invincible; she has her weak parts the same as any other organised body. Take for instance a cricket eleven with a member who can bat and bowl, and the rest absolutely relying on him for a good send off. He goes in first and is bowled second ball. What happens is, that the rest of the side are thrown into confusion resulting in defeat. It is the same with our navy; she has served us well for many years, and looks like doing so for many more. But in the evolution of nations, England will

[p. 14]

have to fight, and fight hard, if she is to retain her position as premier country of the world. Should our fleet be disabled, can we expect a mere handful of soldiers, not only to guard our towns and property, but also to keep in subjection those thousands of men who have never handled a rifle, and have never been disciplined and trained to keep their nerve when trouble of this sort comes.

Take China, for instance. With her 400 millions of people, what is she doing to-day? She is gradually Westernising, gradually drilling into her people all the advantages of modern civilization. It must follow, therefore, that she will expand, and as there is only a limited amount of space on this earth, and the best of that is occupied, she will have to fight for more, unless we reach the ideal state of settlement by arbitration.

Now, what chance should we stand at present, if China took it into her head to attack us? Our ships would naturally keep us secure, but she will not remain for long without ships. The trade of the country will forge ahead, and to have good trade, you must have battleships and cruisers to see that trade protected. Hence she will form her fleet.

Now some of my readers will say, "You are talking

[p. 15]

of years hence" – so I am, but you cannot train an army in five minutes. Of course, conscription is only possible in this country, provided we have a guarantee that in the time of war, our berths will be kept open. This will no doubt be one of the most important articles in any such Bill.

It is therefore, the bounden duty of every Englishmen, if he thinks anything of the future of his country at all, to see that before long, a bill is passed in Parliament compelling every able-bodied man over the age of nineteen, to do a certain amount of military training every year. This will not only strengthen our army, but it will also be a blessing in disguise as regards the physical and moral well-being of every citizen in the country. In closing, let me remind you of Nelson's famous signal: "England expects every man <u>this</u> day will do his duty".

Bontex.

Readers will notice that the magazine does not reach them as a rule at the appointed time. Will Readers, therefore, please return it to the class on Sunday afternoon so that any readjustments in the circulating list may be made.

[p. 16]

T.L.H.C.
When the Cat's away, the Mice play.

The Trinity Spinsters had quite a flutter on the first Saturday afternoon, following the departure of Miss Messent and Miss Johnston for the scene of their holidays. They were inundated with male visitors, and the unusual honour caused such pleasurable excitement that the afternoon passed away in a long series of squeals of delight. We hear from unimpeachable sources that mixed doubles were the only form of the game which yielded satisfaction, and those visitors who played, were run after in a most shameless manner.

It seems that the Major was one of those present, but this will surprise no one. We should like to know, however, what idea he had at the back of his head in allowing the girls absolutely to walk over him? Still, we suppose he knows his own business and we certainly have no right to pry into it.

As the light got bad, we understand that it became necessary to spend a considerable time, very frequently, in seeking lost balls behind the bushes. This is only guess work, but I wonder if we are anywhere near the

[p. 17]

truth in supposing that mixed doubles were the vogue in this branch of the game as well?

The whole story sounds so interesting that it might be advisable to send an official representative who could report in greater detail on a future occasion.

Ed.

OUR SYLLABUS.

You will have noticed in our Leader's Letter that we shall devote an afternoon in September to the consideration of a fresh syllabus. There are many courses we might adopt, and each will doubtless commend itself in different quarters. An Epistle, the Prophecies of the Book of Revelations, the Psalms, the book of Job, the Proverbs, the meaning of the Symbolism of the Temple, the Early Christian Church as portrayed in the Epistles, the Continuity of the Bible, all subjects which can be studied to our great profit.

Might we not also resume our custom of regular opening papers. If these were all treatments of various aspects of one subject, such as Temple Symbolism, we should gain such an intimate knowledge of contemporary history and causes, as would make the series doubly instructive.

[p. 18]

CIRCULATING LIST

Whoever is in possession of the magazine on a Sunday must bring it to the class in the afternoon. The dates underlined indicate Sundays, and every effort should be made to keep to the scheduled dates.

	Date mag. To be passed on.	
Mr. A. H. Evans.	<u>Aug. 3rd.</u>	
Mr. R. S. Rowe.		
Mr. F. Rowe.	Aug. 5th.	
Mr. C. Bedwell.		
Mr. L. Bedwell.		
Mr. N. Bedwell.	Aug. 8th.	
Mr. E. H. Bowler.	<u>Aug. 10th.</u>	
Mr. W. Cramp.		
Mr. P. Coomber.	Aug. 12th.	
Mr. E. Munro.	<u>Aug.17th.</u>	If any reader is away
Mr. F. Perkins.	Aug. 19th.	on holidays the next
Mr. G. Barrett.	Aug. 21st.	in rotation should
Mr. F. Jones		receive the
Mr. A. Jones		magazine.
Mr. H. Jones.	<u>Aug. 24th.</u>	
Mr. A. Carpenter.	Aug. 26th.	
Mr. R. Chippindale.	Aug.28th.	
Mr. A. Austin.		
Mr. F. Rittershausen	<u>Aug. 31st.</u>	
Mr. C. Moxley.	Sep.2nd.	
Mr. M. Davis	Sep. 4th.	
Mr. H. Eagle.	<u>Sep 7th.</u>	
Mr. D. C. Messent.		
Mr. W. Messent.		
Mr. L. Messent.	Sep. 10th.	
Mr. E. Lynch.	Sep. 12th.	
Mr. S. Seymour.	Sep. 14th.	
Mr. A. Gosling.	Sep. 16th.	

Return to Editor.

No. 12

THE

ANGELS' VOICE

EDITOR   JAS. GODDEN

[p. 1]

[A map of western Europe, including the names of several towns in southern England, Paris, Berne, Lausanne, the Italian lakes, Gibraltar, Algiers, Genoa and Milan.]

[p. 2]

THE ANGELS' VOICE.
September.   No. 12.

EDITORIAL.

Dear Readers,

The holiday season is now almost past, and the winter's steady work is close upon us. This should bring a considerable change in our methods of circulating the magazine. Where the slack readers have allowed themselves double the scheduled time, and the unintelligent ones have retained the magazine because their immediate successors were away, we now expect to see an almost business-like celerity, which, after all, will not entail a tremendous effort.

We hope to make our next issue a special number so that it shall suitably mark the commencement of the Winter season. Articles and sketches should reach the Editor not later than the third week in September, by which time we hope that every reader will have sent us of his best.

Ed.

[p. 3]

LEADER'S
LETTER.

"Maxton",
King's Avenue, S.W.
August. 1913.

My dear Fellow members,

Next month was the time appointed for the commencement of our effort to raise the necessary funds for the exterior repairs and decorations of the Church and Manse. In the early days of September, a General Rally Gathering will be held, and at that meeting our scheme is to be introduced to the Church and Congregation. It is expected that every Class Member will make an especial point of being present, for it is quite possible that a considerable portion of the sum required, may be obtained on that occasion.

We are now within measureable distance of the commencement of the Gymnasium and Physical Culture Classes. How much we owe to Mr. Austin for his untiring energies as Hon. Instructor, few, if any, can fully realise. Last season was a great success, being thoroughly enjoyed by a good number, but there are some who did not join in the benefits accruing, and it is hoped that there may

[p. 4]

be an increase in the numbers of those who attend Thursday by Thursday, to indulge in the healthful exercises set by a thoroughly competent instructor.

It has been very encouraging to hear … how satisfactory the arrangements for conducting the Class during the holiday weeks have been, and many thanks are due to those who led the proceedings on the four Sundays in question. One feels that this experiment having proved so successful, may be capable of some developement [sic] …

The attendance of our members at Sunday services … , during the holiday season, has been especially good … As we approach the Winter Season, will some who seldom turn into the sanctuary, think the matter over? Amidst lifes changes and difficulties, we do need the assistance of all the means placed at our disposal, for strengthening our Faith and helping us in life's way. I therefore invite all to … regularly worship with us.

Our Annual Meetings take place early in November and although it is early yet, we are seeking to make

[p. 5]

arrangements that will give entire satisfaction to all. Please do your best to ensure record attendances when the time comes – but of this, more anon.

Believe me to be,

Yours very sincerely,

D. C. Messent.

Our frontispiece shows, in the form of a map, the wide field covered by our Class members, during this holiday season. Although we may at some future date, indulge in long holiday trips, the probabilities are few of a similar map re-appearing for many years.

The Church Rally Day will be the second Sunday in September. Mr. D. C. Messent, will take the chair at the Lecture, and thirty "Angels" present, … Of course!

The Open Air Meeting will be continued through September, unless the raw, chilly evenings set in early. Remember that we have got to make a graceful exit, so as to justify our re-appearance next year.

[p. 6]

JERSEY

It will be an auspicious day for the Class, when its noble band of pioneers sets out for the unknown, semi-barbarous Channel Isles. Those gifted with prophetic vision can see an "Angel" perched on every Alpine peak, breathing out the song of the Robin upon the clear Swiss air.

The party which leaves us on September 6th., will consist of four class members and our church organist, whilst A.H.E. has promised to join the party in Jersey.

As the Jersey police are numerous and addicted to the wearing of plain clothes, the prospect of a speedy reunion, is a hope confined solely to the optimistic.

Mr. Cramp is straining every nerve to be present during the second week. That week's holiday will be badly wanted if he keeps the effort up to the very last.

GENIUS

Two per cent inspiration; ninety eight per cent perspiration.

[p. 7]

WEAK WOMAN.

Each day I used to suffer in a throng
Of fighting, swaying men, around a tram.
The cause of my restraint and patient suffering,
And calmness, as I saw each car pass full,
Was found in my regard for those whom I
Was wont to think of, and accordingly protect,
As my inferiors, a weaker sex.
I sent the Valentines with honeyed words,
And other tributes to their strange attractions,
And though these things would often fail to please,
I took no ire because they were but women.
But, with the hope of sharing with their lords,
The rights and cares which unto them belong,
A subtle change came o'er each female breast,
And madness entered as their reason went.
Their dignity they changed for awkward haste,
And now you see them joining in the rush,
Each morning, to the scene of business strife,
And digging shapely elbows in the ribs
Of those whom Nature made their lawful keepers.
We are thereby absolved from courteous duties,
And I no longer wait to let them pass,

[p. 8]

But with a spring, <u>prove</u> their inferiority,
By getting first my foot upon the step
Which leads to easy punctuality.

Cherub.

8, Bythorn Street,
Brixton, S.W.
August, 1913.

My dear Gym. Boys,

From various remarks I have heard ... several of you are anxious for the Gymnasium to re-open. That is a good healthy sign, and I trust you have all had such an enjoyable holiday that you feel quite ready to work off ... superfluous energy at the Gym. I am hoping for a larger squad than ... last year, and ... I think ... that we shall wind up the season with a display. The material at my disposal is alright, BUT THERE IS NOT ENOUGH OF IT. So buck up ... and help to keep me busy on Thursday evenings ... Some of you can do with the exercise, and so can I, and if you will help me, I will do my best to be of service to you.

Yours very sincerely,

Sgd.   Alfred. P. Austin.

[p. 9]

[Drawing of a young woman, wearing a hat with ribbon.]

[p. 10]

A BACHELOR'S PARTY.

We shall not all remember the 21st. August, for we were not all present at Arlingford Mansion,[1] but the sixteen who managed to obtain entrance will not lose their impressions for many a day. The company arrived in a rather straggling manner, and the full number took over an hour to assemble. A telegram was received from the Stock Exchange, to advertise the fact that its sender would be late. This was a quite unnecessary expenditure, for we knew exactly how the case would be, from previous experience.

There was no lack of musical instruments, and we had an expert in attendance on each. The gramophone was in charge of a personal friend of the host, the banjo was strummed by our professional strong man, the piano was served by our church organist, and "Bedwell's Idol" had an enthusiastic and interpretative worshipper. For a while, the time passed in general conversation but then the ball was set rolling with the "Death of Nelson". Four years have elapsed since some of us heard it in the Reigate Hill Tea Shop, and since then the singer had never tried it over, yet the haunting melody poured forth unfalteringly from that marvellous throat, and we sat spell-bound under its magic charm. It was a superb

[p. 11]

effort, a magnificent triumph. We next had a rollicking sea song from the Clapham Park Warbler, and to most of us his style was an absolute revelation.

The full company had now arrived and the fun began to wax hot. An unoffending acquaintance who happened to pass along the road, was captured and carried in, and being a musician was deposited at the piano. Whilst he was dashing out a banjo accompaniment, four irrepressibles linked arms and indulged in a quadruple waltz.

---

[1]   This may be either no. 76, the Snoswells' ten-room home, or no. 22 where the Bedwells lived.

The interval for feeding was a tribute to the batchelor [sic] skill of those responsible. The waiting was perfection itself, and it was lucky there were no ladies present or their hearts would now be in possession of our handsome waiter. He stood there, a splendid, dark young fellow, wearing his evening clothes with the air of an Italian nobleman. Only one member failed to be impressed, but his rude guffaws were speedily quieted with a sound bumping.

The rest of the evening beggars description. Pipes of all sizes and nationalities, cigars of one uniform excellence, and innumerable "cigarillos" helped to hide us from each other in a pungent blue mist. The songs which followed all had chorouses [sic], but presently the chorouses [sic] claimed the entire field, and with infinite pains and

[p. 12]

finish, the story of the Murdered Robin was rendered by the assembled company.

Time was by now putting a good many obstacles in the way of the further rolling of the ball, so the flamen[2] of the harmonium led us in the National Anthem, and once again in the good old Scotch farewell, which was sung with such emphasis and spirit, that thoughtful persons like myself, could not help wondering what the neighbours' thoughts would be.

After many hand-shakings, accompanied by thanks and congratulations, the company streamed away, many of them promising themselves the pleasure of holding similar "re-unions" in their own homes as opportunities occurred.

THE GIRLS' CLASS.

The Adult School Syllabus is being followed out by our friends in the next room, as well as by ourselves. They treat it much as we do, and have not had any papers. They find the same difficulty with the series as we do. The social problem side of each subject, is so greatly emphasized, that they could hardly be considered a Bible Class.

They intend to keep to the series till the end of the year, but they will then look round for a more satisfactory syllabus.

[p. 13]

THE PRIMARY DEPARTMENT.

Every Sunday afternoon, we see gathered at the bottom of the stairs, a considerable number of children, a rather mixed crowd. This is the

---

[2]   A flamen was a priest to a Roman deity. *Oxford English Dictionary.*

Primary Department, which meets in the Hall directly underneath our room. Since it was instituted ten months ago, it has had very fair success, and the work shown a beneficial effect, not only on the children, but also on those elder pupils of the Sunday School who have given themselves to this work.

The Department was formed from the Infant Classes then in existence, and numbered roughly 75. It has now increased by roughly 33%, making a total of about 100. The teaching staff of nine, proves sufficient to cope with the average attendance of 65. The senior classes are fairly large, containing about twelve children, but the average class should only consist of four or five.

The undertaking involves considerable preparation, and the whole teaching staff assembles at the Manse on Friday evenings to study the lesson together. In the "Chronicle" there is a story specially intended for Primary Department Workers, and this prepared under Mr. Lansdown's guidance, and, together with its Scripture basis, is retold to the children on the following Sunday.

[p. 14]

A close connection is maintained with the families from which the children come, by means of the cradle roll. All additions to the families are carefully noted, with a view to securing the child's attendance as time goes on. Up to the present, 26 names have been enrolled, and two children secured through this channel.

Possibly our readers would be interested in the little scheme they now have on hand. They feel the want of a clock at their end of the Hall, and they are now actively collecting pennies to provide a suitable time-piece. As they will be far from the only ones to benefit, they will be quite justified in approaching everybody, even us.

The Harvest Festival will be held on the second Sunday in October. We hope to publish a photograph of the decorations.

Our Secretary's address is, for the present, Broadleas Prison, Dover.[3]

In the light of this information we think the Jersey party may possibly be reduced by one. Still, … he may be free by the day of sailing.

[p. 15]

TRINITY FOOTBALL CLUB. 2nd. XI.

By the time this Journal has "gone the round", I hope we shall be well under way. Seventeen members have signed on for the coming season … we shall play 18 matches, having received nine permits.

[3]   R. S. Rowe.

One of our halves will be leaving us for voyages on the high seas, and we are also sorry to have to let Mr. F. Rowe go. On the other hand we have the pleasure of securing Messrs. A. Snoswell, and S. Seymour – two of our own …

We are to meet old rivals, such as St. John's, 44th. Boy's Brigade, Reay Old Boys, and St. Luke's Boy Scouts.

We have several open away dates, and if any reader knows of a team which would entertain us on their ground, kindly communicate with the secretary.

As regards the qualities of the players, I will remain silent till the end of the season … But I must not take any more space, yet – what about 2nd. XI versus 1st. XI?

Ref.

[p. 16]

[Drawing of a roof.]

[p. 17]

OFFICIAL NOTICE

Physical   of   Culture

RE-OPENING

Subject to the approval of the Deacons, it is proposed to make the opening night of the season, Thursday, October 6th. Those who attended last year, will of course be with us, and I should be glad to have the names of a good number besides, who will join with them, this season.

Don't put it off … but book it now, and make it a point of honour that you are present … The greater the number of times you attend, the greater benefit will you obtain, not only physically, but morally as well, for a sound body helps to make a sound mind.

BOOK IT NOW! THURSDAY EVENINGS AT TRINITY GYMNASIUM. The hours will be … from 8 to 9.45. Also please note that we start promptly to time!

No waiting!

W. Cramp.
Hon. Secretary.
16, Acre lane,
Brixton, S.W.

[p. 18]

PHYSICAL CULTURE AT HOME

A few years ago a young mother with three
   Bouncing young kiddies, as fat as could be,
Was anxious to get their weight somewhat reduced,
   With this end in view, by a poster induced,

She hied her way to a Culture expert
   For advice as to how she their fat could convert
Into muscle, and make them much healthier boys
   And give them a graceful and easier poise.

He told her that Dumb Bells and Indian Clubs
   Would alter their seeming resemblance to tubs,
And showed her how his patient movements would tend
   To make their young bodies more easy to bend.

If you'll send your boys round, for a modest outlay,
   I'll teach them to do things in THE proper way,
And then they can practise them when they get time,
   Till they rival an athlete who's just in his prime.

The boys trotted round to the Culture Expert,
   And to simplify matters I'll call the first Bert,
The eldest but one I will christen "Young Jim".
   The third was a swanker, so Algy suits him.

It didn't take long just to run through the drill,
   And they got the man's method, though minus his skill
And away they ran home just as fast as they could
   To tell their dear parents they'd learnt what they should.

The noise was too much for poor father, who said,
   "You do that upstairs, but please mind the bed",
So off they all climbed to the top of the house,
   Leaving dear father as quiet as a mouse.

[p. 19]

When dumb bells were mentioned Young Jim said "Right O!"
   But happened to get right against the window,
The result was of course a big hole in the pane
   Which Jim surveyed often, 'cos in came the rain.

On the opposite side of the room was poor Bert
    Who'd gone to the length of removing his collar.
With Indian Clubs he was going first class
    Then bang went one club through a big looking glass.

We'll turn our attention to Algernon now
    Who has been pretty quiet while trying just how
He could fix a developer up on the door,
    But tried it too soon and came bang on the floor.

They thought they'd keep going, it caused so much fun,
    But day after day there was more damage done.
But when pa said sternly "This game you must stop",
    Algy's big Club hit him right on the top.

No more did their father intrude in that den;
    His laddies had now become vigorous men,
And though now and then a big window went smash,
    He said, "What another?" – and paid up in cash.

In due course of time they'd improved such a lot,
    That Bert and Young Jim got engaged on the spot.
Their ma was so pleased with the sturdy young things,
    That she got their poor father to pay for the rings.

Algy, poor chap, has to wait just a while,
    But he strides off to work in a fine manly style,
And not very long will this lad have to wait,
    Before he gets knobbled by his future mate.

Now of course there's a moral attached to all this,
That a healthy young man, finds that health brings him bliss.

                                   A.P.A.

[p. 20]

POLITICAL.
FEMALE SUFFRAGE.

    It is not my aim in this brief article to deal exhaustively with so controversial a subject, nor is it to suggest steps wherein a remedy for present-day anomalies may be found, but to indicate the spirit in which the question should be studied, especially to those who themselves feel keenly and would gladly see the problem solved. Is the modern movement right or wrong? That is a question to be answered before any satisfactory steps can be taken. What is the true, God-intended relation of woman to man? In the light of the answer to this question, has she any grounds for her present day claims?

Whoever boldly proclaims that the sexes are to all intents and purposes equal, reveals the worthlessness of his conclusions, for patently the care is not so. The male and female frames are of the same order, and indisputably of equal importance, but they differ from each other in many ways. In a like manner, their minds and spirits are similar, and they work in harmony, but only because one fits into the other, or, in other words, because they are not identical.

For the purposes of this article we have only to study

[p. 21]

the difference in the masculine and feminine aptitude for government. That both are capable of governing we find no difficulty in admitting, but where does the sphereof the one end, and of the other begin? Judging from their frames, it seems certain that in the simplest state, man, the harder creature, would undertake the rude work, which called for violent effort, and involved turmoil and aggressiveness. Woman, on the other hand, would find her true place in superintending the quieter branches of communal life. From these general terms we may draw a general conclusion. Man is adapted for external, and woman for internal government. Bringing this principle to bear on modern life, we come to the conclusion that man's true sphere is in the management of the general business of the community, and the woman's influence finds its visibly direct, though not final limits, in the home.

A strong plea of the suffrage agitater [sic], is the injustice to which women must submit. The injustice undoubtedly does exist. But it has only been produced by much travelling along wrong lines. Modern industrialism has gradually absorbed women, and woman labour, into its schemes, and by giving them the responsibilities of a man, it has given them the grounds for claiming a man's duties.

[p. 22]

Woman who was intended as "an help meet for man", we now see as his competitor, and the change is unnatural and wrong. The task before those who would put wrongs right, is, therefore, to make it possible for woman to take her proper place as man's equal, in the sense of complement, and not as his rival.

This is the ideal which must be aimed at, and only as we travel towards it, will feminine discontent and unrest, tend to diminish. To meet an actual injustice by travelling still further away from the ideal is foolishness. Woman's claim for a share in external government is certainly not unfounded, but the claim is based upon a state of affairs produced by the false position she has assumed. It is, therefore, very evident that a satisfactory settlement will not be arrived at, by granting what, in the light of modern conditions, she has come to consider as her rights.

? ? ?

[p. 23]

[Drawing of a child with a saucepan stuck on his head, and his concerned mother.]

[Signed:] FLR.[4]

A BLACK OUTLOOK FOR TOMMY.

HIS MOTHER: "You little wretch. How dare you look me in the face and say it was an accident".

[p. 24]

CIRCULATING LIST
GET IT ROUND!

Mr. D. C. Messent.	Sep. 3rd.
Mr. W. Messent.	
Mr. L. Messent.	
Mr. R. S. Rowe.	Sep.6th.
Mr. F. Rowe.	
EDITOR	
Mr. C. Bedwell.	Sep.9th.
Mr. L. Bedwell.	
Mr. N. Bedwell.	
Mr. E. H. Bowler.	Sep. 11th.
Mr. W. Cramp.	Sep.14th.
Mr. P. Coomber.	
Mr. E. Munro.	Sep.16th.
Mr. F. Perkins.	Sep.18th.
Mr. H. Lansdown.	Sep.20th.
EDITOR	
Mr. C. Smith.	Sep.22nd.
Mr. G. Barrett.	Sep.24th.
Mr. F. Jones.	Sep.27th.
Mr. A. Jones.	
Mr. H. Jones	

---

4   Presumably Frank Leonard Rowe. See also *AV* 10 (July 1913), 33, 35.

EDITOR

Mr. A. Carpenter.	Sep.29th.
Mr. A. Austin.	Oct.1st.
Mr. C. Moxley.	Oct.3rd.
Mr. M. Davis.	Oct.5th.
Mr. H. Eagle.	Oct.7th.
Mr. T. Lynch.	Oct.9th.
Mr. S. Seymour.	Oct.11th.
Mr. A. Gosling.	Oct.13th.
Mr. A. H. Evans.	Oct.15th.

The dates are those on which the magazine is to be passed on.

THE ANGELS' VOICE

No. 13

EDITOR: JAS. GODDEN.

[p. 1]

[This consists of three photographs – first, a man 'sleeping' on his front, fully clothed, on a stony beach; secondly, five people climbing rocks (three men and two women); and lastly, two young men outside a beach chalet, in swimwear.]

[p. 2]

THE ANGELS' VOICE.

No. 13.1913.

OCTOBER

EDITORIAL

Dear Readers,

This number does not make its appearance any too early for its purpose – neither is it any too late – it has left the printing room just at the proper time. The bleak winter season with all its recompenses, still seems a good way off, but the dark evenings are already with us, and indoor engagements press close upon each other.

To us, this active season is doubly welcome: it offers something to record, and better still, tiresome holidays do not snatch the indispensable contributors from our grasp.

We are particularly grateful to the artists who have helped to make this number so attractive, and we trust that you will all remember that those whose names succeed yours on the list, are just as eager to receive the magazine as you are loath to pass it on.

Ed.

[p. 3]

LEADER'S LETTER.

"Maxton",
King's Avenue, S.W.
October 1913.

My dear Fellow Members,

We have now entered upon a time which we have all been anticipating. The winter season is upon us. Football and Gymnasium are in full swing, and we ... have settled down, and are, I trust, well satisfied and keen at the prospect of our Winter Programme.

We are hoping ... for a renewal of several of our old friendships. During the summer ... two or three of our old members have allowed themselves to be absent from both Class and Church Service. This of course we greatly deplore but are glad to know that it is their intention to return ...

As a Class, our study of the Epistle to the Galatians should prove most instructive and helpful. It is necessary that the Christian should know his Bible. It is also necessary that his knowledge of it should not be merely of the "patchwork" type, meaning simply choice pieces

[p. 4]

culled from here and there. He should know the various books as Books, and so get a more intelligent understanding of God's Word ...

A recent letter from our friend Will Crosley conveys the glad news that we may expect him home from India somewhere about Christmas time. We all look forward to enjoying his companionship again, and in the meantime let us continue to pray that he may have travelling mercies ...

With every good wish,
Ever yours sincerely,
D. C. Messent.

On the following page will be found a picture of the R.M.S. "Elephanta". This vessel has been the floating home of our friend W.T.C.[1] for many months past, and he shortly looks forward to leaving her for the homeward voyage.

[p. 5]

[A postcard of a ship in dock.]

[1] William Thomas Crosley.

[p. 6]

MANNERS MAYKETH MAN.

On Wednesday evening, the 17th. September, Mr. Lansdown gave a lecture with the above familiar phrase as his subject. A good number were present ... and the Lecture Hall was practically full. Mr. D. C. Messent, the chairman, introduced the speaker with admirable brevity, and the audience settled down to listen to an interestingly developed topic.

The Lecturer pointed out that his subject was the motto of the ancient school of Winchester, the oldest public school in England. But before this school was established, it was the motto of its great founder, William of Wykeham. The words ... were by no means easy to understand; nevertheless, it was important that we should grasp their meaning, for if true, they contained the whole secret of manhood. The phrase separated itself into two parts, each of which presented its own difficulty. What were these manners ... ; and ... how did they make the man? The actual words were not ... connected by sense. "Manners" he said, was a derivative of the Latin "manus", which meant a hand. Manners, therefore, were hand motions; salutes, bowing, hat-raising; all of them general

[p. 7]

external attributes ... Many a "freak gentleman" had all these hand mannerisms, and the result was the fop, which only meant a fool; the dandy, another word of much the same import; and masher, or one who fascinated with his eye. All these types were harmless enough, but the man who had their agreeable exterior and a vicious heart, at once fell under the category of cad.

The cad, he showed us to be a truly contemptible creature. In the first instance, the word itself had no sinister significance, but from meaning those who undertook humble work, it came to designate ... those who had something to be ashamed of. Instead of a builder's assistant, it indicated a jerry-builder's man, and ... one who went from door to door begging. The cad, then, was really a cadger; ... who tried to get something for nothing: and our modern cad would rather ... defraud his own parents than go without his cheap finery.

In deep contrast ... there stood the true man. In his case, it was character that counted. The fine ... motions of the hand might be lacking, but they left the man, "a man for a' that". But as the palace was not complete and perfect until the carved work and the

[p. 8]

gilding were in their place, so the man was still unfinished until …
good manners had been acquired. In this, the world's estimate of
ancestry was far from being the true one. Race and descent might
provide numerous opportunities for the acquisition of all the externals
of the gentleman. "But" said the lecturer, "think of Beau Brummel,
Chesterfield, George IV, the first "gentlemen" of Europe of their day.
Look at them … on the rubbish heap of history".

He then went on to point out the three characteristics of a
gentleman. The most important was sincerity, and so universally was
this acknowledged, that the "word of a gentleman" was … absolutely
reliable. Second in importance came sympathy, for every gentleman
could feel for others, and … show his sympathy wherever possible by
charitable philanthropy. Lastly the gentleman was a man of honour.
The common saying ran, "Every man has his price". But this was not
true, the man of honour could not be bought.

In closing, the speaker pointed out how these characteristics might
be made the personal possession of each one. No man was really "to
the manner born" – until he was born again. The grace to attain to this
high

[p. 9]

dignity must come from God, and then no door worth passing through,
would be shut against us, and kings themselves must own us as their
equals.

After the applause had subsided, the chairman spoke a few words,
and intimated that a silver collection would be taken on behalf of the
Exterior Renovation Fund. At the same time, he briefly introduced the
scheme that had been adopted for raising the necessary sum.

The collection amounted to £2. 7. 6, and hymn and prayer then
brought the meeting to a close.

THE VESPER.

At the last Church Meeting, Mr. D. C. Messent suggested that it
would be well to drop the Sanctus, Amens, and Vesper. Mr. Evans
strongly protested against the use of the present Vesper on account of
its ridiculous wording. He said that it implied that we were afraid of
the dark. Mr. Lansdown contradicted him strongly and … said that
there was not a man on earth who was not afraid of the dark, which is
of course very questionable.

The subject was eventually referred back to the next church meeting, and in moving this step, our Cibby[2] threw out vague threats at anyone who should dare trifle with our music. Well done Cib!

[p. 10]

[Painting of a moonlit sailing boat.]

[signed:] ETJ

[p. 11]

AN OD(OUR) TO A MOTOR BICYCLE.

An "Angel" rode a bicycle,
   The push-bike sort, you know,
But as the motors passed him by
   His pace seemed rather slow.

He therefore pinched and screwed and scraped
   And with no small conceit,
A "Triumph – 1910" he bought,
   Dirt cheap – see his receipt.

Enthusiastic, he discoursed
   Upon his acquisition.
In cheaper locomotion then
   He gave a disquisition.

But still he wasn't satisfied
   Although he went the pace.
The handlebars were not the sort
   To give his figure grace.

He scrapped the old and bought a pair
   Whose slope would be correct:
Then scornfully disdained all those
   Who rode their mounts erect.

[p. 12]

Alas! One very fateful day
   A trap was laid – and he
Was led to open out full speed
   And – nabbed by some P.C.

---

[2]   Cyril Bedwell (C.B.).

When up before the "beak" he came,
    £2 went in a fine,
And this, with many "extras", caused
    His keenness to decline.

PROPHETIC (Written July 1913 and since fulfilled)

If adverts, now you follow up
    This bargain you may choose,
"A Triumph – 1910, for sale,
    No offer I'll refuse".

OVER HEARD AT THE OPEN AIR.

Mr. D.C.M. endeavouring to keep several small boys in order.
    "'ere Bill, come round 'ere. We aint 'arf 'avin a game with
some fat ole man!"
    A case for the T.Y.M.P.C.G.T.C. Eh?

[p. 13]

THE LITERARY SOCIETY

The Literary Society is going to hibernate this season. A committee meeting was held on Wednesday evening, September 24th, after the week-night service, to consider a policy for the coming winter. Mr. W. J. Messent was willing to act as Secretary, but ... there was a general lack of enthusiasm to make a fresh start. Tacit consent seemed to be given to the suggestion that we had too many engagements already, and ... it was resolved to suspend operations for a year, and in the meantime to offer the deacons the services of the committee, for organization purposes in connexion with any special lectures that might be proposed.

Now that the Literary Society has failed to come up to the scratch, it is up to the Class to see what it can do independently ... in view of the opinions expressed on the Sunday when we resolved to change our syllabus, perhaps it would be a good plan to have two or three debates on social subjects on week nights during the winter.

[p. 14]

[Three photographs of beach scenes with young men and women.]

[p. 15]

THE TRINITY BOYS IN JERSEY.

It is not possible in the limited space at my disposal, to give a complete account of our two weeks holiday in Jersey, so I must content myself with endeavouring to give you an idea of our doings, coupled with a short description of the scenery and life of this beautiful island.

Under ordinary conditions, the journey is a very pleasant one and can be made either by L. & S.W.Ry. to Southampton, or by the G.W.Ry. to Weymouth, and thence by boat; the former sea-trip occupies eight hours and the latter six hours. We chose the former, and on arriving at Southampton, promptly turned into our bunks and tried to sleep. I have heard of some wary people who sleep on their screws, but it is quite another matter trying to sleep on the screw of a L. & S.W.Ry. steamer. However, we were fairly successful, and did not rise until half past four the next morning, when we found ourselves just off the famous Casket Rocks. We stayed on deck the rest of the journey and had a very enjoyable trip. R.S.R. was very loath to leave his bunk (fearing the loss of his last meal) but was glad of the fresh air when he did come up from the stuffy cabin, and I am pleased to report that we all retained that which we had eaten.

[p. 16]

[Three photographs, badly faded.]

[p. 17]

When some ten miles from Jersey, the sun came out with great power, and our entry into St. Heliers [sic] Harbour under such glorious conditions, augured well for the success of our holiday. We soon found ourselves on the Esplanade and into "Belle Vue", where we were to be housed by Mr. and Mrs. Hallewell for our two weeks stay. A wash and brush up and a splendid breakfast put us in fine spirits, and we then wandered off along the Esplanade for a short walk before dinner to take our bearings so to speak. After dinner we again found ourselves walking along the Esplanade and eventually we settled ourselves down for the afternoon on the sands, and wrote letters to our respective homes, informing mothers and fathers and pals – and others – of our safe arrival. After tea we were all disposed to retire early to make up for the overnight deficiency, and we did so at a quarter to nine.

I will now attempt to describe some of the scenery to be found in Jersey. The coastline abounds in lovely bays, all of which are very pretty indeed, although I think Portelet Bay and St. Brelade's Bay come first. The train journey to St. Aubins and Corbiere gives one a fair opportunity of seeing some very fine stretches of typical country, as also does the train journey to Gorey, on the other side of the island.

[p. 18]

[Three more photographs of Jersey – St Brelade's Bay Hotel, two men making nets, and a well-loaded charabanc.]

[p. 19]

Tomato and potato farms are to be found in plenty, whilst the famous Jersey cabbages, which grow as high as ten, twelve and even fourteen feet, are to be seen on every side. In most of the fields one sees the beautiful Jersey cows and goats, but it struck me as rather singular that no sheep are reared on the Island.

The valleys of Jersey are magnificent. The most famous and the most picturesque is the Waterworks Valley from Millbrook to St. Lawrence. It's beauty is quite beyond my adequate description, but I really must say that it is the loveliest walk I have yet taken, even beating, in some respects, the famous lanes of Devonshire. The chief industries of the inhabitants seem to be potato and tomato farming, and there are plenty of well-stocked orchards and nurseries, which provide employment for a goodly number of the natives. Fishing occupies the time of some, but there did not appear to be a likelihood of this branch of industry being overcrowded. A snapshot of a fisherman making nets at St. Brelades will be found opposite. There are plenty of shops of all kinds, and they all seem to do a thriving business.

I shall now give you as graphic a description as time and space will allow, of a typical day spent by the six of us. Rising somewhere about seven o'clock (a quarter

[p. 20]

[Three photographs of a beach – two men in a beach hut; rocks with clothes draped over them; one man with wet hair sitting at the entrance to a beach hut.]

[p. 21]

past sharp, is R.S.R's time and we were not allowed to forget it) we would go for a bathe at West Park, some five minutes walk, and then return to breakfast. Whilst the meal was in progress, Mr. Hallewell would come in and announce the trip for the day, and request us to sign our names on a list in the hall before ten o'clock, if we intended to take part. This we did on several occasions, but I am now dealing with one only. At 11 o'clock or thereabouts, the brakes arrived, sometimes four, sometimes five, or even six, according to the number on the list.

Sufficient food for the whole party was placed on board, and when all were seated we started off to the accompaniment of the various "war cries" for which Hallewell's is famous. After an hour or so we stopped to rest the horses, and this done we started off once more. When we arrived at our destination we seated ourselves on the grass, and the food was handed round by the "Captain" and his Lieutenants (Space will not permit of telling how this arrangement is come to, but it will be fully described in a complete and illustrated essay which I propose to get out as soon as possible). The meal consists of sandwiches and tomatoes, buns, pastries, apples, bananas, and whatever you care to drink. When all have been satisfied, we break up into small parties, some for a bathe, some for exploration, and

[p. 22]

[Three more photographs, badly faded.]

[p. 23]

some for "woffling", a term which is fully explained in the accompanying photo. At the sound of the Captain's whistle we return to the brake and start for home, breaking the journey halfway for a cup of tea and a piece of cake. Throughout the trip, songs and choruses are shouted by the happy party, and although the music was not always of the best, it served to show the spirits of those who supplied it. All we had to do at the finish of the day's outing was to pay up – three shillings – a very moderate sum indeed.

A splendid five-course dinner was served at half past six, and the evening was devoted to writing post cards, or a walk to a nice little retreat at the top of West Park, overlooking St. Aubin's Bay and St. Heliers [sic]. As a rule, we retired after coffee and biscuits at ten o'clock.

There are plenty of good walks to be had, or ... you can get a train to most ... places of interest. A feature of the railways (of which there are two) is, that if you take a return ticket, you are allowed to get out at any intermediate station, explore the vicinity, and return from lower down the line, or the same station, just as you like.

Bathing can be indulged in at any time of the day, as there are specially constructed pools, which do not

[p. 24]

empty at low tide. This enables you to choose your own time. There is no special place for men or women, but all bathing, with ... early morning exceptions, is mixed. Living is remarkably cheap, and our own experience has been a huge and pleasant surprise.

To sum it all up, you could do a lot worse than spend a holiday in Jersey, and personally, I can thoroughly recommend any of you to try it for yourselves. The address where we spent such a happy time can be obtained from any of us, together with full details as to how to enjoy yourselves during your stay.

The "Holiday Fund" idea was discussed by us, and voted to be of great assistance to some of our younger fry in obtaining the necessary cash, and so will be adopted again for next year.

When the complete essay is ready, I shall be pleased to lend it any of you who care to read it.

A.P.A.

One of the Six.

Our frontispiece gives a few pictures of our leader on his holidays. There were others but we really could not consent to their publication in this magazine.

[p. 25]

AFRAID HA! HA!

The following letter has reached the Editor with the particular request that it should be published without comment:–

Girls' Club,
Trinity Church,
Brixton.

Dear Mr. Editor,

In reply to your application for the Winter Programme of the Girls' Club, for publication in your magazine, I regret that I am unable to supply same.

The syllabus of <u>THE CLASS</u> not having yet been issued, a Programme cannot yet be expected from the Girls' Club.

May I suggest that you issue yours under the heading, T.L.H.C. Winter Programme, for then your estimate of our club's initiative will give you complete assurance that you cannot possibly be on wrong lines.

Yours sincerely,

CLUB SECRETARY.

Particulars of what the T.L.H.C's are thinking of doing during the Winter, will of course, be found on another page.

Ed.

[A drawing of goblins contemplating a flower growing from the earth.]
[Signed:] I.M.

A BROWNIE STUDY.

[p. 27]

ON THE SUBJECT OF CONSCRIPTION

A reply from a far country.

In reading through the article on Conscription, one or two points have struck me, on which I should like to pass a few remarks. In the first place "Bontex" has taken rather a narrow view ... He says, "Compelling every able-bodied man over the age of nineteen to do a certain amount of military training every year". Is it practicable or fair to the average young man ... ? It would be if England could provide adequate employment for her total population, but ... she cannot, and a fair percentage emigrate at the age of about twenty. If young men are ... compelled to go through a course of military training covering ... three years, what is going to happen? No one between the ages of 19 and 22 will be able to leave the country, the labour market will become congested; wages will be reduced and unemployment materially increased. Employers will not care about engaging men until their period of compulsory training is complete, and therefore, instead of being in a fairly comfortable position at 22, young men will be just starting life.

[p. 28]

"Bontex" hints at a possible Chinese invasion somewhere in the dim future, and I quite agree with him, that it will be "years hence". First of all, China has to get her Navy. But her finances will be controlled by European Powers for some years, so there is at least one considerable obstacle ... He also says, "The trade of the country (China) will forge ahead". Who will be responsible for this? Not the Chinese, but ... mostly Englishmen. Take her shipping for instance. How many Chinese officers are there on board ships trading in Chinese waters? I doubt if you would find one. Chinese shipowners there certainly are, but invariably European Officers, and of those, about 90 per cent. come from Great Britain, and the withdrawal of these would mean that China's trade would be absolutely paralysed.

W.T.C.

The committee of the Literary Society has offered its services to the deacons for the purpose of organising occasional lectures. Oh dear! We remember a year or two ago, when we were treated to a series of lectures ... Nothing but lectures! Not a single social meeting throughout! It is to be hoped that the deacons will make use of this committee, but why not turn them on to the organisation of a Christmas Party?

[p. 29]

THE EXPERIMENT

Taking things all round, affairs went very smoothly during our leader's summer vacation from the chair, and the class showed a good attendance during those four Sundays, considering that holidays were on. The afternoons were taken by Mr. Godden, Mr. Cramp, Mr. Austin, and Mr. Bedwell.

Mr. Godden gave us a very full and interesting afternoon, but of course, something extra is always expected from this young man, whose resources seem to be never ending.

Mr. Cramp got through his facts rather too quickly, but Mr. John Rowe stepped in when things were looking a bit dull and gave us some good sound facts to ponder over. Altogether the afternoon was well spent. Mr. Cramp had evidently studied the subject well, and what he gave us was well worth listening to.

There are occasions when one has the necessary facts but cannot find time to bring them out. This was the case when we saw Mr. Austin in the chair and the return of Mr. Messent from his holidays. Mr. Austin had only given us a few of his many points, when Mr. Messent found a question that took all the afternoon to thrash out. It was rather a pity that the afternoon should have been occupied on this

[p. 30]

one point, but it was of no avail, Mr. Messent clung to the question till 4 o'clock arrived. Doubtless, it was very disappointing to Mr. Austin who had a lot of interesting items to put before us.

With Mr. Bedwell, things went along fairly quietly until he made his closing statement, "God is Nature, and Nature is God". This aroused Mr. Messent and Mr. Godden, who were both of the opinion that our Cibby was inclining to Pantheism. This brought about a fairly lively discussion which was not shared by our "Spearmint" friends, who seem quite content to sit and chew, and laugh when occasion offers. The idea of our fellows taking the chair is, I think, a good one, and I should like to see it tried again.

"Vortex".

It will soon be time for us to fix the date of our Annual Meeting. There is some doubt as to the exact date upon which the anniversary falls, but it is certainly either the first or the second week in November. However, we have held them mostly to suit our own convenience ... Don't forget that the preceding Sunday is invariably a Rally Day. Last year we crammed over forty into our room. There is no excuse for any slackening off. Mr. John Rowe has promised to address the meeting on that occasion.

[p. 31]

[Still life: fruit in a bowl.]

[p. 32]

TRINITY FOOTBALL CLUB (1st. XI.).
Competitions –
Season 1913–14.

Amateur Football Association Junior Cup.
Surrey County A.F.A. Junior Cup.
North Surrey Amateur League. Div. II.

What a Programme our Football Club has before it this season. Can any member fail to be enthusiastic ... ? The only doubt existing is whether it can fulfil all its engagements.

Cup and League Football is very different from the type that our men have hitherto indulged in. It differs from "friendlies" insomuch as it is very strenuous, for rough and tumble games are usually the order of the day.

Our defence is ... good enough to hold any forwards that are likely to come up against it, but what of our gallant forwards? Will they be dashing enough to get the goals that alone win matches? ... It is for them to prove their ability ... They may often be up against a very sound defence; ... and so may be tempted to slacken their efforts; but we are con-

[p. 33]

vinced that they will never give up trying to their <u>utmost</u> but will always endeavour to be worthy of their splendid comrades behind them.

Someone has said that the best defence is a strong attack, and there is great truth in it ... in all walks of life. The idols of so many of our members (the Chelsea team) are a striking example of the truth of this statement. The "Pensioners" lose matches, not because of a weak defence, but because of a slow though "pretty" forward line. Matches

265

are won by dash. The recent triumph of the American Polo Team over ours is an example of this. The Yankees went for it ... while our men were manoeuvring. Let our forwards remember this and we shall have a fine record at the end of the season.

"Hopeful".

The Literary Society has stepped aside. What shall we do to keep the dust from settling in our room? You mostly remember the Picture Palace Debate. Why not a few more on equally controversial topics? They will give us just the exercise we need for our Sunday afternoons ...

[p. 34]

T.L.H.C.

The spirit of change hovers over the weather-worn buildings of our church, and amongst the ... Girls' Club, its work is particularly manifest. They have actually decided ... that they will no longer meet together for sewing. If the club is intended to be a recreative agency no one can take exception to this ... The Hockey Club will continue ... to take its due succession of defeats, but the most marked change will be found in the singing class. Their former performances were undoubtedly enjoyable, but they wish to present an exceptionally attractive programme at the close of this season. They wish to have scenery illustrating the pieces they render, and, further, instead of choir singing they would like soloists and a chorus. In fact, ... the result will be Grand Opera. I did hear ... that the reason for this ... was because they thought the "boys" would like it.

They will meet on Monday evenings, taking singing one week and gymnastics the next. As the "boys" have been a decided factor in determining the season's programme, it is quite probable that they will feel interested in the club's progress, and occasional reports will be supplied if the information is obtainable.

[p. 35]

[Drawing with a male patient in a chair and a doctor arriving while little creatures, named gout, stitch etc., roam around.]

[Signed:] HR.

THE DOCTOR'S VISIT.

[p. 36]

AN IMPORTANT CHANGE.

On the 21st. September, we devoted an afternoon to the consideration of our syllabus. As we have already pointed out, the Adult School Union's series of lessons was not giving satisfaction to the whole of our members, and there was a considerable feeling that some change was desirable.

Mr. Messent spoke briefly on the matter and then left it for class discussion. Most of the members seemed undecided, and not many suggestions were forthcoming, although Mr. Carpenter warmly advocated the continuance of our course of studies.

The suggestion was made that we should devote the time between now and the end of the year to the Epistle to the Galatians, and in the meantime, the new syllabus of the Adult School Union should be examined, and if not approved, another course of study should be prepared. This was agreed to without any dissentient.

Mr. Godden asked if the portions for study would be posted up on the notice board, and Mr. Messent undertook to see that it was done by the following Sunday. It was also decided that the Secretary should arrange for four papers to be given at intervals by class members.

[p. 37]

THE LAND QUESTION

By the time that this article reaches the majority of its readers, ... the Chancellor will have opened his great land campaign. That there is something wrong with the countryside is admitted by all parties. Thousands are flocking to the towns, unable to find work on the land which is rightfully theirs. One fifth of the country is held by members of the House of Lords. Five thousand people own nearly half the land of England ... The whole of the soil is owned by about one million persons altogether. It therefore follows that millions must be landless. I can imagine some ... readers saying, " ... what has this to do with me?" I do not get my living on the land". ... But this ... affects everyone. The well-being of the community is bound up with that of the agricultural worker.

HOW NOT TO DO IT

There are many remedies suggested ... for the evils arising from the present system of land tenure. One is to make the land the sole object of taxation. The advocates of this policy say that if the land is made the sole object of taxation, everyone will contribute ...

[p. 38]

to the national exchequer. The Chancellor's scheme will not embrace this policy of the Single Tax; it is not supported by public opinion ... ; it is only advocated by a few irresponsibles who have learned to mouth phrases about freeing the land. As a matter of fact it is not land reform at all, but fiscal reform, an entirely different thing. The policy of the single tax is little understood, and it seems to me ... that those who understand the least about it are its advocates.

Another body of men who would turn this place from a landlord-ridden country into a land flowing with milk and honey, are those whose policy it is to make more landlords. When we ... examine their scheme of peasant proprietorship, we find that it is ... bare-faced impudence. They say that we should encourage men to become owners of small plots of land to be used for agricultural purposes. But one has to remember that the proposal came from the landlords themselves. What does their scheme really mean? It seems that they may sell the land that they would rather be without, and that they can sell it at any price they like to ask. We all know that that is so, especially if the State purchases it. I have a case before me where a landlord asked 4,800 years purchase for

[p. 39]

land wanted for public use.

The disadvantages from the small-owners point of view are overwhelming. The chances of a successful small-owner being able to buy land adjoining his own, are very remote. Then again, in the majority of cases he would be owner in name only. In all countries where this policy has been tried, the owner has been in the clutches of the moneylender, and often pays more in interest than the fair rent of the land.

Perhaps one of the greatest difficulties ... is a financial one. If only one fifth of the agricultural land of England were ... bought for small ownerships, the cost would be ... about £200,000,000. This is based upon the average price (£32) paid per acre for land for small holdings. But it is safe to say that the land bought under the Unionist policy would be very much higher in price. Lastly, ... small ownerships are not wanted ... Only two per cent of the applicants under the Small Holdings Act, apply for ownership.

THE ONLY WAY

Whatever the Chancellor's policy may be, there is only one way whereby the land problem can be finally solved. That way is to nationalise the land. There is a fairly strong body of land nationalisers in this country, and the "Land Nationalisation Society" has nearly one hundred vice-

[p. 40]

presidents in the present parliament. Its advocates do not suppose that all the land can become public property at a given moment on a certain day. But they would welcome anything that would give the people the power to buy land whenever it was wanted for use. They ask that it shall be bought at the price on which it is taxed. That would be fair to the landlord, and possible to the community. No four thousand years purchase for us! Where is the money coming from, you say? No money will be required. The landlords will not be paid in golden sovereigns. They will be given Government Land Stock to the amount of the value of their land. This policy was adopted when the London Docks were bought, and also when the water companies became public property. Millions of pounds worth of private property was bought by the public without a single penny being paid in cash.

Another important point to remember is that when the nation takes over the land, thus incurring new liabilities, it will take over assets of at least an equal amount. And as time goes on, the liabilities will diminish and eventually disappear, but the assets will grow daily more valuable. Eventually, all the rent coming from the land will be available for the public use, thus reducing taxation to a minimum.

[p. 41]

THE PEOPLE'S BIRTHRIGHT.

Whatever objections may be urged against public ownership of other forms of property, they cannot be urged against the public ownership of land. Unlike industries, land is not the result of human effort. The land was here before man came. No one can add to it, neither can any portion of it be taken away. Land is an essential to life, quite as necessary as the water we drink and the air we breath. Land was given for the use of all. It is the people's birthright.

A.C.[3]

THE PEACE PALACE.

Who is the Prince of Peace? Not Carnegie[4] I am very certain. Here is a great capitalist, financing a numerous body of men who are longing for what Christianity alone will give. They build their palace, they invite each people of the world to do some small part, and the great Prince of Peace has a small statue on a stairway, sent by a South American Republic.

---

[3]   Algernon Carpenter.
[4]   For Andrew Carnegie see *ODNB*.

The work will be vain, ... the cause of Christ is not going to be won on earth by the money which is the outcome of exploited labour. No! The Carnegie Millions will not suffice.

[p. 42]

CIRCULATING LIST.
GET IT ROUND!

Mr. D. C. Messent.	Oct. 3rd.
Mr. W. Messent.	
Mr. L. Messent.	
Mr. R. S. Rowe	Oct. 6th.
Mr. F. Rowe.	
Mr. A. H. Evans.	Oct. 8th.
Mr. C. Bedwell.	Oct. 11th.
Mr. L. Bedwell.	
Mr. E. H. Bowler.	Oct. 13th.
Mr. A. Austin.	Oct. 15th.
Mr. W. Cramp.	Oct. 18th.
Mr. P. Coomber.	
Mr. A. Carpenter.	Oct.20th.
Mr. A. Munro.	Oct.22nd.
Mr. C. Smith.	Oct.24th.
Mr. F. Perkins.	Oct.26th.
Mr. H. Lansdown.	Oct. 28th.
Mr. G. Barrett.	Oct. 30th.
Mr. F. Jones.	Nov.2nd.
Mr. A. Jones.	
Mr. H. Jones.	
Mr. C. Moxley.	Nov.4th.
Mr. H. Messent.	Nov.6th.
Mr. F. Butcher.	Nov.8th.
Mr. M. Davies.	Nov.10th.
Mr. H. Eagle.	Nov.12th.
Mr. T. Lynch.	Nov.14th.
Mr. S. Seymour.	Nov. 16th.
Mr. A. Gosling.	Nov. 18th.

The dates are those on which the magazine is to be passed on.

THE ANGELS' VOICE

No. 15.

Editor: Jas. Godden.

[p. 1]

FOREWORD

There is a rumour of a rumour that the "Angels' Voice" is a journal run ... for the benefit of Trinity as a whole. Let us ... correct the impression by stating that it is produced solely for a little group of boon companions who chuckle together over ... its pages; it is a private enterprise under the control of nobody but its editor.

You ladies, who much against our wishes, insist on skimming through the magazine, be not surprised because you find it not actually to your taste.

You others whose names are on our list, and yet who do not like the conversation of the company you mix with, why not cross out your names and thus secure uninterrupted peace?

[p. 2]

[Drawing of a puppy standing on two legs.]

PLEASE!

[p. 3]

THE ANGELS' VOICE.

NO. 15.   December   1913.

EDITORIAL

Dear Readers,

This is our last issue before Christmas, and to such as we can reach in time, we wish all the compliments of the season. The others, we hope, will find themselves no worse for their period of feasting when they too receive the magazine.

Our cover artist we particularly thank for her sustained and practical interest, and ... in closing, may we call the attention of the squeamish ones to the recommendations in our Foreword.

Ed.

[p. 4]

LEADER'S LETTER.

"Maxton",
King's Avenue, S.W.
November 29th. 1913.

My dear Fellow Members,

After a review of our doings during the past month we are all conscious of much ... to be thankful for. Although our Football ... has not been as successful as we ... desired, it must be said that we have not experienced any debacle, but quite on the contrary, have usually just failed by the odd goal.

In the great event of the month – our Annual Meetings – records were both broken and set up, and it should be ours to raise a pean [sic] of thankfulness for the numbers, spirit and helpfulness attending them.

We are more than glad that we can claim as our associates the members of the Junior Bible Class with their leader, Mr. James Rofe, and we all look forward to the Sunday, not far hence, when he will occupy OUR CHAIR at the quarterly joint meeting.

The study of the Epistle to the Galatians has been proceeding steadily. The great doctrine of Justification by Faith has arrested our attention anew and led us into fresh visions of the freedom that is in Christ.

[p. 5]

During the coming year the Life of Moses will probably be before us, and we may look forward to some ... helpful studies of the doings ... of this most wonderful man.

It is good to be able to report once more that all abroad are well. Perhaps before this issue has gone the round, Will Crosley will have returned, and Harold Eagle[1] be on his homeward voyage, whilst the Munros who landed in Australia on November 25th. will undoubtedly be settling down to farm or bush life.

We are all glad that our neighbours had ... a successful ... Anniversary, and trust that their Class may grow in numbers and influence ...

Yours very sincerely,
D. C. Messent.

---

[1] Harold Eagle was a merchant seaman.

The Girl's Bible Class are taking an active interest in ... missionary work in China. They contemplate withdrawing their support from the London Missionary Society.[2]

[p. 6]

[Two photographs – one a hostel corridor; the other shows a family with several men, one woman and two children.]

[p. 7]

LAS PALMAS.

Our readers will be very glad to see that H.S.R.[3] has sent us over the photographs of the Seamen's Institute which appear in this issue.

The view along the corridor shows that it is by no means a dull and insignificant building, whilst the views of the recreation rooms give a good idea of the attractions that can be offered to those sailors who spend a short time in the port.

The group shows Mr. and Mrs. Hiley[4] entertaining the stewards of a passenger boat at tea. Mr. Hiley is right in the centre wearing spectacles, and I am sure the group could only have been improved had H.S.R. been sitting next to him.

HAVE A GLASS OF PORT OLD DEAR?

It sounds most horribly vulgar, and yet we suppose it is alright since it occurs in connection with the T.L.H.C.'s. In a recent fixture their opponents opened the proceedings by singing "Onward Christian Soldiers" and then re-inforced their physical strength by quaffing Fine Old Port. The quantity was sufficient to make them forget all ladylike dignity, and they were unkind enough to run quite fast. This was fatal to Trinity who lost the game by 18 – 0.

[p. 8]

[Two photographs of men playing snooker.]

---

[2]   This is also discussed by the young men. See *AV* 7 (Nov. 1911), 35; *AV* 9 (Dec. 1912), 9; *AV* 15 (Dec. 1913), 44.

[3]   Henry S. Rowe.

[4]   The Hileys may have been known to Trinity folk because she had been connected with the neighbouring Congregational church at Stockwell Green or because her father was a master butcher who may thus have known the Messents.

[p. 9]

ANNIVERSARY SUNDAY

For many weeks, all of us had been looking forward to our Anniversary; our leader has been putting all his energy into the arrangements and some ... had tried to follow in his example. These efforts culminated in our breaking all previous records ...

It did one good ... to see numerous chairs and forms placed round the table, and forming a second and third line of defence.

We were very glad to see again such old friends as George Harper, Arthur Holman, Fred Handy and Percy Calcott. They have left us for various reasons ... but we trust to have them back ... in course of time.

We opened the afternoon with our Brotherhood Hymn, after which Mr. James Rofe led us in prayer, for he ... had come up to join us on this afternoon. After one or two more hymns we listened to an address from Mr. John Rowe. He based his remarks on the report which was brought back to the Israelites by those ... sent out to spy out the Promised Land,[5] and by linking the incident up with the New Testament, gave us a memorable half hour.

After the notices from the Secretary, we had another

[p. 10]

hymn and the benediction was pronounced.

A little later we assembled for tea downstairs ...

It was suggested that we should partly occupy the time until 6.45 by having some of the favourite hymns of the class ... The Major was allowed to rest and Miss Lansdown served us at the piano. Several hymns were suggested such as "For all the Saints" and "The sands of time are sinking". We had also in memory our friends across the seas, so we sang "Eternal Father strong to save".

Mr. Bedwell made a few remarks between the second and third verses of this hymn, stating how much he regretted the departure of Harold Eagle, and asking us to have him specially in our minds.

The sing-song ... lasted for an hour, and the interest was well sustained by the remarks offered by one or two present. Mr. Godden ... urged the fellows to make a point of being present at the evening service, and after we had come out for a stroll, we assembled on our side of the gallery in as strong a muster as we have ever presented.

C.F.B.

---

5   Numbers 13.

[p. 11]

[Postcard] Genova – Panorama da Corso Carbonara.
[Photograph of a classical building behind a feminine statue holding a cross.]

[p. 12]

AN OCEAN CRUISE AND CONTINENTAL TOUR.
(Continued)[6]

In the last issue of this periodical, I related my experiences during the sea trip; in this issue I have endeavoured to tell you of my over-land journey to London. As stated in my last account, we arrived at Genoa on the 1st. October. I was sorry to leave the boat for it seemed quite tame and altogether too steady on land for me, but the change had to be made, so we took our baggage up to the Customs. Here a very funny little incident took place. A thorough young Irishman, one of our party, had purchased a box of cigars in Gibraltar and was wonderfully pleased at the price he had given for them. But on arriving at the Customs he was requested to open his bag; the officer at once spotted his cherished cigars and explained that he must either pay the usual duty or they must be confiscated, whereupon poor Pat's ... tail went between his legs. However, after some consideration he decided to give them up. The officer at once proceeded to do his duty, but Pat was not to be beaten and politely asked if he might keep a few. The officer replied with a nod and Pat thereupon seized two great handfuls of cigars; ... and retired smiling. You will hear more about this gentleman as I proceed.

[p. 13]

[A postcard and a photograph of Milan cathedral.]

[p. 14]

From the Customs we went to our Hotel and after depositing our bags, took the Polytechnic carriage drive to the Campo Santo. This is the general burying place of Genoa and ... contains thousands of most beautifully carved marble tomb stones; one ... a minature [sic] of the summit of Milan Cathedral.

During our stroll round this place we came across a sculptor working on a beautiful figure of a man, and he informed us that he had been at this one thing three years and he did not expect to finish it for a considerable time.

---

6   The earlier magazine, *AV* 14, is no longer extant.

We then proceeded ... to the City, and visited the church of the Annunciation ... On entering, our attention ... turned toward the ceiling. It was absolutely gorgeous, being covered completely with 18 carot [sic] hammered gold ... The only breaks were some magnificent paintings 500 years old, which were as bright as if they had been painted the previous day. We then turned to the altar and on either side of this were most magnificent twisted alabaster columns. This also was studded with gold ... exquisitely wrought. This is not the only place of its kind, for the cathedral is similar in one half of the ceiling, the other half having been destroyed

[p. 15]

[Postcard of Milano – Porta del Duomo.]

[p. 16]

by fire.

The main street is ... a wonderful sight, for the shops protrude over the pavement and are supported by polished marble columns, and as one walks down this arcade, overhead are beautiful paintings and mosaic work, whilst the shops themselves are almost better than ours in the West End.

... The following morning we departed for Milan, and during the day visited the Cathedral which is built entirely of marble.

...

On paying 1 franc, we were allowed to enter a room which contained the preserved remains of St. Charles, a friend of the poor. The room containing them was lined with beautifully carved silver, and the rock crystal coffin was edged with the same metal. The remains were very well preserved considering that they were 500 years old, but it was the robes, studded all over with the most costly of stones, the beautiful crown over the head and the magnificent diamond rings, which most attracted our attention.

After having ascended to the highest point ... we returned to lunch at our hotel, after which four of us took a taxi drive round the

[p. 17]

[Postcard of Milano – Corso Vitt. Emanuele.]

[p. 18]

City. I say a drive but I think it was more like a flight, for we only had a short time to do it all, as the driver knew, and I am certain that round most of the corners our cab went on two wheels. However, we saw all the most important sights in Milan, including the Cemetery, Arena, Arc de Triomphe and a funeral, and at 4 o'clock we left for Lugano on the Italian Lakes. But alas! No beautiful blue waters, nothing but ugly grey mountains and dirty water at their base.

On arising the following morning we were delighted to find beautiful sunshine and lovely blue lakes, and after breakfast we were informed that an excursion round the Lakes of Lugano and Como was the programme for the day. We proceeded to the pier where the Lake Steamer was waiting and after steaming along Lugano for about an hour we reached the end of the lake and took the mountain railway across to Lake Como. Here the weather was beautiful and the scenery far beyond my power of description. We sailed along ... calling at the most beautiful little stopping places. As we went along we passed high mountains covered from top to bottom with beautiful foliage, sometimes we passed a mountain waterfall working the wheel of a power station, and here and there a few pretty little houses would nestle high up the hills among the trees.

[p. 19]

[Two postcards of Italian Lakes – Axenstrasse and by moonlight.]

[p. 20]

Later in the afternoon we called at the Villa d'Este where Napoleon stayed several times. From here we took a tram along the frontier to Chiasso and thence took train back to Lugano, thus ending one of the most delightful days I have ever spent.

After dinner in the evening several of us took a stroll round the town and among us was Pat. Arriving at a tobacconist's we saw some huge cigars quite twelve inches long, and promised the Irishman that we would treat him to one if he would smoke it. We were rather dismayed at his acceptance of the offer, for the thing cost 2d. and there were only four of us. However, carefully choosing the best and straightest, amid shrieks of laughter, he endeavoured to light it with one match, but this was much too hard a job, for it would have needed a steam pump to draw any smoke through. We accordingly made a small bonfire with newspapers and trip bills (Sacrilege. Ed.) and eventually, after much pulling and puffing and blowing and gasping, he accomplished his task. But poor old Pat could not stick it long and had to put it on one side for a bit, and I believe it took him three solid days to finish that cigar.

On the following morning it was Saturday, and a topper too, raining as hard as possible, and not a mountain to be seen. However, after breakfast, several of us

[p. 21]

[Three photographs.]

[p. 22]

decided to ascend Mont Brè. We reached the top at about 12.15 and looked round to see … only clouds.

Next morning we were … catching the 9.25 train to Fluelen. This journey is through most magnificent scenery, huge mountains, rushing torrents and terrific waterfalls …

Alighting at Fluelen we took a lake steamer to Lucerne but the view was completely cut off by rain and mist. That day we had chocolate and rusks (not husks) and butter for our Sunday dinner on board a lake steamer. The thing that struck me most in Lucerne, not being able to see the scenery, was the lion monument, carved out of solid rock, about 30 to 50 feet high, in memory of the Swiss guard of the French King who all perished during the wars.

We at last got so absolutely sick of the incessant rain that … we decided to start for Paris by the 9 o'clock express that night, thus spending one night in the train.

Well, we spent a night in the train but sleep was out of the question, for just as we had taken off our boots … the collector came to clip our tickets and … he got most ridiculous-

[p. 23]

[Two postcards – one of Kulm-Hotel Monte Brè, Lugano and the other of Le Trocadero, Paris.]

[p. 24]

ly excited … However, after searching all over the compartment he left us to ourselves. But we were not left thus for long. The next visitor was the Customs Officer at one o'clock in the morning who made us get every bag and package down and open it, then quietly said, "Alright". We tried once more … to sleep, but … it was not long before our old pal came in again still awfully excited. I was excited too and would have forfeited my chances of sleep that night for the privilege of giving him a punch on the nose … However, he again withdrew until about 5.30 a.m., when in he came again, and after lying on the floor and poking about for some time, he all at once jumped up holding up a pair of ticket clippers.

In Paris we took one of Cook's Motors all round the city and in a day saw all the interesting buildings, including the Opera House, Eiffel Tower, Invalides, Tomb of Napoleon, Notre Dame and the Pantheon.

On the following day we took the same car to Versailles and saw many wonderful and luxurious things there, more especially the fountains. They only play five times a year and two of them play for no more than three quarters of an hour, but even this short period costs £200. In the time of the Kings of France these fountains were constantly playing, day and night.

[p. 25]

[Postcard of Tour Eiffel.]

[p. 26]

The following morning we left for Dieppe, and ... we reckoned on an easy crossing. We had not been out of the harbour five minutes before the wind sprang up and our boat pitched and rolled frightfully. But <u>still</u> my friend and I ... enjoyed a cigarette or two during the voyage. We landed at Newhaven after an exceedingly rough crossing through which only six of us kept fit; even some of the crew were queer.

When we arrived home we ... had had a really fine time. We had travelled in all, 4,000 miles, and in fifteen days had visited five countries and a continent.

L.H.M.[7]

RENOVATION FUND.

The promises are coming in, some slowly, some promptly, according to the characters of those who secured them.

A recent committee found that the £30 was certainly obtainable, but not a stone must be left unturned if £50 is to represent the final result of our efforts.

[p. 27]

THE LAST RECORD

(Tune: "The Lost Chord".[8])
A lament over T.L.H.C.
Doloroso.
Defeated one day at our hockey,
We were weary and ill at ease,

[7] Lewis H. Messent.
[8] This 'archetypal Victorian drawing-room ballad' was composed by Sir Arthur Sullivan in 1877. *The Oxford Dictionary of Music*.

For our players wandered idly
And only hit shins and knees.
We know not what we were playing!
Or what we were doing then,
But we struck at the ball so wildly
That it went to the other men.

And flooded and crimson our eyes were,
We wished for the "Angels" balm.
The loss rested sore on our spirits
Unlike an infinite calm.
No solace was there for our sorrow,
But bruised and broken with strife,
A most harmonious echo
To our now discordant life.

We tried some perplexing meaning
Into the score to squeeze.
We trembled and all vowed silence
And were not loth to cease.

[p. 28]

We had fought, but we sought quite vainly,
The ball through their goal to force,
For it came from the stick of their forwards,
And volleyed through ours, of course.

It may be "The Voice of the Angels"
Will speak of this loss in rhyme.
It may be – with Major's assistance –
We shall beat them another time.
It may be "The Voice of the Angels"
Will tease us all, just for fun.
It may be we'll soon be forgotten,
But never that eighteen none.

M.E.

BOXING

The deacons are not easy to get at and nothing further has been heard in the matter of boxing in the Gym. The deputation appointed has by no means lost sight of the matter, and hopes to bring things to a satisfactory issue ...

YOUR HOLIDAYS

The Holiday Club Committee has drawn up alternative schemes for visits to Jersey, North Wales, Belgium or the Lake District. All are most attractive and do not vary greatly in price.

[p. 29]

NORTH SURREY LEAGUE. DIV.II.
TRINITY V. DULWICH GROVE RESERVES.
Nov. 1st. 1913.

Having made such a disastrous start in our League Programme in the game with L.C. & W. Bank, great interest naturally centered [sic] round this second encounter. Harry Lansdown stood down in favour of E. H. Bowler, who thus bowed his entry into serious football, making a very favourable impression. L. H. Messent ... was unable to play, and so the remainder of the team was the same as on the previous Saturday.

The "Reserves" are a good bustling side ... but we inflicted upon them their first defeat ... and so became entitled to two valuable points.

The game itself was not good ... For Trinity, Collins was the best man, with Chippindale, Barrett, Linge,[9] and McCormick following on behind. The backs were very shaky ...

The first goal was recorded after 20 minutes. It was scored from a very good centre from E.H.B., the ball being ... headed in by Chippindale.

Unfortunately the whole game was poorly refereed,

[p. 30]

for although both sides suffered through bad judgements, it must be confessed that Trinity had the better of this handicap, for one goal awarded was at least doubtful, and on several other occasions we appeared to be the favourites. However, the result did not materially suffer, for ... the better side won.

The only Dulwich goal was a bad one ... for H. Jones allowed himself to be badly beaten when it looked as though he could easily have cleared ...

The Trinity forwards could not get together, being much too individualistic, an old fault of theirs. Rutter ... did not put in a decent centre during the whole game, whilst Linge was hardly up to his usual dash.

The only redeeming feature about this mediocre performance was the "bagging" of the two points already referred to.

---

[9]   Probably a mis-spelling of Lynch.

Result:– Trinity 3   Chippindale 2
                             Barrett 1
Dulwich Grove Res. 1

[p. 31]

A.F.A. Surrey Junior Cup.
TRINITY v. SURBITON HILL RESERVES.
November 8th. 1913.

The fact that a team cannot afford to make mistakes … was amply exemplified to our sorrow in this the second round of the above Cup Competition. That up to the last fifteen minutes Trinity had all the best of the play, nobody will deny, but … they made two very bad mistakes which brought about their downfall.

As may be gathered, the match … was bitterly disappointing, but in football one must be ready for heartburns, and especially in Cup Ties, for the knock-out system … allows no quarter.

As previously stated, Trinity had the best of the play for fully threequarters of the match; the forwards … and the halves were in fine form. E.H.B. was played outside right … but … his efforts to centre were just as bad as they were good the week before. Yet, as the only goal we scored came from one of his runs, to a certain extent he retrieved his character.

Surbiton were not long in getting together. They had

[p. 32]

pace and weight, and although always fair, used both. But our defenders were always a match for them, and had not the two calamities occurred, Surbiton would certainly never have scored.

Their first goal came fifteen minutes from the kick-off and was the result of a nasty "hands" much too near the "area" … It is seldom that our Captain infringes the rules but … the Ref. had no alternative but to award a free kick. It took the form of a lifting shot, and aided by a stiff breeze, the ball … sailed into the far corner of our goal … A goal-keeper can never go backwards, but must always be ready … to go forwards.

After this … Trinity continued to press but always lacked the finish which is so necessary to netting the ball. Right up to half time our men were continually in the Surbiton area, and on several occasions, such as when Chippindale's head got in the way of a stinging shot from McCormick … , were most unlucky. Had not the "Ref". miscalculated the

[p. 33]

time, and been seven minutes short in the first half, a time when our fellows were pressing most hotly, it is possible that a replay might have ensued.

Soon after the change of ends, a good pass to E.H.B. and a splendid centre by him enabled Rutter to score with a fine ground shot which put us on equal terms. This we remained till ... the second catastrophe took place. From a concerted movement ... a good straightforward shot was put into our goal mouth. It ... should have given Fred. Handy no trouble, but the ball twisted out of his hands and rolled into the net. How so good a goal-keeper could have blundered thus cannot be explained, but must be put down to the chances of the game.

From this blow Trinity never recovered, and soon after Barrett twisted a muscle and Chippindale got damaged, ... in a gallant effort to retrieve our fortunes. Thus weakened, Surbiton ... dispelled all prospects of a replay by monopolising the game until the whistle went.

Result:–
SURBITON 2.
TRINITY 1. (Rutter)

[p. 34]

NORTH SURREY LEAGUE. DIV. II.
TRINITY v. CROYDON SOUTHEND.
November 15th. 1913.

A goal conceded by each of the "backs" and a penalty missed, is the doleful tale of this game. Trinity will never climb the League Table until there is a vast improvement ... The "backs" persistently hamper the goal-keeper and mis-kicks are almost the rule ... The "halves" ... need much more precision in passing to their "forwards", and the latter must acquire ... understanding of one another's play ...

It was painful to watch the pitiable exhibition of mere individualism, ... the utter absence of ... concerted action. All worked "on their own" and all failed. In an endeavour after the ball, Trinity never got there first, and in a tackle were always easy to beat. Even when in possession they were hopelessly at a loss to know what to do, ... until robbed by an opponent. Such is the unexaggerated criticism, and ... each must study his weaknesses ... before much improvement can be recorded.

[p. 35]

Serious complaint was justifiably made concerning the shape of the ball, and ... we have never been asked to play with a worse one, but ... it cannot excuse the miserable display.

The "Southend" ... are ... not too difficult to beat. Their great feature is the rapidity with which they get "on the ball" ... Our men, apparently, were also infused with ... this spirit, but they always "got there" second which was ... quite useless. The hard working "Chip" who was at centre owing to Barrett being ill, did the best among our attackers, but he failed to distribute the ball to his "wings" and consequently there was little ... swinging of the ball which is so disquieting to a defence. Lansdown ... showed signs of improvement both in pace and in ball control but he was not supported well by his partner Linge ... E.H.B. playing at outside right was too timid ... Coomber did some good work, but his "throwing in" might have been more judicious, whilst Handy had no chance with the goals scored ...

[p. 36]

...

R. S. Rowe's penalty kick was weak ... , and although these penalties are not easy to take, to score from them is the rule rather than the exception.

Our position in the League cannot be far from the bottom. Out of a possible six points we have scored two, but one cannot help thinking that when next we meet our vanquishers ... a different result will ensue.

RESULT:– CROYDON SOUTHEND 2
TRINITY   1 (Linge)

TRINITY v. LARCOM
November 22nd. 1913.

After the "strain and stress" of Cup and League Football, a "friendly" with our old opponents came as a welcome relaxation. McCormick and Barrett were absentees.

Larcom have about the same strength as in former seasons. Their ubiquitous centre forward is still the outstanding feature of the attack, but one noticed several new faces, each one ... strengthening of the team.

[p. 37]

Trinity ... should have been several goals up by half time instead of which our visitors had the only point scored before change of ends. This was due to our poor centering and shooting. The centering of H. Lansdown left much to be desired ... whilst the marksmanship of Linge and Bowler was grievously at fault ...

On the change of ends things improved. Chippendale at centre led his men well, and ... one could catch some faint vision of concerted action. The "timid one" got going on several occasions, and ... was usually dangerous, whilst Rutter reminded us that in spite of "anno domini" he still has some of his old form left.

The halves all did well. The continued improvement of Coomber is very satisfactory, but the backs again showed an utter lack of understanding of one another ... But ... when pressed, they managed to come out with honours.

Attention must be drawn to the bad habit of both halves and backs in obstructing their goalkeeper during "corner" kicks ... Several goals have been given away and matches lost through this mistake.

[p. 38]

A custodian must have plenty of room to work in, his vision must not be impeded, and ... no goalkeeper will thank either "back" or "half" for standing nearly under the cross bar.

RESULT   TRINITY 3   Chippindale
                               Bowler
                               Rutter
          LARCOM 1

November 29th, 1913.
NO MATCH.

A PROTEST.

The habit of smoking is open to debate, but ALL will agree that there cannot be two minds concerning the propriety of "lighting up" almost before the Benediction has been pronounced.

A great improvement ... is that all who apparently must smoke immediately after services would wait a respectful time as it is not expedient that knots of offenders should violate the susceptibilities of their many friends.

"UNSELFISH"

Belgium for 'bacca. Enquire re Holiday Club.

[p. 39]

[Notes on sport: two newspaper cuttings about Trinity's football team.]

[p. 40]

ANNUAL BUSINESS MEETING.

On the 2nd. Sunday in November, 1907, a band of youngsters under Mr. D. C. Messent's leadership, assembled in what is now the room of the Girl's Bible Class, and stood up together … and sang the opening hymn at the first meeting of the Trinity's Young Men's Bible Class.

On November 13th. 1913, the same class met together to hold its Sixth Annual Business Meeting …

As has been our custom for five years past, we assembled for light refreshments and lighter chatter at a quarter past eight. Three quarters of an hour later we took our places in the Lecture Hall, and our chairman, Mr. Snoswell, offered up the opening prayer.

On either side of Mr. Snoswell were Mr. D. C. Messent, our leader, and Mr. R. S. Rowe, our secretary. Letters of apology for absence first claimed our attention, and Mr. Messent announced that Messrs. Carpenter, Barrett and Perkins had written to him, whilst Mr. Lansdown, our president, was very disappointed at not being with us …

[p. 41]

The chairman then called upon our Secretary for his Report. The opening note was rather a mournful one; we had lost more members than we had gained. This could be explained … by the emigration of several … , and made the drop from 23.5 to 22 in our average attendance … less alarming. During the year only one member had joined the church although our connection with it as a class had been greatly strengthened. We had had a considerable share in the cleaning of the church; we had run a successful stall at the Bazaar, and latterly we had associated ourselves with the Renovation Fund. It was satisfactory to note that … during our Leader's summer holiday it was possible to conduct our meetings without any outside help. For some time past the Adult School Union's Syllabus had not given complete satisfaction, and a change had recently been made, resulting in our present study of the Epistle to the Galatians. Our various athletic activities were briefly touched upon and the trip to Jersey was … a pattern upon which to mould … next season's holidays. The report closed with an exhortation to each individual member to do what lay in his power for the increased … success of our weekly meetings.

[p. 42]

The report was received with considerable applause, after which Mr. Snoswell called for a motion for its adoption.

Mr. Godden ... commented upon several points. He dwelt chiefly on our diminished numbers and turned the attention of the meeting to the record attendance of the previous Sunday. These numbers were in some degree due to the presence of the Junior Bible Class, who by their attendance at both our Anniversary Gatherings showed an interest which we were perfectly justified in assuming would eventually lead them to join us. With a brief reference to our share in the Open Air Meetings of the past summer, ... he moved the adoption with great pleasure.

The motion was seconded by Mr. A. Austin ...

Mr. C. Bedwell ... urged particularly that members should seriously consider ... church membership. He also complained that ... he did not receive a mark when he was downstairs teaching, and he suggested ... that if he were counted present when he was

[p. 43]

absent, our average attendance would be improved.

The motion was then put and the report adopted unanimously.

(At this point the Major entered. Prolonged cheers.)

The Treasurer's report was satisfactory, for our average contributions had increased from 2s. 11½d. to 4s. 4d. per month. The total amount collected for class purposes was £2. 12. 1. and after expenses had been met, a balance of £1. 6. 8½d. remained to be carried forward. The report was moved and seconded, and carried unanimously.

Mr. F. Rowe next presented his report as Missionary Treasurer. The total collections for the year had amounted to £6. 8. 11., an increase of £1. 8. 4½. over the previous year's aggregate. The largest amount collected on one Sunday was 5s. 2d. as against 5s. 2½d. in 1912, and the lowest amount was 1s. 6d. as against 1s. 4d. The average weekly contribution for the year had been 3s. 7d., and the report was concluded with the hope that during the current year it would reach 4s. 0d.

The adoption was moved by Mr. C. Bedwell, seconded by Mr. E. H. Bowler, and carried without any dissentient.

Arising out of Mr. F. Rowe's report was the matter of the disposal of the funds in hand. Mr. Godden moved that they

[p. 44]

should be divided equally between the two missionary stations with which we are personally connected and Mr. C. Bedwell seconded. But Messrs. Austin, Cramp & D. C. Messent ... brought forward an amendment that the money should be divided equally between the London Missionary Society, Mr. Rowe and Mr. Fairman. The amendment was ... carried with three dissentients.

287

At this point, Mr. John Rowe, who was received with great enthusiasm, gave a brief account of what our previous year's money had done, and put before us the alternative schemes to which our present contribution might be devoted.

Owing to ... the nomination papers given out on the previous Sunday, the election of officers took ... little time ... The officers for the ensuing year are therefore:-

Leader:	MR. D. C. MESSENT.
Secretary:	MR. R. S. ROWE.
TREASURER:	MR. L. H. MESSENT.
Missionary Treasurer:	MR. F. ROWE.
Prayer Meeting Sec.	MR. W. CRAMP.
Organist:	MR. C. MOXLEY.
Auditors:	MESSRS. C. SMITH
	& G. BARRETT.

Committee: Mr. D. C. Messent.   Mr. R. S. Rowe.
Mr. L. H. Messent.   Mr. F. Rowe.
Mr. W. Cramp.   Mr. A. Austin.
Mr. C. Bedwell.   Mr. M. Davies.

[p. 45]

Whilst waiting for the results of ... the election of committeemen, the members of the 2nd. XI. through Mr. M. Davies, presented their secretary with a token of their appreciation of the trouble he takes on their behalf.

Mr. Bedwell replied suitably, and ... investigated the nature of the gift, which to the great delight of those assembled, proved to be a pair of razors.

When the merriment had subsided, Mr. A.H.E. strolled to the front and produced a typewritten speech. Its opening words,

"Quite diffident and ill at ease
As all the meeting plainly sees", threw

his hearers into a paroxysm of laughter, ... which lasted throughout the reading of this rhymed matter ... The occasion of the outburst was the presentation to the Editor of an enormous model of a blue pencil. When the article was handed over, ... the happy recipient ... required many minutes to recover sufficient composure ... to express his thanks and appreciation.

The next business ... was the suggested holiday club mentioned in the

[p. 46]

Secretary's report. Mr. Evans and Mr. Cramp spoke enthusiastically of the project, and our leader expressed his pleasure that ... the initiative was to be found amongst the members themselves. He suggested that a committee should ... frame a suitable scheme and the following gentlemen consented to serve, Messrs. A. H. Evans, A. P. Austin, J. G. Godden, W. Cramp, and R. S. Rowe.

The last motion was brought forward by Mr. Godden, who suggested all meetings which might be in any way due to our Class, should be opened and closed with prayer. The proposal met with sympathetic consideration ...

Our chairman concluded the meeting with a few words, in which he pointed out that we should ... be on our guard against ... slackness ...

He then offered the closing prayer ...

[p. 47]

AN AEROPLANE TRIP

I have been asked to give an account ... of my first aeroplane trip, but as that was about a year ago and I have made several flights since, my first impressions are rather dimmed. However, I will do my best ...

Having got a promise of a trip from our Aviator ... I took the opportunity of reminding him ... He gave his consent so I clambered into the machine, and while I was strapping myself in, "Contact" was shouted, and I heard the roar of the engine, whilst the propeller started revolving at a terrific speed. The ... machine began to move very slowly. The speed gradually increased until I felt the ground slipping away from me. By this time the engine was full out and the propeller was doing about 900 revolutions per minute, and being a Tractor Biplane[10] the wind cut through me like a knife and absolutely took my breath away at times. I might say I had already lost my cap, and my hair, never being noted for its curliness, was standing up on end like wire. I won't say it was fright but will put it down to the wind from the tractor. After I had got over the first peculiar feeling

[p. 48]

of being in the air, I began to get – shall I say – my "Air Legs", and could look about me. The Aerometer was showing a speed of between fifty and sixty miles per hour, varying according to the wind, for we were flying against it. I was looking down at the people who ... at an altitude of about 1300 feet ... appeared pretty small. You have seen

---

[10] In a tractor biplane, the engine and propeller are placed in front. *OED*.

a fly walking across a high ceiling, and if you were to imagine for a minute that the ceiling and yourself were reversed and that you were looking down at the fly instead of up at it, you will have some idea of my impressions.

Whilst meditating over these "dots", my heart nearly came into my mouth; I felt as though I were being thrown over the side, and that the machine was going to turn turtle. I saw our left plane rise and the right drop until we were at an angle of about 80 degrees, but – false alarm – we were only banking so as to turn, and the machine righted itself almost immediately. This happened in less time than it takes to write, as it only needs a few seconds to turn. We were then flying with the wind which increased our speed to about 65 miles an hour, and the sensation of travelling at such a rate was simply splendid … If I had been the pilot myself I believe I should have gone as fast as ever the machine would let me. I have always looked upon "Speedmen" upon the road and track

[p. 49]

as being just a little "loose up above", but I can quite understand the fascination of speed now. The faster you go the faster you want to go.

I noticed that we had reached an altitude of about 1350 feet and were getting near to the flying ground. We now had another bank, for which I was prepared after the shock of the first, but … it made me feel a little "groggy". We had hardly got righted … before we had another at an opposite angle, and I guessed that we were going to do a spiral and descend. I was right and we did about twelve spirals, and you can hardly imagine what a pleasant feeling it is to rise about 75 to 80 degrees on one plane, drop to normal, and then rise on the other one. It is the most fascinating sensation I have ever had. We landed quite safely after a flight of about 15 to 20 minutes which seemed as if it had only been five, and I must say I was very pleased with my trip, and anxious to make another.

G.H.[11]

In our last issue it was stated that the Girls Bible Class was studying Galatians. We are now informed that this is not so. Although they may have touched on the Epistle, it was only in the course of the study of St. Paul as outlined in the Adult School Syllabus.

[11]   Probably George Harper.

[p. 50]

ODE TO MY NEW BLUE PENCIL.

Cut and alter, stubby thing,
Swift on criticism's wing.
Do not be afraid to strike;
Leave in only what you like.

Thou wert given by the men
Who shall thy power when
They have courage to submit,
For correction, what they've writ.

If the doings of a maid
Are before thy glance displayed,
Check the grammar of the "par",
Doing nought the sense to mar.

Let no thought of dull complaint
Make thy livid strokes grow faint.
In the end thy work gives pleasure
O thou editorial treasure.

J.G

[p. 51]

THE CHRISTMAS FIRE.

After more than a week's cycling we had reached the little town of Wrexham in North Wales, and not far off was the Rhosddu Coal Mine. We found our lodging for the night and then walked out to the pit head. The few people we had spoken to about the matter, held out very little hope of a chance of visiting the bottom, so we had quite made up our minds to rest contented with watching operations above ground. The shaft was interesting enough and we strolled about till it was dark. On our way back we passed the manager's office and saw someone inside talking to a miner. We ... went up to tackle him on the subject of a trip to the bottom. For a while we could scarcely understand each other; his English savoured strongly of Welsh and we were at cross purposes. But at last we managed to make out, "Where have you been working before?" he evidently thought we were after a job so we hastened to give him to understand that we were only tourists. After a few minutes ... he ... said we might go down with him at 10 o'clock on the following morning. Before we left he showed us round the operating machinery. The fan and pumps claimed most of our attention.

[p. 52]

The former was a huge affair, thirty feet in diameter with blades four feet wide. The latter were very fascinating to watch, making five strokes a minute and drawing up 150 gallons each time. The pumps were two in number, and if either were to stop working, it would mean that all activity in the mine must cease.

The next morning we cycled over to the mine and got there comfortably about three minutes before the appointed time. The tidy manager of the previous evening was dressed more like a navvy, and when he saw our rig-out he took us into his office, told us to take off our collars, and gave us each a dirty old cap and a miner's lamp.

The mine is in two sections. One is quite dry, the other taps several underground streams which necessarily make it rather wet. We decided to visit the dry part and walked up to the shaft head. Our previous experience of lifts was confined to those on the "Underground" system, clean and steady. But these lifts were iron cages, dripping with water and covered with rust. They are quite small, measuring 3½ feet wide by eight feet long, and are designed primarily to take two trucks lengthwise. The lifts have two tiers so as to accommodate four trucks, and as one cage descends, another is drawn up, thus reducing the necessary working power to a minimum.

[p. 53]

As soon as a lift came up, the manager told us to get in, but to take care not to let our clothes touch the sides, and to press our heads against the roof so as to keep it upright. No sooner had we taken our positions than a bell rang and the lift dropped six feet so as to take in two trucks in the upper tier. The bell rang again and then ... After a second or two our feet seemed to catch up with the floor again, and the horrible sensation of falling through space was somewhat abated. The guides upon which the lift slides appear to be bent, and throughout the journey the cage is swaying and jolting. As there are no barriers at either end, it would be quite easy to fall out if you did not hold tight.

Soon the floor felt as if it were being pushed up towards us, and the lift came to a standstill. The journey seemed to have lasted about five minutes, but in reality was only thirty seconds. The depth of the shaft is a quarter of a mile so you will see that our average speed was 30 miles per hour.

We got out, and ... followed our guide along the main avenue. Everything was black, oppressively black, although the tunnel was well furnished with electric lights. This lasted for about two hundred yards, but the Authorities will not allow it any further from the shaft for fear of fusing or sparks. The wide road then became narrower, and whereas formerly, there was a double set of rails, now there was only a single set of rails, and the roof was slightly lower.

It may be interesting to note that the haulage in the mine is done mostly by stationary engines worked by compressed air and the ponies are being superseded. The engines wind and unwind steel cables, one of which runs along the ground through the coal dust, whilst the other travels along pulleys fastened to the roof.

The standing room was becoming less and less, and we who were not used to this class of work, were continually bumping our heads. It felt much like walking about with back and head bent down, and bumping into a lamp-post at every turn.

Along every road, at intervals of ten yards, are niches into which the men may get out of the way of the trains. These trains are made up of about 24 trucks, and as a truck is often almost as big as the tunnel, it can be easily understood that before the refuges were made compulsory by law, men were frequently losing their lives through being overtaken by a train.

After another twenty minutes we turned sharp round to the right and crawled on our hands and knees to where

some men were working. They were mostly small but wonderfully strong, and seemed to pick up pieces of coal weighing about half a hundredweight and throw them into the trucks with ease. They were lying on their sides, picking away at the shale underneath a seam of coal. After this had been dugout to a depth of about four feet, explosives were inserted in the top, and the explosion left a tremendous heap of coal all in good sized lumps.

Whilst sitting here I dropped my lamp and for a while was "in the dark" as the miners say. We next wriggled through a small hole not quite big enough to crawl through and found ourselves once more in a fairly decent road. The manager at this point sent my lamp to be re-lighted. The lamps are opened and closed by a powerful electro-magnet so that it is impossible to tamper with them. As no matches are allowed in the mine, several lighting stations are provided. The lamp is pressed on two small buttons and the current causes the oil to take fire at once.

Nearly half an hour later we came to a working where special trucks only eight inches high are used and the men looked like snakes as they wriggled along behind.

The roads are everywhere most irregular, with frequent gradients of 1 in 6 so as to get at seams forty feet above or below the old working. The roads are dug out considerably

[p. 56]

wider than seems necessary at first sight, but the sides are afterwards packed with the loose shale, making the sides closer together and fairly even.

By this time we had come back to the main avenue with its electric lights, and during the whole trip we had only seen two ponies. There are 65 of them in the mine altogether so it shows what a small portion of it we visited. As a matter of fact the whole mine has a diameter of nine miles. The ponies are not blind ... and the men appear to be rather fond of them. We paid a visit to the stables and this brought us back to the shaft with its lifts. As soon as one came down we jumped in and were whirled back to daylight. After a wash and many grateful thanks to the manager, we rode off south, thinking of the figures we should always see in the dancing flames as we gathered round the blaze on a winter's evening.

[p. 57]

HOW THE COOLIE WORKS.
By Our Indian Correspondent.

One often hears the expression "Working like a nigger" and by it we usually mean to infer that someone has been throwing his whole energy into the work in hand. The ludicrousness of this expression is not understood until niggers have actually been seen at work, and for the benefit of those who cannot do this, we will renew our acquaintance with Messrs. Appolosawmy, Munasawmy, Rungasawmy and Coopasawmy, who are now employed on a road repairing job in Rangoon. First of all let us ... find out the meaning of "Work" according to them. We find it defined as "Something at which one is always present, but which one seldom does".

It is a nice warm day in Rangoon and work has already commenced, the coolies having been mustered and told off to their various jobs. Luckily Ramasawmy and Appolosawmy are working together, carrying earth, so we shall be able to keep an eye on them ... Appolosawmy has been at work for two minutes during which time he has dislodged enough earth to fill Ramasawmy's basket. Ramasawmy strolls up, basket on his head, and Appolasawmy rakes in the earth, drops his mamootie, helps to lift the

[p. 58]

mighty burden and Ramasawmy staggers off with his ten pound load. Appolosawmy slowly recovers his mamootie. What is the use of hurrying.? Ramasawmy has not reached the dumping ground. Time enough to commence digging when he is coming back, so Appolosawmy has a rest. Ah! There is Rungasawmy, I wonder if he will ever pay back that two annas he borrowed at the toddy shop last night. What's that? It's mud on the mamootie! Nothing must impair the might of the next blow. He looks around for a stick. Stay! Wasn't there a piece of iron somewhere about. He will go and look for it. Cooperasawmy is using it so he will have to wait. Surely that wasn't an ant I felt. Yes it was – but no, it can't have been – well I might as well make sure. Fancy missing the chance of catching an ant for the sake of filling Ramasawmy's basket. What! He is back again? Well, he must wait, that's all.

Thus the day continues until evening comes, and with the walk home the excitement begins. Before Appolosawmy came to Rangoon he was used to walking home in single file through the jungle, where the largest living thing to be seen was probably an army of ants marching along. In towns it seems to be the fashion to walk in groups of three, two in front and one behind. In the town also there are devil cars which often drive one into the ditch

[p. 59]

or if two of them meet, make you dance from one side of the road to the other. He eventually reaches home and there has his dinner consisting of dall and rice, or only rice. Appolosawmy is no connoisseur in food, but he knows a thing or two about toddy and betel. Occasionally he purchases a few rotten vegetables which is his only luxury, and he very often dies from it. Dinner is over and after a visit to the toddy shop, or perhaps being a spectator to a quarrel between Poabathy and his wife, he suddenly feels sleepy and so lies down on his mat, first of all taking care to cover up his head, and is off into log-like insensibility for nine solid hours.

W.T.C.

BEAUTY EXERCISES

There recently appeared an article in a popular evening paper, telling its lady readers how they could increase their beauty by means of exercises.

The cutting has been circulated round the Girl's Gym, and it is rumoured that these exercises are far more popular than those which are simply circulated to render them physically fit.

[p. 60]

IS IT TRUE

That the niece of a Jersey Pastor has captured the heart of a
    patriarch "Angel"?

That boxing is to be permitted at the gym?

That "gloves" will be worn more frequently this winter if the
    rumour is true?

That A.P.A. has ordered a new "First Aid" outfit in anticipation.

That there is still an outstanding sub. for last years gym?

That prospective housekeeping expenses prohibit the purchase
    of a new mac?

That D.C.M. has been seen taking lessons in the "Tango" from
    E.H.B. in King's Avenue?

That A.P.A. possesses a pair of sky blue socks with white stripes?

That he is afraid to wear them for fear of cutting out a fellow
    chorister?

That the last four numbers of the "Angels' Voice" have had a
    close season?

That C.F.B. has confessed to being speechless?

That J.G. was moved to tears by the kind presentation made to
    him at the A.G.M?

That Mr. S.A.S. proposes to turn out in plaid trousers at the
    next A.G.M?

That Wally's bag is lined with suitable material for such garments?

Contributions under this heading will be required next month.

[p. 61]

CIRCULATING LIST
GET IT ROUND!NO TIME TO WASTE!

Mr. D. C. Messent.	
Mr. W. J. Messent.	
Mr. L. Messent.	Dec. 6th.
Mr. R. S. Rowe.	
Mr. F. Rowe.	Dec. 9th
Mr. E. H. Bowler.	Dec. 11th.
Mr. F. Perkins.	Dec. 13th.
Mr. C. Bedwell.	
Mr. L. Bedwell.	
Mr. N. Bedwell.	Dec. 16th.
Mr. A. H. Evans.	Dec. 18th.
Mr. A. Austin.	Dec. 20th.

Mr. W. Cramp.	Dec. 22nd.
Mr. P. Coomber.	Dec. 24th.
Mr. A. Carpenter.	Dec. 26th.
Mr. C. Smith.	Dec. 28th.
Mr. H. Lansdown.	Dec. 30th.
Mr. G. Barrett.	Jan. 1st.
Mr. R. Chippindale.	Jan. 2nd.
Mr. F. Jones.	
Mr. A. Jones.	
Mr. H. Jones	Jan. 5th.
Mr. C. Moxley	Jan. 7th.
Mr. H. Messent.	Jan. 9th.
Mr. F. Butcher.	Jan. 11th.
Mr. M. Davies.	Jan. 13th.
Mr. T. Lynch.	Jan. 15th.
Mr. S. Seymour.	Jan. 17th.
Mr. A. Gosling.	Jan. 19th.
Mr. C. Oke.	Jan. 21st.

The dates are those on which the magazine is to be passed on.

APPENDIX: LIST OF NAMES

Those listed as subscribers appear on one or more of the circulation lists in *AV*.

Details of employers, where given, are derived from telephone numbers, published in *AV*.

The names on Trinity's war memorial are included even where not mentioned in *AV*. In several cases it has proved impossible to obtain biographical information.

First World War service has been noted where it can be confirmed from those records which survive.

Armston, Miss – TLHC rambler 1912.

Austin, Alfred Phipps – subscriber, amateur actor, gymnasium instructor, one of four older class members.[1]
1881 and 1891 censuses: Alfred was in an orphanage in Wanstead, Essex.
1911 census: 8 Bythorn Street, aged 33, solicitor's clerk.
Employer 1912: Whatley and Son, solicitors, 27 Lincoln's Inn Fields.[2]
Before full-time army service, was clerk with Employers Liability Assurance.
Reservist in Royal Fusiliers until 29 Oct. 1905. Rejoined 6 Dec. 1909 in Royal Army Medical Corps. War service: sergeant (sanitary inspector) in France and Salonika. Discharged Oct. 1918 due to malaria.[3]
Died 26 Oct. 1933 when living in Streatham Vale, with wife Nellie.[4]

Austin, Harold – footballer, 'a Faversham man'.[5]
1911 census: 57 Shakespeare Road, aged 22, printer's reader, b. Faversham, Kent.
Boarded with Fanny Cross (59, widow) as did Harry Reeves (see below).

Barrett, Arthur William Guy – subscriber, footballer, cricketer, auditor of class accounts.
Sister, Elizabeth Nellie, married at Trinity 1904.[6]
1911 census: 61 Dulwich Road, aged 19, clerk.
Family: widowed mother, Harriet, 53 (became church member 1908[7]); sisters: Edith Annie Daisy, 29; May, 22 (became church member 1908[8]) and Rose 16 (became church member 6 Dec. 1914[9]).

---

[1] *AV* II (Aug. 1913), 12.
[2] *POLD 1910*, i. part 3, p. 1292.
[3] TNA, War Office: Soldiers' Documents from Pension Claims, WO 364/ 95. Service no. 527011.
[4] PPR *Calendar* (1933).
[5] *AV* 5 (March 1911), 31.
[6] TCC Marriage, 2 July 1904.
[7] TCC Meeting, 25 Mar. 1908.
[8] TCC Meeting, 12 Feb. 1908.
[9] TCC Meeting, 2 Dec. 1914.

Trinity's War Memorial

Employer 1912 and 1913: Frederick E. Potter Ltd, advertising agents, Koh-i-noor House, Kingsway.[10] (Ernest Bowler had same employer – see below)
War service: acting corporal Royal Army Ordnance Corps.[11]
Was living in Brixton during the 1920s.[12]
Died 1978, Hillingdon.[13]

Beagley, H. – subscriber. (Also once as Bealey – presumably a misprint.)

Bedwell, Cyril Francis – subscriber, 1912 rambler, also known as **Cibby** (C.B.).
1911 census: 22 Arlingford Road, aged 20, drapery warehouseman.
Sister: Maud Beatrice Bedwell, 18 (became church member 1910[14]). Brothers: see below.
Employer 1912: Fore Street Warehouse Co., 104 to 107 Fore Street, Moorgate and 30 Milton Street, Moorgate.[15]

---

[10] *POLD 1914*, part 3, p. 1184.
[11] TNA, First World War service medal and award rolls, WO 329/2108. Service no. 016817.
[12] LMA, electoral registers, LCC/PER/B/1643, 1765.
[13] General Register Office, *England and Wales Civil Registration Indexes*.
[14] TCC Meeting, 1 June 1910.
[15] *POLD 1910*, i. part 3, p. 886.

Employer 1913: Stuart, Sons and Co. wholesale milliners, 32, 33, 36 and 37 Old Change, Ludgate Hill.[16]

Cyril had a heart condition and did not join up in the First World War. He was a fire watcher in Brixton to guard against bombing.[17]

1918 married Clarissa Lansdown at Trinity. Cyril's profession: buyer (export trade).[18] Bernard J. Snell, minister of Brixton Independent Church, witnessed the marriage.[19]

Died 1967, Bournemouth.[20]

Bedwell, Leslie John Hunter – subscriber, 1912 rambler.

1911 census: 454–6 Brixton Road, aged 16, boarder at Bon Marché (tailoring dept.),[21] gentlemen's hosier's assistant.

Employer 1912: Arding and Hobbs, drapers and house furnishers, Clapham Junction.[22] Arding and Hobbs' shop was destroyed by fire in 1909. The present buildings, built 1910, were the largest department store south of the Thames.[23]

War service from 2 Sept. 1914 in 21st Battalion, The London Regiment. Was a corporal when he became a casualty in 1917. Reverted to private on transfer to the army pay office in Exeter.[24]

Seriously ill in the 1920s. An occasional lay preacher. Died 1973, Gloucestershire.[25]

Bedwell, Norman Sidney William – subscriber, 1912 rambler.

1911 census: 22 Arlingford Road, aged 14, clerk to Health Department, Corporation of the City of London.

Employer 1913: Thomas Dunlop Young, MRCVS, veterinary inspector for City of London and chief meat inspector for Corporation of London, 502, 503 and 504 Central Markets, Smithfield.[26]

War service: private in Manchester Regiment, followed by Labour Corps.[27]

May have fought in 3rd battle of Ypres, July to Nov. 1917. In Dec. hit by shrapnel which entered his lungs. In England for the rest of the war. After discharge, qualified as accountant.

Treasurer of Herne Hill Congregational Church for about 20 years. Died 1979, Croydon.[28]

Berry, Frederick H. – victim of typhoid.

1901 census: 98 Acre Lane, aged 9.

Died 5 Nov. 1910.[29]

---

[16]   *POLD 1914*, part 3, p. 1284.
[17]   Information from Carolyn Bedwell (grand-daughter).
[18]   Information from Carolyn Bedwell.
[19]   TCC Marriage, 20 May 1918.
[20]   General Register Office, *England and Wales Civil Registration Indexes*.
[21.] *POLCSD 1911*, part 1, p. 40.
[22]   *POLCSD 1911*, part 1, p. 328.
[23.] <http://www.britishlistedbuildings.co.uk/en-488213-arding-and-hobbs-store-non-civil-parish->, accessed 25 June 14.
[24.] TNA, War Office: Soldiers' Documents from Pension Claims, WO364/ 201. Service no. 15875.
[25]   Information from David Bedwell (nephew).
[26]   *POLD 1914*, part 3, p. 1370.
[27]   TNA, Medal Rolls index card, WO 372/2/72421. Service nos 41809 and 595523.
[28]   Information from David Bedwell (son) and Herne Hill United Church.
[29]   *AV* 2 (Dec. 1910), 10.

Biggins, Fred – subscriber, footballer. Sometimes given as Biggin or Biggens.
1911 census: possible match – 69 Ballater Road, Charles Frederick Biggin, aged
15, clerk in wallpaper merchants, b. Sheffield. Sister: Jessie Lee, aged 17, shop
assistant, boots and shoes.
In Nov. 1911 Miss J. Biggin (or Biggen) applied for church membership and in
Dec. she was nominated as a Sunday school teacher.[30]
Employer 1912: Emil Goldstein, silk agent, 5 Gutter Lane, Cheapside.[31]
War service of C. F. Biggin: private in the Essex Regiment. Died 19 Sept. 1918 in
Palestine. Parents' address 40 Acre Lane, Brixton.[32]

Bishop, Jack – footballer.

Black, Mr – has a deep voice and long whiskers.

Boud, E. J. – war memorial.

Bowler, Ernest Henry – *AV* sub-editor, 1912 rambler.
1911 census: 68 Dalberg Road, aged 19, junior clerk at an advertising agents,
boarder with Harper family.
Employer 1912: Frederick E. Potter Ltd, advertising agents, Koh-i-noor House,
Kingsway[33] (same work address as Guy Barrett).
Employer 1913: G. Street and Co. Ltd., British, Foreign and Colonial Advertising
and Newspaper Agents, 8 Serle Street, Lincoln's Inn.[34]
War service from 9 Nov. 1914: rifleman in 9th (Reserve) Battalion, The London
Regiment, Queen Victoria's Rifles. Discharged 27 Aug. 1915 due to wounds. Left
leg amputated.[35]
1916 married Rose Edith Gale at Trinity. Ernest's profession: advertising agent's
clerk. Address: 12 Morval Road, Brixton.[36]

Butcher, Frederick Albert – subscriber, war memorial.
1911 census: 45 St James's Road, aged 18, telephone operator in stockbrokers.
Brothers: Harry (see below), Sydney Lewis, 14, and Reginald Frank, 10; sister:
Nellie Grace, 12.
Employer 1913: R. Nivison and Co., stock and share brokers, 1 Bank Buildings,
Princes Street, Bank.[37]
Sidney Butcher became a church member in 1914[38] and Leonard (cousin, 22
Appach Road) in 1915[39].
Artillery reservist in the Territorial Force. Enlisted 13 Sept. 1910. War service:
Gunner in Royal Horse Artillery and Royal Field Artillery. Killed in action on
Western Front, 21 Aug. 1916.[40]

---

30   TCC Meeting, 29 Nov. 1911, 31 Jan. 1912; TCC Sunday School Teachers Meeting minute
     book 1891–1914, 14 Dec. 1911, 18 Jan. 1912, 17 Apr. 1912.
31   *POLD 1910*, i. part 3, p. 911.
32   CWGC. Service no. 43211.
33   *POLD 1914*, part 3, p. 1184.
34   *POLD 1914*, part 3. p. 1283.
35   TNA, War Office: Soldiers' Documents from Pension Claims, WO364/326. Service no.
     3388.
36   TCC Marriage, 25 Dec. 1916.
37   *POLD 1914*, part 3, p. 1145.
38   TCC Meeting, 21 Apr. 1914.
39   TCC Meeting, 3 Feb. 1915.
40   CWGC. Service no. 758.

Butcher, Harry John – subscriber.
1911 census: 45 St James's Road, aged 16, telephone call office attendant for National Telephone Company.

Calcott, Percy – among those present on Nov. 1913 anniversary Sunday who 'left us for various reasons' (his sole mention).[41]

Calloway, A. – subscriber, 'Emmigrates [sic] so that his riches may grow.'[42]

Carpenter, Albert Victor
1911 census: 17 Railton Road, aged 15, boot trade assistant, brother Algernon William (see below).
1930 married Maud Marion Benson at Trinity.[43]

Carpenter, Algernon William – subscriber, favoured women's suffrage and was probably *AV* socialist writer 'Politician'.
1911 census: 17 Railton Road, aged 20, boot trade assistant.
1924 married Hilda Mary Perkins, sister of Frank Perkins (see below), at Trinity.[44]

Castle, Mr – one-time footballer.

Chippindale, Richard John – sometimes given as Chippendale – subscriber, footballer.
1911 census: 321 Camberwell New Road, aged 17, shipping clerk.
Employer 1913: Relph, Darwen and Pearce, paper agents, 76 Finsbury Pavement, Moorgate.[45]
War service from 28 Oct. 1915: private in 60th Battalion Royal Army Medical Corps.[46]
1919 married Flora Amy Radford at Trinity. Richard's profession: paper agent's manager.[47]

Cloak, C. – subscriber.

Collins, E. M. – footballer.

Coomber, Phillip J. – subscriber, 1912 rambler, footballer.
1911 census: 16 Acre Lane, aged 18, boarder with Cramp family (see below), engineer, electrical switchman, b. Portsmouth.
Employer 1912: L. Kamm and Co., electrical engineers, 27 Powell Street, Goswell Road, Clerkenwell.[48]

Cotsworth, Edward – new member of Bible Class, Christmas 1912.

Cramp, Walter Robert – subscriber, 1912 rambler, footballer.
1911 census: 16 Acre Lane, aged 21, clerk, stockbrokers.
Phillip J. Coomber (see above) boarded with Cramp family.

---

41   *AV* 15 (Dec. 1913), 9.
42   *AV* 3 (Jan. 1911), 30.
43   TCC Marriage, 22 Feb. 1930.
44   TCC Marriage, 11 Sept. 1924.
45   *POLD 1914*, part 3, p. 1202.
46   TNA, First World War 'Burnt Documents' (Microfilm Copies), WO363. Service no. 77225.
47   TCC Marriage, 6 Sept. 1919.
48   *POLD 1910*, i. part 3, p. 997.

1921 married Elsie Joan Parnell at Trinity. Walter's profession: managing clerk to stockbrokers.[49]

Crosley, William Thomas – subscriber, auditor of class accounts.
1911 census: 31 Branksome Road (see James Godden below), aged 18, clerk, granite merchants.
Became church member Mar. 1911.[50]
Moved to 'warmer climes' (India); departed for Bombay, 14 Sept. 1912; wireless operator.[51]
Returned on holiday Christmas 1913.
War service: driver in Royal Field Artillery.[52]
Later became a merchant/mercantile assistant alternating between the Straits Settlements and Streatham. His employer's address 149 Leadenhall Street.[53]
Died 11 Oct. 1957, Southend-on-Sea, Essex.[54]

Cummings, E. G. – war memorial.

C.V.M. – artist.

Davies, Gwilym John – junior footballer (mentioned once).
1911 census: 6 Barnwell Road, aged 12. Brothers: Montague (see below), Gwynne Richard, 7. Sisters: Frances Mary, 16, Doris Annie, 10.

Davies, Montague Howell – subscriber, junior football team captain, war memorial. Sometimes listed as Davis.
1911 census: 6 Barnwell Road, aged 14.
Employer 1913: Dollond and Co. Ltd., opticians, manufacturers of telescopes, spectacles, barometers, 35 Ludgate Hill.[55]
Became church member 1914.[56]
War service: private in 14th Battalion Royal Welsh Fusiliers. Died 29 Dec. 1917.
Son of John Howell and Frances Louisa Davies.[57]

Eagle, Frank Walter – junior footballer.
1911 census: 21 Kellett Road, aged 16, scholar. Brother of Harold (see below).
Oct. 1911 became a student of mechanical and electrical engineering at the Northampton Polytechnic Institute, London, where he joined the University of London contingent of the Officers' Training Corps. War service from Sept. 1914. Lieutenant in the Royal Engineers. Died at Foncquevillers, 6 June 1916.[58]

Eagle, Harold Burnham – subscriber, 1913 rambler.
1911 census: 21 Kellett Road, aged 14, scholar.

---

49 TCC Marriage, 17 Sept. 1921.
50 TCC Meeting, 28 Mar. 1911; TCC Deacons, 23 Mar. 1911.
51 *AV* 9 (Dec. 1912), 6; TNA, Board of Trade passenger lists, BT27/772/1. Now Mumbai.
52 TNA, First World War service medal and award rolls, WO 329/52. Service no. 12814.
53 TNA, Board of Trade passenger lists, BT26/698/73, BT26/1052/23, BT27/1514, BT27/1410/10/1, BT27/1120. The Straits Settlements was a British crown colony on the Strait of Malacca comprising four trade centres, Penang, Singapore, Malacca and Labuan. <http://www.britannica.com/EBchecked/topic/567981/Straits-Settlements>, accessed 19 Mar. 2015.
54 PPR *Calendar* (1957).
55 *POLD 1914*, part 3, p. 883.
56 TCC Deacons, 24 Mar. 1914; TCC meeting, 25 Mar. 1914.
57 CWGC. Service no. 21595.
58 *The Roll of Honour of the Institution of Electrical Engineers* (1924), 121–3.

Employer 1913: District Chemical Co. Ltd., chemical manufacturer, 1 Fenchurch Avenue.[59]

His departure overseas regretted by Bedwell but Messent expected him home soon.[60]

Became apprentice 25 Oct. 1913 on merchant ship.

War service from 1 Nov. 1914 in Royal Naval Reserve until 20 Feb. 1920. Sub-lieutenant.

14 Sept. 1920 returned to merchant shipping, becoming master mariner 13 Sept. 1921.[61]

Served in Merchant Navy during the Second World War.[62]

Died 6 Jan. 1961, Leigh-on-Sea, Essex.[63]

Evans, Albert Howard – subscriber, rambler,[64] holiday planner, one of four older class members,[65] participant in gym club 'which existed some 10 years ago'.[66]

1911 census: 35 Mount Pleasant Villas, Stroud Green, Hornsey, aged 42, boarder, journalist.

His father and sister lived at 4 Winterwell Road.

Evans, W. – subscriber.

Probably Albert Evans's younger brother, **Walter Morley**, also a journalist.

Fagan, Will – footballer.

Fairman, Walter Trotter (1874–1941) and Mary A. (1867–1942)[67]

Missionaries in Egypt at Shebin-El-Kom in the Nile delta with the North Africa Mission (NAM).

Walter invited to preach at Trinity 20 Aug. 1911, morning and evening (paid 42*s.*).[68]

Missionary meeting at request of NAM on 4 Oct. Requested they send Walter to speak.[69]

Their son, Prof Herbert Walter Fairman of Liverpool University, was an Egyptologist.[70]

Walter's brothers, Wallace Frederick and Donald Hyma, married at Trinity[71] and his father (or brother), George, was instructor to the Girls' Guild[72] and among re-elected deacons 1905.[73]

Finch, W. – war memorial.

---

[59]   *POLD 1914*, part 3, p. 880.

[60]   *AV* 15 (Dec. 1913), 5, 10.

[61]   National Maritime Museum, Greenwich, Master's Certificates, no. 0015107; TNA, Navy Department medal rolls, ADM 171/92.

[62]   TNA, Database of Second World War Medals issued to Merchant Seamen, BT 395/1/27658.

[63]   PPR *Calendar* (1961).

[64]   Participates in all three rambles listed in *AV* and recalls others he has done.

[65]   *AV* 11 (Aug. 1913), 12.

[66]   *AV* 9 (Dec. 1912), 19, 20.

[67]   TNA, Board of Trade passenger lists, BT26/1178/118, BT27/923/12/1. *The Trinity Magazine*, iii. no. 30 (June 1905).

[68]   TCC Deacons, 27 July 1911.

[69]   TCC Deacons, 14 Sept. 1911.

[70]   <http://www.ukwhoswho.com/view/article/oupww/whowaswho/U164038>, accessed 25 Feb. 2015.

[71]   TCC Marriage, 17 Nov. 1906, 6 Apr. 1912.

[72]   *The Trinity Magazine*, iii. no. 27 (Mar. 1905).

[73]   *The Trinity Magazine*, iii. no. 29 (May 1905).

Fouracre, L. – subscriber, 1912 rambler, footballer.
Employer 1912: John Heathcoat and Co., lace manufacturers, 13 Ironmonger Lane, Poultry.[74]

French, John Morgan – war memorial.
1911 census: 282 South Lambeth Road, aged 20, compositor, printer.
War service: gunner in 1st/5th Glamorgan Brigade, Royal Garrison Artillery. Died 31 Aug. 1916 aged 25.[75]

Giggs, Richard George – subscriber, 'new chap' Dec. 1910.[76]
1911 census: 65 Arlingford Road, aged 15, clerk, stockbrokers.

Gladwin, M. – artist.[77]

Godden, Graham Orchard – war memorial.
1911 census: 80 Holsworthy Square, Grays Inn Road, aged 15. Brothers: James (see below) and Alfred.
War service: private in 7th Battalion Somerset Light Infantry. Died of sickness 6 Dec. 1914 aged 19. Grave Reference: Q. 174938, Brookwood Cemetery.[78]

Godden, James George – *AV* editor, 1912 rambler, secretary of Bible Class. Educated at City of London School.[79]
1911 census: 80 Holsworthy Square, Grays Inn Road, aged 17, junior clerk, Port Sanitary Authority.
1911 became church member.[80] From mid–1913 lived at 31 Branksome Road (see W. T. Crosley above).
Instrumental in saving a man from drowning on Bible Class Whitsun excursion near Guildford.[81]
Employer 1912 and 1913: Port of London Sanitary Authority (Herbert Williams MD, medical officer), 51 King William Street, Greenwich.[82]
War service: acting corporal in 3rd Battalion Queen's (Royal West Surrey) Regiment.[83]
1919 applied for freedom of the City of London.[84]

Goodwin, G. – participant in gym club 'which existed some 10 years ago'.[85]

Gosling, A. S. – subscriber, war memorial. Appears either with initial A. or S.
S. and A. Gosling probably the same person. S. appears three times, lastly in *AV* 10 (July 1913). A. appears four times commencing in *AV* 11 (Aug. 1913). In *AV* 9 (Dec. 1912), S. Gosling is pencilled into the subscribers' list and has been initialled ASG.
1911 census: possible match – 7 Richmond Place, Stockwell, Arthur Sydney Gosling, aged 14.

74 *POLD 1910*, i. part 3, p. 947.
75 CWGC. Service no. 668.
76 *AV* 2 (Dec. 1910), 19.
77 *AV* 7 (Nov. 1911), 42.
78 CWGC. Service no. 14935.
79 LMA, Freedom admissions papers, COL/CHD/FR/02/2650/51.
80 TCC Meeting, 28 Mar. 1911.
81 TCC Meeting, 3 June 1914; TCC Deacons, 23 Mar. 1911.
82 *POLD 1911*, i. part 3, p. 444.
83 TNA, First World War service medal and award rolls, WO 329/ 646. Service no. G/11554.
84 LMA, Freedom admissions papers, COL/CHD/FR/02/2650/51.
85 *AV* 9 (Dec. 1912), 19, 20.

Employment 1913: Irongate and St Katharine Steam Wharf, St Katharine, near the Tower.[86]

Habergrutz, J. – 1912 rambler.

Handy, Fred – footballer, 'came back' for anniversary in Nov. 1913.[87]

Harper, George – subscriber, 1912 rambler, 'came back' for anniversary in Nov. 1913.[88]
May have taken aeroplane trip in late 1912.[89]

Hayley, Beatrice (Trissie) May – TLHC rambler 1912, hockey player, sang at children's tea.
'It is rumoured that during the absence of the chosen one in Canada, Miss Hayley has engaged a Locum Tenens to perform his duties.'[90]
1911 census: 116 Branksome Road, aged 18, hairdresser.
1914 Beatrice Healey became a church member.[91]
1917 married George Frederick Gardner, a sapper in the Canadian Engineers, at Trinity. Her address: 18 Winslade Road.[92]

Hayman, H. – 'a dark horse … in the mile race' in summer 1910 or 1911.[93]

H.E.C. (probable reading) – artist.

Hiley, Harold Gladstone (1881–1956) and Lizzie May (1880–1977)
1905 Harold qualified as a master mariner.[94]
Ran the British and Foreign Sailors' Society Seamen's Institute in Las Palmas from 1907.[95]
23 Nov. 1907 they married at Stockwell Green Congregational Church. Her father, Charles Punter, was a master butcher.[96]
War service: from 1916 Harold was in the Merchant Navy. Torpedoed and sunk 17 June 1917.[97]
1926 Harold became a lay evangelist of the Congregational Union of England and Wales, serving churches in Berkshire and Buckinghamshire.[98]

Hill, Stella – TLHC rambler 1912, hockey player.
1911 census: possible match – 12 Winterwell Road, aged 19, milliner.
Became a church member 4 Dec. 1912.[99]

86 *POLD 1914*, part 3, p. 1020.
87 *AV* 15 (Dec. 1913), 9.
88 *AV* 15 (Dec. 1913), 9.
89 *AV* 15 (Dec. 1913), 47.
90 *AV* 8 (July 1912), 11.
91 TCC Deacons, 24 Mar. 1914.
92 TCC Marriage, 8 Sept. 1917.
93 *AV* 7 (Nov. 1911), 48. It is not clear whether by 'last summer' the writer means the immediately previous summer or that of 1910.
94 National Maritime Museum, Greenwich, Master's Certificates, no. 036817.
95 The Surman Index Online, Dr Williams's Centre for Dissenting Studies, <http://surman.english.qmul.ac.uk>, accessed 21 Mar. 2015. *CYB* (1956).
96 Marriage certificate.
97 National Maritime Museum, Greenwich, Master's Certificates, no. 036817.
98 The Surman Index Online, Dr Williams's Centre for Dissenting Studies, <http://surman.english.qmul.ac.uk>, accessed 21 Mar. 2015. *CYB* (1956).
99 TCC Deacons, 31 Mar. 1912; TCC Meeting, 8 May 1912.

Holman, Arthur – subscriber, footballer, 'came back' for anniversary in Nov. 1913.[100]

Hooper, W. T. – war memorial.

Irons, B. – war memorial.

Johnson, W. – subscriptions collector for gym club 'which existed some 10 years ago'.[101]

Johnston, Elizabeth Taylor – TLHC rambler 1912, artist ETJ.
1911 census: 70 Arlingford Road, aged 30, LCC elementary teacher.
1915 married D. C. Messent (see below) at Trinity.[102]
Died 11 Oct. 1962, St Bartholomew's Hospital, Smithfield – residence Beckenham.[103]

Johnston, William – war memorial, his brother and sisters married Messent sister and brothers (see above and below).
1911 census: 70 Arlingford Road, aged 25, LCC school board clerk.
Sisters: Elizabeth (Bessie), a long-haired chum, and Rachel J.
Married Beatrice Abbott at St Jude's C. of E., Brixton, 27 July 1912.
Children: William b. 20 June 1913, Kenneth David b. 3 Apr. 1915, Marjorie Beatrice b. 6 Jan. 1917.
War service: gunner in Royal Garrison Artillery, from 19 Nov. 1915. British Expeditionary Force, France, 30 Sept. 1916–19 Apr. 1917. 16 Dec. 1916 admitted to hospital; 19 Apr. 1917 admitted to field hospital and died from wounds. Buried Faubourg D'Amiens Cemetery, Arras. On headstone 'Ready Aye Ready'.[104]

Jolly, Miss W. – TLHC rambler 1912.
1911 census: possible match – 39 Arlingford Road, **Winifred Annie Jolly**, aged 16, no occupation.

Jones, Arthur Edmund – subscriber.
1911 census: 41 Rattray Road, aged 24, pianoforte maker. Brothers: Frank and Harry (see below).

Jones, Frank Clifton – subscriber, footballer, deacon after the Second World War and church treasurer.
1911 census: 41 Rattray Road, aged 17, apprentice in engineers.
Employer 1913: A. W. Penrose and Co. Ltd., electrical engineers, electrotypers' plant and machinery, photo engravers' plant and machinery, lithographers' plant and machinery, 109 Farringdon Road.[105]
Became a church member 1914.[106]
Died 1960, Lambeth.[107]

---

[100] *AV* 15 (Dec. 1913), 9.
[101] *AV* 9 (Dec. 1912), 19.
[102] TCC Marriage, 27 Feb. 1915.
[103] PPR *Calendar* (1963).
[104] TNA, First World War 'Burnt Documents' (Microfilm Copies), WO363. CWGC. Service no. 90856.
[105] *POLD 1914*, part 3, p. 1170.
[106] TCC Deacons, 24 Mar. 1914; TCC Meeting, 25 Mar. 1914.
[107] General Register Office, *England and Wales Civil Registration Indexes*.

Jones, Henry William – known as Harry – subscriber, footballer.
1911 census: 41 Rattray Road, age 21, pianoforte maker.

Jones, Lionel – 1912 and 1913 rambler, entertained at children's party, wore brown (probably not related to the other three Joneses).

Lansdown, Clarissa – hockey player, pianist at Nov. 1913 anniversary Sunday.
1911 census: The Manse (21) Church Road, aged 21, office clerk, Imperial Protestant Foundation.
1918 married Cyril Bedwell (see above) at Trinity.[108]

Lansdown, Mathias – minister, Bible Class president.
1911 census: The Manse (21) Church Road, aged 52, b. Cardiff. Wife, Fanny, 57, b. Bodmin.
Daughters: Clarissa (see above) and Kathleen, 20, office clerk, Imperial Protestant Foundation, b. Bournemouth. Son: Harry (see Mathias Henry below).
Left Trinity and retired after his wife died in 1920 but had a number of temporary pastoral oversights, mostly in the West Country.[109]
Died 17 Dec. 1932, Wellington, Somerset.[110]

Lansdown, Mathias Henry – known as Harry – subscriber, 1912 rambler, footballer.
Became a church member 1910.[111]
1911 census: The Manse (21) Church Road, aged 18, electrical engineer's apprentice.
War service: temporary second lieutenant in Royal West Surrey Regiment.
1917 awarded Military Cross for conspicuous gallantry and devotion to duty. He assumed command, and gallantly led his company to their objective, maintained his position there, and conducted the withdrawal from the farthest point in the enemy's lines with marked skill.[112]
11 June 1917 Capt. M. H. Lansdown MC … was admitted to … hospital, Boulogne, on June 9th with slight debility. His condition was considered 'satisfactory'.[113]
May have been in Royal Victoria Hospital at Netley, near Southampton, having been gassed.[114]
1919 married Kathleen Margaret Unwin at Trinity. Harry's profession: fruit grower.[115]
Died 1952, south-west Surrey.[116]

Lidstone, Alfred Morgan – war memorial.
1911 census: 39 Arodene Road, aged 22, carpenter, b. Swansea, Glamorgan.
Sister: Alice, 17, became a church member 6 Dec. 1914.[117]
War service: rifleman in 13th Battalion King's Royal Rifle Corps. Died 14 Nov. 1916, aged 28. Thiepval Memorial.[118]

---

[108] TCC Marriage, 20 May 1918.
[109] Surman index card at Dr Williams's Library, London.
[110] *CYB* (1934), 267.
[111] TCC Meeting, 28 Sept. 1910.
[112] *Supplement to the London Gazette*, 17 Apr. 1917, p. 3683 (pdf from Carolyn Bedwell).
[113] Photo of letter to Rev. M. Lansdown (from Carolyn Bedwell).
[114] Information from Carolyn Bedwell.
[115] TCC Marriage, 25 Dec. 19; information from Carolyn Bedwell (Fanny Lansdown's diary).
[116] General Register Office, *England and Wales Civil Registration Indexes*.
[117] TCC Meeting, 2 Dec. 1914.
[118] CWGC. Service no. R/17223.

Lynch, Edward T. – subscriber, war memorial (E. Lynch), junior footballer (may be Linge in senior team).
Appeared variously with the initials E. T., E., T. and F.
1911 census: 29 Kellett Road, aged 15, office boy (poor law).
Employer 1912: Lambeth Guardians' Offices, 128 Brook Street, Kennington.[119] Workhouse which became Lambeth Hospital.
War service: private in C Company, 7th Battalion London Regiment. Died 17 June 1915, aged 19. Fosse 7 Military Cemetery (Quality Street), Mazingarbe.[120]

McCormick, Thomas Luckin – footballer.
1920, aged 30, married Annie Messent (see below). Thomas's profession: master builder. Address: Windermere Lodge, Windermere Avenue, Finchley.[121]
Died 13 May 1935, Bexhill.[122]

Marr, Charles Wesley – war memorial.
1911 census: 45 Arlingford Road, aged 14, clerk in Australian merchants.
War service: rifleman in London Regiment, First Surrey Rifles. Died 11 Sept. 1916. Louez Military Cemetery, Duisans.[123]
Marriott, A. – subscriber, Scottish.

Maynard, Miss – TLHC rambler 1912.

Messent, Annie – hockey player, TLHC rambler 1912.
1911 census: 16 King's Avenue, aged 15.
Became a church member 1910.[124]
1920 married Thomas McCormick at Trinity (see above).[125]
Died 6 Dec. 1965, Hastings.[126]

Messent, Daniel Cockerill – subscriber, 1912 rambler, Bible Class leader, one of four older class members.[127]
Lived at Maxton, King's Avenue, Clapham Park, Wandsworth.[128]
Became assistant deacon 1907.[129]
1911 census: 16 King's Avenue, aged 31, meat salesman.
Employer 1912 and 1913: Daniel Messent, meat salesman, 107 Central Markets, Smithfield.[130]
1915 married Elizabeth Taylor Johnston, 34, sister of William (see above), at Trinity.[131]
1915 his sister Elizabeth married Harry Reeves (see below) at Trinity.[132]

[119]   *POLD 1910*, i. part 3, p. 1013.
[120]   CWGC. Service no. 1986.
[121]   TCC Marriage, 27 Apr. 1920.
[122]   PPR *Calendar* (1935).
[123]   CWGC. Service no. 2288.
[124]   TCC Meeting, 4 May 1910.
[125]   TCC Marriage, 27 Apr. 1920.
[126]   PPR *Calendar* (1966). (Having been widowed and remarried to Horace Lee.)
[127]   *AV* 11 (Aug.1913), 12.
[128]   *AV* 9 (Dec. 1912), 14.
[129]   TCC Meeting, 6 Feb. 1907.
[130]   *POLD 1910*, i. part 3, p. 1068.
[131]   TCC Marriage, 27 Feb. 1915.
[132]   TCC Marriage, 15 Apr. 1915.

Died 27 Nov. 1936, Beckenham.[133]

Messent, Henry – subscriber.
1911 census: 2 Stile Hall Parade, High Road, Chiswick, aged 25, butcher.
1911 church membership transferred from Trinity to Gunnersbury Congregational Church.[134]
Moved to Australia. Departed London, 24 Sept. 1929.[135]

Messent, Isabella – artist.
1911 census: 16 King's Avenue, aged 29, no occupation.
1923 married David James Johnston, brother of Elizabeth and William (see above), at Trinity.[136]
Died 25 Dec. 1936, Finchley.[137]

Messent, Lewis Hunt – subscriber, Bible Class treasurer, footballer.
Became a church member 1910.[138]
1911 census: 16 King's Avenue, aged 18, single, meat salesman.
1921 married Gladys Maud Way at Trinity. Address: 30 Stradella Road, Herne Hill.[139]
Died 24 July 1957, 105 Burbage Road, Herne Hill.[140]

Messent, William Joseph – not Bible Class member but subscriber, secretary of Literary Society and participant in gym club 'which existed some 10 years ago'.[141]
1907 married Rachel Jamieson Johnston, sister of William (see above), at Trinity.[142]
1911 census: 1 Hollingbourne Road, aged 30, meat salesman. Rachel, aged 26, sons Alan and Daniel both aged two, two servants.
Employer 1912: Daniel Messent, meat salesman, 107 Central Markets, Smithfield.[143]
Died 22 July 1957, Eastbourne.[144]

Miller, Leonard – new at Bible Class Christmas 1912.

Morse, A. or C. or F. – subscriber, unclear which initial is correct or if there was more than one Morse.
(An Edwin Morse became a church member 1914.[145])

Morton, S. – war memorial.

Moxley, Richard Charles – subscriber, 1912 rambler, Bible Class organist, nicknamed 'the Major', one of four older class members.[146]

---

133 PPR *Calendar* (1939).
134 TCC Meeting, 2 Aug. 1911.
135 TNA, Board of Trade passenger lists, BT27/1246/21/22.
136 TCC Marriage, 12 Sept. 1923.
137 PPR *Calendar* (1937).
138 TCC Meeting, 1 June 1910.
139 TCC Marriage, 1 June 1921.
140 PPR *Calendar* (1957).
141 *AV* 9 (Dec. 1912), 19, 21.
142 TCC Marriage, 2 July 1907.
143 *POLD 1910*, i. part 3, p. 1068.
144 PPR *Calendar* (1957).
145 TCC Meeting, 25 Mar. 1914.
146 *AV* 11 (Aug. 1913), 12.

1903 Annie Kate Moxley married John Jacob Gething at Trinity.[147]
1911 census: 65 Trent Road, aged 34, stationers shop assistant. Sister: Annie Kate Gething, 36, married, boarding house keeper.
Died 4 Apr. 1949, 65 Trent Road.[148]

Munro, Edward Charles – subscriber, sometimes typed as A. Munro. 'Munros' go to Australia.[149]
1911 census: 58 Helix Road, aged 14.
War service from 10 Sept. 1915: Lance Corporal 5th Australian Field Ambulance. 2 July 1917 awarded Military Medal for bravery in the field at Bullecourt. Discharge approved 21 Aug. 1918 because of the deaths in action of two of his brothers. Family farm: Dunbeath, Burpengary, North Coast Line, Queensland.[150]

Nobbs, Miss B. – hockey player.

Noble, Alec – moved to Zurich, Switzerland.
1901 census: 73 Arlingford Road, aged 12.
His move to Switzerland on 17 Feb. 1911 from their home, then in Streatham, was noted in the margin of the family's 1911 census return.
War service from 21 June 1916 in Royal Navy, leaving on 25 Jan. 1918 possibly on transfer to the RAF.[151]

Oake, E. – 1913 rambler. Oke, C. – subscriber. Presumably the same person.

Osland, Miss K. – TLHC rambler 1912.
1911 census: possible match – 55 Geneva Road, **Kathleen Osland**, aged 14.

Osland, Miss N. – TLHC rambler 1912.
1911 census: possible match – 55 Geneva Road, **Norah Osland**, aged 13.

Perkins, Frank – subscriber.
1911 census: 35 Talma Road, aged 19, pianoforte maker.
Sisters: Helen F., aged 31, toy saleswoman at retail drapers (married A. W. Carpenter – see above), and Ethel.
1919 married Mary Ann Louisa Lake at Trinity. Frank's profession: piano fitter. Witnessed by A. W. Carpenter (see above).[152]
Still attending Trinity in 1960s.

Probart, Mr – quoted Shakespeare.

Randall, H. – junior footballer.

Redman, Mr – 'our' Mr R. being claimed by the Long Haired Chums.[153]

Reeves, Harry – artist, footballer.
1911 census: 57 Shakespeare Road, aged 27, boarder (see Harold Austin above), LCC science master, b. Whitstable.

147 TCC Marriage, 6 Mar. 1903.
148 PPR *Calendar* (1949).
149 *AV* 15 (Dec. 1913), 5.
150 National Archives of Australia: B2455, First Australian Imperial Force Personnel Dossiers, 1914–20. Service no. 13629.
151 TNA, Royal Navy registers of seamen's services, ADM 188/594.
152 TCC Marriage, 20 Sept. 1919.
153 *AV* 9 (Dec. 1912), 22, 33.

1915 married Elizabeth Harriet Messent, sister of D. C. and W. J. Messent (see above), at Trinity. Harry's profession: Insurance Society's sub-manager. Address: 23 St Saviour's Road.[154]

Ri/(?) (last initial illegible) – artist.

Rittershausen, Ferdinand Ernst von – subscriber.
1911 census: 78 Bedford Road, aged 22, merchant's clerk, chemical works, b. Tulse Hill.
Father: Stefan, b. Austria. Mother: Edith May, b. Worcester. Brother: Percy (see below).
War service: private in Duke of Cambridge's Own (Middlesex) Regiment.[155]

Rittershausen, Percy von – artist (PvR).
1911 census: 78 Bedford Road, aged 16, merchant's clerk, cloth merchants, b. Germany, British subject by parentage.
Became a furrier. Died 9 Sept. 1965, Newton Abbot, Devon.[156]

Rofe, James – leader of the Junior Bible Class.
Rofe family: caretakers, came from Tolmers Square Congregational, recruited by Mathias Lansdown, joining Trinity on 24 Feb. 1903.[157]
1911 census: 31 Hayter Road, aged 22, estate clerk.
Became Congregational minister 1919.[158]
Died 14 Mar. 1963, having retired to Fleet, Hampshire.[159]

Rowe, Frank Leonard[160] – subscriber, possible artist.
1911 census: 2 St Saviour's Road, aged 16, railway clerk, Great Northern Railway.
Brothers: Henry Shepard, Robert Stanley (see below).
Also half-brother John Langland (see below).
Employer 1913: Great Northern Railway Co., Accountants Dept., King's Cross.[161]
1919 married Dorothy Gertrude Gibbs and gives his occupation as soldier.[162]
Had various occupations including gold mining in Australia and chicken farming.
Became totally blind.
Died 3 Jan. 1963, Gussage All Saints, Dorset.[163]

Rowe, Henry Shepard – subscriber, 1912 rambler, cricketer, war memorial.
1911 census: 2 St Saviour's Road, aged 18, bank clerk.
Employer 1912: Lilley and Skinner Limited, boot and shoe manufacturers and leather merchants, 275 and 276 High Holborn.[164]
Became church member Feb. 1913.[165]
Lived for a time in Las Palmas.

---

154   TCC Marriage, 15 Apr. 1915.
155   TNA, First World War service medal and award rolls, WO 329/1506. Service no. G/75042.
156   PPR *Calendar* (1965).
157   TCC Register of Candidates for Church Fellowship 1898–1903.
158   *CYB* (1964–65), 447.
159   PPR *Calendar* (1963).
160   Full name from 1901 census.
161   *POLD 1914*, part 3, p. 955.
162   LMA, Holy Trinity, Tulse Hill, Register of marriages, P85/TRI2, 23 June 1919.
163   Information from Christine Snape (great-niece).
164   *POLD 1910*, i. part 3, p. 1029.
165   TCC Meeting, 22 Jan. 1913.

War service: rifleman in 1st/16th Battalion London Regiment, Queen's Westminster Rifles. Died 19 Sept. 1916. Thiepval Memorial.[166]

Rowe, John Langland – not Bible Class member but present or mentioned at some meetings.
1901 census: 73 London Road, aged 22, Southwark, shopman, butcher.
Working with China Inland Mission, travelling to and from Shanghai.[167]
Also travelled from Las Palmas (see Henry S. Rowe).[168]
Died 1933, China.[169]

Rowe, Robert Stanley – known by his middle name. Subscriber, 1912 rambler, football captain, secretary of Bible Class.
1911 census: 2 St Saviour's Road, aged 20, clerk, engineers.
Became a church member 1911.[170]
Became a tenant farmer in Gussage All Saints, Dorset, where he died 4 Mar. 1966.[171]

Rutter, D. – footballer.

Seymour, S. – subscriber, new member of football team in Sept. 1913.
July 1913 worked in costumes dept.

Shearer, L. – brother of P. Shearer below.

Shearer, P. – subscriber.

Sherman, W. – war memorial.

Smith, C. – subscriber, 1912 rambler, auditor of class accounts.
Employer 1913: Metropolitan Water Board, 41 Commercial Road, Pimlico.[172]

Snoswell, Arthur Cecil – war memorial, 1913 rambler, 2nd XI footballer, new member of football team in Sept. 1913.
1909 older sisters Florence and Alice married Clarence Brazil and Arthur Edwards respectively at Trinity.[173]
1911 census: 76 Arlingford Road, aged 13, scholar.
Father: Samuel Henry Snoswell, 57, manager printer and pattern card maker, b. Ramsgate. Deacon and Sunday school superintendent.[174]
Mother: Elizabeth Amelia Snoswell, 14 of 15 children were still living.
Sisters: Mabel Rose, 25, became church member 1913;[175] Hilda Grace, 22, long-haired chum (see below); Lilian Edith, 20; Winifred Eva, 18, became church member 1910;[176] Dorothy Kate, 15.
Brother: Archibald Frederick, nine; others see below.

166   CWGC. Service no. 4189.
167   TNA, Board of Trade passenger lists, BT27 27/985; Library and Archives Canada, Canadian passenger lists, RG 76-C. See *AV* 15 (Dec. 1913), 43–4.
168   TNA, Board of Trade passenger lists, class BT26/581/45.
169   Information from Christine Snape (great-niece).
170   TCC Meeting, 28 Mar. 1911; TCC Deacons, 23 Mar. 1911.
171   Information from Christine Snape (great-niece).
172   *POLD 1914*, i. part 3, p. 1112.
173   TCC Marriage, 26 June 1909.
174   TCC Deacons 1906–20, title page.
175   TCC Meeting, 22 Jan. 1913.
176   TCC Meeting, 1 Jun. 1910.

1915 sister Ethel married Eric Bangs at Trinity.[177]
War service: rifleman in 9th Battalion London Regiment, Queen Victoria's Rifles.
Died 11 Mar. 1917 aged 19. Gommecourt Wood New Cemetery, Foncquevillers.[178]

Snoswell, Ernest Edgar – war memorial.
1911 census: 76 Arlingford Road, aged 24, buyer's clerk, shipper's.
1915 married Lily Beatrice Nash, 26, at Trinity. Ernest's profession: private Royal
Army Medical Corps (civilian profession: shipping clerk).[179]
War service: rifleman in 9th Battalion London Regiment, Queen Victoria's Rifles.
Died 25 Apr. 1918. Bouchoir New British Cemetery.[180]

Snoswell, Hilda Grace – TLHC rambler 1912.
1911 census: 76 Arlingford Road, aged 22, no employment recorded.
1926 married Edward Rampley.[181]
Died 11 July 1944.[182]

Snoswell, Laurence Sidney – subscriber.
1911 census: 76 Arlingford Road, aged 16, assistant in haberdashery, draper's
warehouse.
War Service: Royal Navy 1912–19.[183]
Moved to Australia. Departed London, 1 Nov. 1923.[184]

Squires, F. – subscriber, had strong Cockney accent.

Stripp, Austen – Mrs Lansdown's nephew and brother of Herbert (see below).
Became a church member 1909.[185]
1911 census: 32 Fore Street, Moorgate, aged 19, draper's assistant.
War service from 14 July 1915: private in 2nd Battalion the Devonshire Regiment.
Missing, presumed killed in action at Ploegsteert, 9 Nov. 1917. Ploegsteert
Memorial.[186]

Stripp, Herbert William – subscriber, 'nice curly hair',[187] once noted as B. Stripp,
but always bracketed with Harry Lansdown in subscriber lists. Mrs Lansdown's
nephew.
1911 census: East Looe, Cornwall, aged 21, assistant in the family shop dealing in
stationery, grocery and drugs.
War service 1915–19: sergeant in Somerset Light Infantry.[188]

---

[177]   TCC Marriage, 4 Dec. 1915.
[178]   CWGC. Service no. 391332.
[179]   TCC Marriage, 23 July 1915.
[180]   CWGC. Service no. 392540.
[181]   General Register Office, *England and Wales Civil Registration Indexes*.
[182]   PPR *Calendar* (1945).
[183]   TNA, Royal Navy registers of seamen's services, ADM 188/995.
[184]   TNA, Board of Trade passenger lists, BT 27/1023/3/10.
[185]   TCC Meeting, 29 Sept. 1909 (name given as Austin Stripp).
[186]   M. A. H. D. H. de la C. de Massue de Ruvigny, *The Roll of Honour: a Biographical Record of all Members of His Majesty's Naval and Military Forces who have Fallen in the War*, iv. 201; CWGC. Service no. 290498.
[187]   *AV* 3 (Jan. 1911), 32
[188]   TNA, First World War service medal and award rolls, WO 329/896. Service nos 2259, 200541.

In 1930s lived in Battersea and Wandsworth.[189] Died 1956, Plymouth.[190]

Swan, Alan – treasurer of gym club 'which existed some 10 years ago', one of three brothers involved.[191]

Vale, Madge – moved to Bexhill.[192]
Became a church member 1910.[193]

Williams, Mr – 'comic song with actions, given by that patron of infantile life'.[194]

Wright, F. – war memorial.

Wright, P. – war memorial.

Yates, E., F. or N. – each is only mentioned once as subscriber, 1913 rambler and 1912 rambler respectively. Unclear which is correct or if there was more than one.

York, Frederick Charles – subscriber, 1912 rambler, footballer.
1911 census: 23 Branksome Road, aged 18, engineer's junior clerk.
War service: occupation on marriage certificate given as soldier.
1916 married at St Saviour's C. of E., Brixton, whilst soldier. E. H. Bowler (see above) was witness.[195]

[189]   LMA, electoral registers LCC/PER/B/2042, 2240.
[190]   General Register Office, *England and Wales Civil Registration Indexes*.
[191]   *AV* 9 (Dec. 1912), 19, 20.
[192]   *AV* 10 (July 1913), 34.
[193]   TCC Meeting, 4 May 1910.
[194]   *AV* 3 (Jan. 1911), 4.
[195]   LMA, St Saviour, Brixton Hill, Register of marriages, P85/SAV1, 28 Nov. 1916.

BIBLIOGRAPHY

PRIMARY SOURCES HELD AT TRINITY CONGREGATIONAL CHURCH, BRIXTON

The Angels' Voice issues 1–3, 5–13 and 15.
Church Meeting minute book 1906–20.
Deacons' Meeting minute books 1906–20, 1920–26.
Dorcas and Benevolent Society account book 1846–97.
Dorcas and Benevolent Society minute book 1846–98.
Marriage registers 1899–1918, 1918–50.
Register of Candidates for Church Fellowship 1898–1903.
Sunday School Teachers' Meeting minute book 1891–1914.
The Trinity Magazine, iii.

PRIMARY SOURCES ACCESSED ONLINE THROUGH ANCESTRY and LIVES OF THE FIRST WORLD WAR

General Register Office *England and Wales Civil Registration Indexes*
Library and Archives Canada, Canadian passenger lists.
LMA, Freedom admissions papers.
LMA, Marriage registers.
National Archives of Australia First Australian Imperial Force Personnel Dossiers
    1914–1920
National Maritime Museum, Greenwich, Master's Certificates.
TNA, Board of Trade passenger lists.
TNA, Census Returns of England and Wales 1881, 1891, 1901 and 1911; RG 11, 12,
    13, 14.
TNA, Database of Second World War Medals issued to Merchant Seamen
TNA, First World War 'Burnt Documents' (Microfilm Copies).
TNA, First World War service medal and award rolls.
TNA, Medal Rolls index cards.
TNA, Navy Department medal rolls.
TNA, Royal Navy registers of seamen's services.
TNA, War Office: Soldiers' Documents from Pension Claims.

In addition, accessed online through the London School of Economics: British
    Library of Economic and Political Science, London School of Economics,
    the Booth MS Collection

PRINTED PRIMARY SOURCES

Bradshaw's General Railway and Steam Navigation Guide (July 1913).
Congregational Year Book.
LMA, electoral registers.
Post Office London County Suburbs Directory.
Post Office London Directory.
Priestley, Joseph, *Report on the Vital and Sanitary Statistics of the Borough of Lambeth During the Year 1910* (1911), *1912* (1913), *1917* (1918).
Principal Probate Registry, *Calendar of the Grants of Probate and Letters of Administration made in the Probate Registries of the High Court of Justice in England.*
Surman, C. E., *Index of Congregational Ministers at Dr Williams's Library, London*: The Surman Index Online, <http://surman.english.qmul.ac.uk>.

SECONDARY SOURCES

Argent, Alan, 'Some Memorials of Bernard J. Snell', *Congregational History Circle Magazine*, v. no. 1 (Spring 2005), 5–10.
—— *The Transformation of Congregationalism 1900–2000* (Nottingham, 2013).
Arlott, John, 'Sport', in *Edwardian England 1901–1914*, ed. Simon Nowell-Smith (1964), 447–86.
Bebbington, D. W., *The Nonconformist Conscience: Chapel and Politics, 1870–1914* (1982).
Benedictus, Leo, 'A Brief History of the Passport', *The Guardian*, 17 Nov. 2006.
Besant, Walter, *London South of the Thames* (1912).
Binfield, J. C. G., *So Down to Prayers: Studies in English Nonconformity 1780–1920* (1977).
Booth, Charles, *Life and Labour of the People in London* (1902), 3rd series.
Brixton Free Press, *Brixton's Churches* (1904).
Brockway, Fenner, *Inside the Left: Thirty Years of Platform, Press, Prison and Parliament* (1942).
Chaplin, Charles, *My Autobiography* (1964).
Cherry, Bridget, and Pevsner, Nikolaus, *The Buildings of England, London 2: South* (1983).
Cox, Jeffrey, *The English Churches in a Secular Society. Lambeth, 1870–1930* (Oxford, 1982).
Donoghue, Bernard, and Jones, G. W., *Herbert Morrison: Portrait of a Politician* (1973).
Dyos, H. J., *Victorian Suburb: A Study of the Growth of Camberwell* (Leicester, 1966).
Evans, Y. A., 'History of Trinity' (typescript c.1978), held at the church.
Fisher, H. A. L., *An Unfinished Autobiography* (1940).
Harris, H. W., and Bryant, Margaret, *The Churches and London: An outline survey of religious work in the metropolitan area. With a full directory of places of worship in the County of London* (1914).
Haw, G. (ed.), *Christianity and the Working Classes* (1906).
Hendy, John, *Folkestone for the Continent 1843–2001* (Ramsey, Isle of Man, 2014).

Bibliography

Howson, H. F., *London's Underground* (Shepperton, 1981).

Kent, William, *Testament of a Victorian Youth* (1938).

'London Typhoid and London Water', *British Medical Journal* (25 Apr. 1896), 1046–7.

McLeod, Hugh, *Class and Religion in the late Victorian City* (1974).

Masterman, C. F. G., *The Condition of England* (1909).

Morgan, K. O., *Consensus and Identity: The Lloyd George Coalition Government 1918–1922* (1979).

Morrison, Herbert, *Herbert Morrison: An Autobiography by Lord Morrison of Lambeth* (1960).

Mudie-Smith, Richard (ed.), *The Religious Life of London* (1904).

Munson, James, *The Nonconformists: In Search of a Lost Culture* (1991).

Ogg, David, *Herbert Fisher 1865–1940: A Short Biography* (1947).

Oxford Dictionary of National Biography.

Paterson, Alexander, *Across the Bridges or Life by the South London River-Side* (1928).

Pember Reeves, Maud, *Round About a Pound a Week* (2008).

Pennell, Catriona, *A Kingdom United: Popular Responses to the Outbreak of the First World War in Britain and Ireland* (Oxford, 2012).

Pugh, Martin, *Speak for Britain! A New History of the Labour Party* (2011).

Robinson, David, *Chaplin: His Life and Art* (1985).

Roll of Honour of the Institution of Electrical Engineers (1924).

Rook, Clarence, *London Side-Lights* (1908).

Ruvigny, M. A. H. D. H. de la C. de Massue de, *The Roll of Honour: a Biographical Record of all Members of His Majesty's Naval and Military Forces who have Fallen in the War* (n.d.).

Selbie, W. B. (ed), *The Life of Charles Silvester Horne* (1920).

Taylor, A. J., 'The Economy', in *Edwardian England*, ed. Simon Nowell-Smith (1964), 103–38.

Walker, H. W., *Mainly Memories 1906–1930* (1986) <http://www.walthamstowmemories.net/pdfs/walker13.pdf>.

White, Jerry: *London in the Nineteenth Century: 'A Human Awful Wonder of God'* (2007).

—— *London in the Twentieth Century: A City and its People* (2001).

—— *Zeppelin Nights: London in the First World War* (2014).

In addition, war deaths, where traceable, have been checked on the Commonwealth War Graves Commission website, < http://www.cwgc.org/>.

INDEX

accountancy, 8, 9, 31, 221, 301, 313
advertising (agents), 25, 31, 91, 168, 230,
    258, 300, 302
aeroplanes, 28, 289–90, 307
age of class members, 20, 217, 235
alcohol, 10, 22, 25–6, 137, 164, 212, 218
'Alpha', 107
Antwerp, 27, 135, 165–6
Ardennes, 165–9, 174, 178, 182
Arlingford Road, 7–9, 45n, 214, 243,
    300–1, 306, 308, 310, 312, 314–15
Armston, Miss, 175, 299
artwork, 20, 30, 33, 43, 51, 61, 64, 67, 68,
    72, 74, 76, 79, 80, 87, 95, 97, 99,
    107, 112–13, 115–16, 128, 130, 132,
    134, 137, 139, 144, 145–6, 149–50,
    157, 173, 180, 185, 194, 209, 221,
    223–5, 239, 243, 246, 250, 257, 263,
    265, 266, 271
Ashburton Park football team, Croydon,
    99
Asquith H. H., 12, 82, 102
Austin, Alfred Phipps, 3, 17, 20, 27, 44,
    47, 53, 62, 84, 92, 94, 101, 119, 125,
    140, 149, 151, 154, 156, 170, 173, 181,
    182, 184, 191, 201, 206, 214–15, 219,
    228, 230, 235, 238, 240, 242–2, 248,
    251, 262, 264, 270, 287–9, 296, 299
Austin, Harold, 99, 123, 299, 312
Australia, 28, 31, 129, 211, 272, 310, 311,
    312, 313, 315

Balfour, A. J., 5
banking, 313
barbers and hairdressers, 8, 124, 196, 307
Barrett, Arthur William Guy, 41, 47, 50,
    51n, 59, 60, 62, 69, 70, 71, 77, 98,
    99, 122, 123, 125, 142, 146, 154, 156,
    170, 184, 186, 188, 190, 206, 217,
    219, 221, 228, 238, 250, 270, 281–4,
    286, 288, 297, 299, 302
basket makers, 8
Battersea, 23, 120, 316

Beagley, H., 47, 62, 84, 125, 300
Bedwell, Cyril Francis, 31, 43, 47, 50,
    60–1, 62, 72, 77, 84, 99, 123, 125,
    142, 147, 149, 156, 162, 170, 173, 184,
    186, 189–90, 192–3, 202, 204, 206,
    213, 215, 219, 221, 224, 227, 230,
    238, 243, 250, 257, 264, 270, 274,
    287–8, 296, 300–1, 305, 309
Bedwell family, 8, 12n, 243n
Bedwell, Leslie John Hunter, 3, 162, 170,
    184, 192, 204, 206, 213, 215, 227,
    238, 250, 270, 296, 301
Bedwell, Norman Sidney William, 31,
    162, 170, 184, 206, 214, 221, 227,
    238, 250, 296, 301
beer, 136–7, 181
behaviour and manners, 58, 255–6
Belgium, 27, 165–9, 195, 281, 285
Bermondsey, 4, 22
Berne, 239
Berry, Frederick H., 11, 29, 50, 54–6,
    142, 301
Besant, Sir Walter, 6, 7n
Bible Class annual meeting, 3, 50–1,
    141–4, 187–190, 192, 240, 265, 272,
    286–9
Bible study, 3, 20, 39, 56, 211, 230, 237,
    244, 254, 258, 262, 264, 267, 272,
    286, 290
Biggins, Fred, 31, 60–1, 69, 70, 77, 98,
    99, 122, 123, 149, 170, 184, 206, 302
bill poster, 9
birds, 24, 115–19
Bishop, Jack, 40, 41, 42, 60, 302
Black, Mr, 77, 302
Blackheath, 7n, 82
boarders, 299, 301, 302, 303, 305, 312
'Bontex', 236, 263
book-keeping, 9
boot trade worker, 31, 102, 303, 303, 313
Booth, Bramwell, 30
Booth, Catherine and William, 15
Booth, Charles, 5, 7, 13–17, 23

Boud, E. J., 302
Boulogne, 26, 33–5, 37, 225, 309
Bowler, Ernest Henry, 3, 25, 31, 33, 49,
    50, 52, 64, 77, 127, 142, 148, 156,
    162–3, 170, 183, 184, 190, 192, 206,
    214, 217, 221, 224, 227, 238, 250,
    270, 281, 285, 287, 296, 300, 302,
    316
Boxhill, 163, 165
Bradford, W. H., 17, 19
brake, horse-drawn, 27, 260–1
Brè, Mont, 278
bridges over the Thames, 3, 11, 130, 178,
    206
Brixton, 5–11, 14–18, 31, 130, 193–4, 209,
    210, 242, 246, 262, 300–2, 308, 316
Brixton Hill Congregational Church, 15
Brixton Independent Chapel, 14–15, 17,
    301
Brockway, Fenner, 23
Brockwell Park, 44, 226
Brotherhood hymn, 161, 178, 196, 203,
    274
Bruges, 27, 165, 221
Brussels, 27, 165–7, 169
builders, 7–9, 255, 310
Burbage Road, 42, 59, 69, 71, 95, 99, 311
Burns, John, 23, 119–20
buses, 11, 100–1, 179
Butcher, Frederick Albert, 3, 30, 47, 62,
    77, 84, 92, 121, 125, 149, 156, 217,
    221, 228, 270, 297, 302
Butcher, Harry John, 62, 77, 84, 92, 121,
    125, 137, 144, 156, 303
butchers and meat tradesmen, 31, 36,
    273n, 307, 311, 314, 310

cabinet makers, 8
cafes and restaurants, 36, 117, 129, 164,
    216, 243
Calcott, Percy, 274, 303
Calloway, A., 47, 62, 77, 303
Campbell, R. J., 13, 23
Canada, 55, 165, 307
Canary Islands, 25, 28, 211
Carlile, Wilson, 15
Carlisle, H. H., 177
Carman, 9
Carnegie, Andrew, 269–70
Carpenter, Albert Victor, 247–8, 303
Carpenter, Algernon William, 23, 31, 47,
    62, 77, 84, 92, 125, 156, 170, 184,

    190, 206, 214, 216, 221, 224, 228,
    238, 247–8, 251, 267, 269, 270, 286,
    297, 303, 312
carpentry, 309
Casino, football team, 69, 70
Casino House, 41
Castle, Mr, 41, 303
'Chaffer', 114
Chaplin, Charlie, 6, 11, 13, 26
Charing Cross station, 34, 100
chauffeurs, 9
Chelsea Football Club, 22n, 171, 176, 265
chemistry, 152–3
'Cherub', 242
Chilworth railway station, 215
China, 4, 31, 232, 236, 263, 273, 314
Chippindale, Richard John, 31, 154, 190,
    199, 214, 217, 221, 228, 238, 281–5,
    303
choir, 17, 19, 55, 91, 186, 196, 218, 222,
    232, 266
Christchurch football team, Streatham,
    59, 121–2
Christ Church, Westminster Bridge Rd,
    13, 22
Chulalongkorn, King of Siam, 44
cigar dealer, 8
cigarettes and cigars, see smoking
City of London, 3, 5, 7, 11, 22, 68, 128,
    178–9, 301, 306
City Temple, Holborn Viaduct, 3, 13, 23
Clandon, Surrey, 216
Clapham, London, 5–6, 11, 40, 71, 161n,
    226
Clapham Junction, 301
Clapham Park, 96, 192, 243, 310
Clapham Villa, football team, 60–1
classes in society, 1, 3, 5–7, 14–17, 22,
    23–4, 25, 35, 135, 213
clerks, 1, 3, 7, 8–9, 31, 299, 301–6,
    308–10, 313–16
Cloak, C., 149, 184, 206, 303
cloakroom attendant, 9
clock repairer, 8
clothes and fashions, 17, 22, 35, 52, 58,
    79, 121, 136, 137, 144, 150–1, 163,
    195, 200, 220, 224, 231, 244, 292,
    296
coachmen, 9
coal mining, 28, 291–4
coats of arms, 43, 51–2, 79–80, 95, 107

Coldharbour, Surrey, 164
Collins, E. M., 199, 281, 303
Como, Lake, 277
company secretary, 9
Congregationalism, 3, 4, 11–18, 23, 25–6,
    30, 31, 161n, 177n, 273n, 301, 307,
    311, 313
conscription, 136, 229, 235–6, 263
cooks, 9, 16
Coomber, Phillip J., 154, 162, 170, 184,
    190, 202, 206, 214, 221, 228, 238,
    250, 270, 284, 285, 297, 303
Cotsworth, Edward, 192, 303
Cramp, Walter Robert, 27, 31, 41, 62, 70,
    84, 122, 124, 125, 141, 142, 148, 156,
    162, 164–5, 170, 182, 184, 189–90,
    192, 197, 206, 213–15, 219, 221, 228,
    230, 238, 241, 246, 250, 264, 270,
    287–9, 297, 303
'C.Ra. N.K.', 179
cricket, 22, 52, 78, 88, 146, 148, 171, 176,
    189, 192, 226, 235, 299, 313
Crosley, William Thomas, 29, 31, 47, 50,
    51, 62, 77, 84, 92, 125, 142–3, 147,
    156, 182, 183, 187, 190, 254, 263,
    272, 295, 304, 306
Croydon, 99, 301
Croydon Southend football team, 283–4
Crusaders football team, Clapham, 40,
    70–1, 98, 154
Cummings, E.G., 304
C.V.M., 30, 134, 139, 209, 304
cycling, 1, 22–3, 28, 87–8, 108–10, 257,
    291–2

'Dan Hymen-Cupid', 165
Davies, Gwilym John, 171, 304
Davies, Montague Howell, 30–1, 171,
    206, 214, 221, 228, 238, 251, 270,
    288, 297, 304
deacons, 13–14, 19, 31, 93, 174, 181, 193,
    206, 218–19, 246, 258, 264, 280,
    305, 308, 310, 314
decorators (house painters), 8–9
delivery workers, 8–9
Dieppe, 279
Dinant, 27, 167–9, 174
Dorking, 164–5
Dover, 27, 73, 165, 219, 245
drawings – see artwork
dressmakers, 8–9
Dulwich Grove football team, 281–2

Eagle, Frank Walter, 31, 171, 304
Eagle, Harold Burnham, 3, 31, 206, 214,
    221, 228, 238, 251, 270, 272, 274,
    304–5
Eastbourne, 7, 311
Egypt, 4, 106, 134, 305
elections, municipal and national, 6, 12,
    24, 56–7, 81, 154
electricians, 8, 303, 308, 309
engravers, 8, 308
'Esau', 124
Evans, Albert Howard, 20, 26, 27, 34,
    36, 47, 73, 84, 101, 125, 148, 155,
    162–3, 175, 177, 181, 184, 189, 195,
    206, 213, 215–16, 218, 219, 221, 228,
    231, 235, 238, 241, 251, 256, 270,
    288–9, 296, 305
Evans, W., 47, 62, 305
'ex officio', 72

Fabians, 5, 81
Fagan, Will, 42, 59, 70, 71, 99, 122, 123,
    154, 305
Fairman, Walter Trotter and Mary A, 4,
    134, 141, 189, 287, 305
farrier, 8
Finch, W., 305
Fisher, H. A. L., 5
fishing, 27, 37, 87,108, 260
fishmonger, 8
'Flapdoodle', 177, 203
Fluelen (Flüelen), Switzerland, 278
Folkestone, 26, 34n, 73
football, 22–3, 39–43, 50, 52–3, 59–61,
    69–71, 79, 88, 95, 109, 110–12, 113,
    114, 121–4, 134, 146–7, 149, 154, 155,
    170–1, 176, 189, 192, 198–9, 201,
    222, 245–6, 254, 265–6, 272, 281–5
Fouracre, L., 162, 170, 184, 199, 206, 306
France, 3, 26–7, 33–7, 73, 149, 181, 226,
    278–9, 299, 308
French, John Morgan, 306
Friday Street, Surrey, 164

gambling, 22
garden party, 182–3, 192, 230–1
gardeners, 5, 8–9
gas engineer, 8
Genoa, 28, 135, 239, 275–6
George V, 26, 56, 118
Germany, 3, 82, 87–8, 108–9, 135, 313

Ghent, 27, 165, 219–21
Gibraltar, 239, 275
Giggs, Richard George, 45–6, 47, 58, 62, 77, 84, 306
ginger beer, 89, 175, 215
Girls' Bible class (see also long haired chums), 2, 21, 89, 178, 191, 196, 203–4, 244, 262, 266, 273, 286, 290, 295, 305
Gissing, George, 7, 10
Gladwin, M., 30, 145, 306
Godden, Graham Orchard, 3, 31, 306
Godden, James George, 1, 6, 20, 25, 26–7, 30, 33, 37, 49, 59, 64, 68, 72, 73, 74, 75, 77, 79, 82, 88–90, 92, 93, 94, 98, 105, 118, 119, 127, 131, 132–3, 134, 139, 141–3, 147, 148, 152, 159–60, 162, 165, 169, 170, 174, 178, 181, 185, 189, 194, 200, 205, 209, 213, 216, 217, 219, 220, 221, 229, 230, 234, 237, 239, 253, 262, 264, 267, 271–2, 274, 277, 283, 287, 289, 291, 296, 304, 306
Goodwin, G., 195, 306
Gosling, A.S., 206, 221, 228, 238, 251, 270, 297, 306
Grayson, A. Victor, 24, 68, 75, 102–3
Great Yarmouth, 183
Gresford Colliery, north Wales, 28
'Guibolles, Le Vicomte des', 94
Guildford, 216, 306
Guinness Rogers, James, 26
gun maker, 8
gymnastics, 136–7, 147, 181–2, 189, 190–1, 192, 194–5, 197–8, 199, 201, 240, 242–3, 246, 254, 266, 295, 296, 299, 305–6, 308, 311, 316

haberdashery, 315
Habergrutz, J., 162, 307
hairdressers, see barbers
Handy, Fred, 41–2, 59–60, 69–71, 77, 98–9, 122, 154, 274, 283–4, 307
Harper, George, 28, 47, 62, 77, 84, 125, 162, 274, 289–90, 302, 307
Hayley, Beatrice [Trissie] May, 66, 114, 165, 175, 307
Hayman, H., 149, 307
H.E.C. (probable reading), 30, 144, 157, 307
Herne Bay, 120

Herne Hill, 11, 31, 40n, 41n, 42n, 170, 301, 311
Hiley, Harold Gladstone and Lizzie May, 28, 31, 273, 307
Hill, Stella, 114, 175, 307
'Hobbett', 176
hockey, 22, 85–6, 89, 111, 112–14, 132, 145, 148, 150, 163, 215, 266, 279–80, 307, 309, 310, 312
Holman, Arthur, 47, 62, 77, 84, 92, 98, 125, 156, 190, 274, 308
Holmwood, Surrey, 164
'Homo', 76
Hooper, W.T., 308
'Hopeful', 266
Horne, C. Silvester, 12, 13, 23, 16ιn
Horsley railway station, 215
Horton, R. F., 13, 25
Hunter, John, 16

Independent Labour Party, 23–4, 81
India, 28–9, 211, 216, 254, 294, 304
insurance workers, 8–9, 31, 313
Irish Home Rule and Nationalism, 12, 82
Irons, B., 308
Italy, 239, 275–7

Jersey, 27, 225, 241, 245, 259–62, 281, 286, 296
jeweller, 8
Johnson, W., 194, 308
Johnston, Elizabeth Taylor, 17, 30, 31, 115, 128, 137, 150, 175, 193–4, 237, 257, 308, 310
Johnston family, 8, 31, 311
Johnston, William, 31, 308
Jolly, Miss W., 175, 308
Jones, Arthur Edmund, 62, 78, 84, 92, 122, 125, 140, 156, 170, 184, 206, 228, 238, 250, 270, 297, 308
Jones, Frank Clifton, 31, 41, 47, 50, 62, 78, 84, 92, 99, 125, 140, 149, 156, 184, 190, 199, 206, 222, 228, 238, 250, 270, 297, 308
Jones, Henry William, 42, 59, 78, 84, 92, 98, 122, 125, 140, 156, 184, 199, 206, 228, 238, 250, 270, 281, 297, 309
Jones, Lionel, 66, 149, 162, 214, 224, 308
journalism, 9, 15, 30, 72, 128–30, 185, 195–6, 305
Junior Bible class, 272, 287, 313

Kennington, 6, 24, 26, 120, 310
Kent, William, 14
King's Weigh House (Congregational)
    Church, 16

Labour Party, 4, 12, 23, 26, 57, 81, 82n,
    102, 119–20, 161n
lace manufacturer, 220, 306
Lake District, 281
land reform, 23, 57, 90, 267–9
Lansdown, Clarissa, 112, 274, 301, 309
Lansdown, Fanny, 10, 18, 31, 315
Lansdown, Mathias, 10, 18, 50–1, 55, 77,
    87, 141–4, 174, 182, 186, 187, 190,
    218, 230, 245, 255, 256, 286, 309,
    313
Lansdown, Mathias Henry, 31, 40, 41, 42,
    47, 60, 62, 69–70, 78, 84, 92, 98,
    114, 122–3, 125, 149, 162–4, 183, 184,
    199, 206, 214, 227, 250, 270, 281,
    284, 297, 309, 315
Larcom Football Club, Beckenham Hill,
    42, 123–4, 284–5
Las Palmas, Grand Canary, 211–13, 216,
    226, 227, 273, 307, 313, 314
Lausanne, 239
Lawrence, Sir Alexander and Lady, 19
Leith Hill, 164
'Liberal', 68
Liberal party, 12, 19n, 23, 46, 56–7, 75,
    81–2, 90, 102–3, 119–20
Lidstone, Alfred Morgan, 309
Liège, 27, 166–7
'Linesman', 113
Literary society, 10, 23, 39, 56, 63, 76,
    92–3, 96–7, 119, 143, 176–7, 188,
    191, 199, 234, 258, 264, 266, 311
Lloyd George, David, 3, 43n, 81, 128–30,
    191, 267–8
London Bridge station, 11
London County and Westminster Bank
    football team, 277
London County Council, 6, 11, 15, 308,
    312
London Missionary Society, 4, 141, 189,
    196, 273, 287
'Long Ear', 176
long haired chums, 30, 85–6, 90, 110–11,
    131–3, 150–1, 173, 175, 177, 183, 196,
    203–4, 212, 237, 262, 266, 273, 279,
    308, 312, 314

Loughborough Park Congregational
    Church, 15
'Lucem Demonstrat Umbra', 196, 203
Lucerne, 135, 278
Lugano, 277–8
Lynch, Edward T., 31, 170, 171, 184, 206,
    214, 222, 228, 238, 251, 270, 281,
    284, 297, 310
Lyndhurst Old Boys football team, 41,
    97
Lyndhurst Road Congregational Church,
    Hampstead, 13

McCormick, Thomas Luckin, 281, 282,
    284, 310
manager, 8, 31, 291–4, 303, 313, 314
Marr, Charles Wesley, 310
marriage, 8, 15, 17, 20, 31
Marriott, A., 47, 62, 78, 84, 95, 125, 133,
    310
Masterman, Charles, 6, 13, 25
Maynard, Miss, 175, 310
Merchant Navy, 28, 31, 254, 272, 305,
    307
messenger, 9
Messent, Annie, 112–14, 175, 237, 310
Messent, Daniel Cockerill, 2, 6, 17, 19,
    20, 31, 47, 50, 56, 62, 74, 78, 83, 92,
    95–6, 97, 99, 124, 141–3, 146–7, 155,
    160–2, 164, 165n, 170, 175, 177, 178,
    183–4, 186, 187, 189–90, 192–3, 199,
    206, 210–11, 213, 218–19, 222, 224,
    226, 227, 229–30, 235, 237, 238,
    240–1, 250, 254, 255, 256, 258, 262,
    264, 267, 270, 272, 274, 286–9, 296,
    305, 308, 310, 313
Messent family, 11, 17, 19, 31, 150n, 273n,
    313
Messent, Henry, 31, 206, 270, 297, 311
Messent, Isabella, 30, 31, 74, 132, 263,
    311
Messent, Lewis Hunt, 28, 42, 47, 50, 60,
    62, 70, 72, 78, 83, 92, 98, 99, 122–4,
    141–2, 148, 155, 170, 183, 188, 190,
    199, 206, 217, 222, 227, 238, 250,
    270, 275–9, 281, 287–8, 296, 311
Messent, William Joseph, 17, 19, 31, 47,
    62, 83, 92, 93, 124, 155, 170, 183,
    195, 206, 227, 238, 250, 258, 270,
    296, 311, 313
Meyer, F. B., 13, 22, 161n
Milan, 239, 275–6

Miller, Leonard, 192, 311
milliner, 301, 307
milkman, 9
missionaries and missions overseas, 3–4,
    23, 28, 31, 134, 141–2, 188–90, 196,
    273, 287–8, 305, 307, 314
Morrison (Lord), Herbert, 4, 5–7, 8, 10,
    13, 26
Morse, A. or C. or F., 78, 149, 182, 184,
    206, 311
Morton, S., 311
motorcycling, 173, 227, 257–8
moustaches, 170
Moxley, Richard Charles, 20, 25, 27, 31,
    47, 62, 78, 84, 86, 97, 110, 125, 142,
    148, 156, 162–5, 170, 183, 184, 187,
    188, 190, 206, 213–14, 216, 219–21,
    222, 226, 227, 230, 235, 237, 238,
    251, 270, 274, 280, 287–8, 297, 311
Mundania Athletic Club, Honor Oak
    Baptist Church, football team, 41
Municipal Reform Party, 6
Munro, Edward Charles, 28, 30, 31, 78,
    149, 184, 206, 214, 228, 238, 250,
    270, 272, 312
music hall, 9–10, 22

Napoleon Bonaparte, 37, 167, 277–8
Newhaven, Sussex, 279
Nobbs, Miss B, 114, 312
Noble, Alec, 28, 134–7, 312
Normandy, 181
North Wales, 28, 281, 291–4
Nunhead Cemetery, 54–5
nursing, 9

Oake, E./Oke, C., 214, 297, 312
office boys, 9, 22, 68, 118, 310
Osborne, W. V., 82
Osland, Miss K., 175, 312
Osland, Miss N., 175, 312
Ostend, 27, 165, 219
'Otherwise Satisfied', 95

Palmer, J.D., MP, 90
Pantheism, 109, 264
Paris, 149, 186, 239, 278–9
Parker, Joseph, 12–13
Parliament, Houses of, 46, 56–7, 81, 82n,
    102–3, 120–1, 236, 267, 269
Pat (Lewis Messent's friend), 275, 277
Paterson, Alexander, 4–5, 9–10, 22

Pember Reeves, Maud, 25
pensions, old age, 57, 75, 90
Perkins, Frank, 31, 38, 78, 79–80, 91,
    93, 125, 149, 156, 170, 183, 190, 206,
    217, 224, 226, 228, 238, 250, 270,
    286, 296, 303, 312
photographs, 24, 44–5, 54, 73, 92, 94,
    134, 137, 142, 145–9, 151, 177, 182,
    211–13, 215, 245, 253, 258–61, 273,
    275, 278
piano making, 8, 31, 308–9, 312
poetry, attempts at, 1, 37–8, 43–4, 52–3,
    58–9, 68, 77–9, 88–90, 100–1,
    110–11, 118–19, 121, 131, 139–40,
    144, 154, 155, 171, 185–6, 195–6,
    197–8, 200, 231, 242, 247–8, 257–8,
    279–80, 291
Police, 7, 35, 65, 67, 82–3, 92, 101, 223,
    241
politics and politicians, 1, 4, 12, 18, 19n,
    23–4, 46–7, 51, 56–8, 68, 75–6,
    81–2, 90, 96–7, 102–3, 119–21, 163,
    216, 248–50, 303
'Politician', 23–4, 46–7, 56–8, 68, 75,
    81–2, 90, 96, 102–3, 119–21, 303
postcards, 34–7, 138–9, 166–9, 211–13,
    220, 226–7, 254, 275–8
postman, 9
Pratt, Kathleen, 17, 19
preaching, 13–15, 23, 25, 109, 230, 301
printers, 7, 8–9, 299, 306, 314
Probart, Mr, 195, 312
Progressive Party, 6

'Q. Pid.', 228

racism, 29, 294–5
railways, 5, 7, 11, 26–7, 36, 46, 89,
    101, 132, 135, 148, 163, 166–7, 195,
    214–16, 219–20, 225, 259–61, 277–8,
    293, 313
rambling, 1, 23, 24, 25, 27, 33, 55, 73,
    115–18, 130, 143, 146, 148, 162–5,
    169, 174, 175–6, 189, 192, 205,
    213–16, 233, 259–61, 299–316
Ramsgate, 26, 34n, 314
Randall, H., 171, 312
Rangoon, 294–5
Ranmore Common, 163
'Rasselas', 51, 82
Raynes Park, 59, 123, 226
Redman, Mr, 196, 203, 312

Reeves, Harry, 24, 30, 31, 64–5, 68, 87, 97, 107, 115–18, 130, 152–3, 154, 199, 266, 299, 310, 312
'Ref', 97, 171, 242
Reigate Hill, 109, 243
restaurant staff, 3, 9, 36, 67, 216
Rhosddu coal mine, north Wales, 28, 291–4
Ri/, 61
Rittershausen, Ferdinand Ernst von, 72n, 84, 92, 125, 149, 156, 184, 206, 228, 238, 313
Rittershausen, Percy von, 30, 31, 72, 313
Rofe, James, 31, 272, 274, 313
roller skating, 22, 58, 112–13, 164
romance and flirtation, 89, 107–8, 121, 155, 164, 201, 216, 231, 237, 242, 266
Rosendale Sports Ground, Herne Hill, 40, 70, 98
Rowe family, 10, 11n, 30, 182
Rowe, Frank Leonard, 30, 31, 47, 62, 78, 83, 92, 124, 149, 155, 183, 189, 206, 213, 221, 223–5, 227, 238, 246, 250, 270, 287–8, 296, 313
Rowe, Henry Shepard, 25, 28, 41, 47, 60, 62, 69, 70, 78, 83, 92, 122, 124, 141–2, 148, 155, 162, 169–70, 183, 188, 190, 206, 211–13, 227, 273, 313–14
Rowe, John Langland, 4, 31, 141, 189, 230–1, 264–5, 274, 287–8, 314
Rowe, Robert Stanley, 27, 31, 40, 41, 47, 50, 62, 78, 83, 92, 98, 99, 111–12, 122, 124, 141–3, 147, 154–5, 162, 164, 170, 181–2, 183, 187–90, 188–9, 190, 199, 206, 213, 219, 221, 224, 227, 238, 245, 250, 259–60, 267, 270, 274, 284, 286, 288–9, 296, 314
Rutter, D., 199, 281, 283, 285, 314

'Sabbatarian', 110
St Andrew's (Kennington deanery) football team, 42, 60, 69
St Andrew's C of E School, 4
St Bartholomew the Great, Smithfield, 138–9
St George the Martyr, football team, 59, 123
St James's Church, Clapham Park, 83rd Boys Brigade, Old Boys, football team, 71
St Martha's Hill, Surrey, 215

St Matthew's Church, Brixton, 18
St Paul's Cathedral, 107, 138, 178–9
St Paul's Church, Herne Hill, football team, 170
St Saviour's Church, Brixton, 18, 316
Samuel, Sir Harry and Lady, 19
servants, 5–6, 8–9, 16, 311
school(s)/education, 4–5, 24
schoolteacher, 4, 8–9, 118n, 308, 312
Seymour, S., 221, 238, 246, 251, 270, 297, 314
Shearer, L., 149, 314
Shearer, P., 47, 62, 79, 84, 92, 125, 314
Shere, Surrey, 215, 233
Sherman, W., 314
ships and boats, 26–9, 34, 36–7, 73, 106–7, 167–9, 212, 233, 236, 254, 259, 263, 273, 275, 277–9, 303, 305, 315
shop worker, 1, 7–9, 15, 31, 301–2, 312, 315
Smith, C., 47, 62, 78, 84, 92, 125, 149, 156, 162, 182, 184, 190, 206, 221, 227, 250, 270, 288, 297, 314
smoking (tobacco), 1, 24–5, 73, 79–80, 93, 100, 137, 159, 171, 212, 227, 244, 275, 277, 279, 285
Snell, Bernard, 15, 301
Snoswell, Arthur Cecil, 214, 246, 314–15
Snoswell, Ernest Edgar, 315
Snoswell family, 8, 10–11, 17, 19, 30, 243n, 314
Snoswell, Hilda Grace, 175, 315
Snoswell, Laurence Sidney, 31, 47, 62, 79, 84, 125, 132–4, 149, 156, 187, 190, 286, 315
Socialism, 5, 23–4, 46, 51, 57–8, 68, 75–6, 81–2, 90, 96, 119–21, 303
Southampton, 27–8, 259, 309
Southwark Cathedral, 180–1
Spicer, Sir Albert, 26
Squires, F., 6, 78, 184, 315
stand maker, 8
Stead, W.T., 30
Stockwell Green Congregational Church, 15, 273n, 307
Stockwell Road Board School, 4
Stripp, Austen, 31, 315
Stripp, Herbert William, 47, 62, 79, 84, 315–16
'Sunday Cyclist', 88, 108–9

Sunday school, 17–18, 20, 22, 50, 55, 109, 141, 149, 178, 245, 302, 314
Surbiton Hill football team, 282–3
Swan, Alan, 194–5, 316
swank and swanking, 25, 43, 72, 100, 110, 133–4, 144, 212, 227, 247
Switzerland, 28, 127, 134–7, 312

Tate, Sir Henry, 9–10
Teetotalism, 10, 25–6, 91
'Telephone', 201
telephones, 33, 169–70, 221
telephonist, 302–3
theatre, 3, 7, 9–10, 15, 94
Thomas, David, 15
Thorne, Guy, 96
'Topper', 179
Tories, 46, 56, 75, 102, 154
Townley Park football team, 198–9
trade unions, 1, 23, 82, 102–3, 120
trams, 11, 36, 89, 112, 130, 135, 220, 242, 277
Trinity Congregational Church, Brixton, 1–4, 7–8, 10, 12, 15–19, 20–1, 30–1, 44, 51, 54, 80, 93, 130n, 151, 174–5, 177–8, 190, 192–3, 203–4, 210, 218–19, 222, 230, 240, 245, 256–7, 271, 286
Typhoid, 29, 54, 301
typists, 9

underground railways, 100, 292
'Unselfish', 285

Vale, Madge, 155, 224, 316
Versailles, 279
Victoria station, 11, 27, 219
'Vortex', 264

war, see also conscription, 1, 3, 12, 15, 19, 22, 24, 26–7, 30–1, 161n, 216n, 235–6, 263, 278, 299–316
warehouseman, 9, 300
Waterloo station, 27, 214
'Welshman', 76, 90, 102–3, 119–20
Weymouth, 259
Wheatsheaf Congregational Church, Vauxhall, 14
wheelwright, 8
whist, 101
White City, 114
Whitefield's Tabernacle, Tottenham Court Road, 13
Williams, Mr, 66, 316
Wimereux, 26, 36–7
Winchester School, 255
wine and sherry, 91, 212
women at Trinity, 17, 19, 20–1, 178
women's suffrage and rights, 1, 21, 23, 216, 248–50, 303
Wren football club, 70, 123
Wrexham, 28, 291
Wright, F., 316
Wright, P., 316

'X. Lea', 172

Yates, E., F. or N., 162, 214, 228, 316
York, Frederick Charles, 41, 47, 60, 62, 79, 84, 92, 107–8, 125, 141, 149, 156, 162–3, 183, 316
Young People's Meeting, 173, 188

Zurich, 28, 135–6, 312

LONDON RECORD SOCIETY

The London Record Society was founded in December 1964 to publish transcripts, abstracts and lists of the primary sources for this history of London, and generally to stimulate interest in archives relating to London. Membership is open to any individual or institution; the annual subscription is £18 (US $22) for individuals and £23 (US $35) for institutions. Prospective members should apply to the Hon. Membership Secretary, Dr Penny Tucker, Hewton Farmhouse, Bere Alston, Yelverton, Devon, PL20 7BW (email londonrecordsoc@btinternet.com).

The following volumes have already been published:

1. *London Possessory Assizes: a Calendar*, edited by Helena M. Chew (1965)
2. *London Inhabitants within the Walls, 1695*, with an introduction by D. V. Glass (1966)
3. *London Consistory Court Wills, 1492–1547*, edited by Ida Darlington (1967)
4. *Scriveners' Company Common Paper, 1357–1628, with a Continuation to 1678*, edited by Francis W. Steer (1968)
5. *London Radicalism, 1830–1843: a Selection from the Papers of Francis Place*, edited by D. J. Rowe (1970)
6. *The London Eyre of 1244*, edited by Helena M. Chew and Martin Weinbaum (1970)
7. *The Cartulary of Holy Trinity Aldgate*, edited by Gerald A. J. Hodgett (1971)
8. *The Port and Trade of Early Elizabethan London: Documents*, edited by Brian Dietz (1972)
9. *The Spanish Company*, edited by Pauline Croft (1973)

10. *London Assize of Nuisance, 1301–1431: a Calendar*, edited by Helena M. Chew and William Kellaway (1973)
11. *Two Calvinistic Methodist Chapels, 1748–1811: the London Tabernacle and Spa Fields Chapel*, edited by Edwin Welch (1975)
12. *The London Eyre of 1276*, edited by Martin Weinbaum (1976)
13. *The Church in London, 1375–1392*, edited by A. K. McHardy (1977)
14. *Committees for the Repeal of the Test and Corporation Acts: Minutes, 1786–90 and 1827–8*, edited by Thomas W. Davis (1978)
15. *Joshua Johnson's Letterbook, 1771–4: Letters from a Merchant in London to his Partners in Maryland*, edited by Jacob M. Price (1979)
16. *London and Middlesex Chantry Certificate, 1548*, edited by C. J. Kitching (1980)
17. *London Politics, 1713–1717: Minutes of a Whig Club, 1714–17*, edited by H. Horwitz; *London Pollbooks, 1713*, edited by W. A. Speck and W. A. Gray (1981)
18. *Parish Fraternity Register: Fraternity of the Holy Trinity and SS. Fabian and Sebastian in the Parish of St. Botolph without Aldersgate*, edited by Patricia Basing (1982)
19. *Trinity House of Deptford: Transactions, 1609–35*, edited by G. G. Harris (1983).
20. *Chamber Accounts of the Sixteenth Century*, edited by Betty R. Masters (1984)
21. *The Letters of John Paige, London Merchant, 1648–58*, edited by George F. Steckley (1984)
22. *A Survey of Documentary Sources for Property Holding in London before the Great Fire*, by Derek Keene and Vanessa Harding (1985)
23. *The Commissions for Building Fifty New Churches*, edited by M. H. Port (1986)
24. *Richard Hutton's Complaints Book*, edited by Timothy V. Hitchcock (1987)
25. *Westminster Abbey Charters, 1066–c.1214*, edited by Emma Mason (1988)
26. *London Viewers and their Certificates, 1508–1558*, edited by Janet S. Loengard (1989)
27. *The Overseas Trade of London: Exchequer Customs Accounts, 1480–1*, edited by H. S. Cobb (1990)
28. *Justice in Eighteenth-Century Hackney: the Justicing Notebook of Henry Norris and the Hackney Petty Sessions Book*, edited by Ruth Paley (1991)
29. *Two Tudor Subsidy Assessment Rolls for the City of London: 1541 and 1582*, edited by R. G. Lang (1993)
30. *London Debating Societies, 1776–1799*, compiled and introduced by Donna T. Andrew (1994)

31. *London Bridge: Selected Accounts and Rentals, 1381–1538*, edited by Vanessa Harding and Laura Wright (1995)

32. *London Consistory Court Depositions, 1586–1611: List and Indexes*, by Loreen L. Giese (1997)

33. *Chelsea Settlement and Bastardy Examinations, 1733–66*, edited by Tim Hitchcock and John Black (1999)

34. *The Church Records of St Andrew Hubbard Eastcheap, c.1450–c.1570*, edited by Clive Burgess (1999)

35. *Calendar of Exchequer Equity Pleadings, 1685–6 and 1784–5*, edited by Henry Horwitz and Jessica Cooke (2000)

36. *The Letters of William Freeman, London Merchant, 1678–1685*, edited by David Hancock (2002)

37. *Unpublished London Diaries: a Checklist of Unpublished Diaries by Londoners and Visitors, with a Select Bibliography of Published Diaries*, compiled by Heather Creaton (2003)

38. *The English Fur Trade in the Later Middle Ages*, by Elspeth M. Veale (2003; reprinted from 1966 edition)

39. *The Bede Roll of the Fraternity of St Nicholas*, edited by N. W. and V. A. James (2 vols., 2004)

40. *The Estate and Household Accounts of William Worsley, Dean of St Paul's Cathedral, 1479–1497*, edited by Hannes Kleineke and Stephanie R. Hovland (2004)

41. *A Woman in Wartime London: the Diary of Kathleen Tipper, 1941–1945*, edited by Patricia and Robert Malcolmson (2006)

42. *Prisoners' Letters to the Bank of England 1783–1827*, edited by Deirdre Palk (2007)

43. *The Apprenticeship of a Mountaineer: Edward Whymper's London Diary, 1855–1859*, edited by Ian Smith (2008)

44. *The Pinners' and Wiresellers' Book, 1462–1511*, edited by Barbara Megson (2009)

45. *London Inhabitants Outside the Walls, 1695*, edited by Patrick Wallis (2010)

46. *The Views of the Hosts of Alien Merchants, 1440–1444*, edited by Helen Bradley (2012)

47. *The Great Wardrobe Accounts of Henry VII and Henry VIII*, edited by Maria Hayward (2012)

48. *Summary Justice in the City: A Selection of Cases Heard at the Guildhall Justice Room, 1752–1781*, edited by Greg T. Smith (2013)

49. *The Diaries of John Wilkes, 1770–1797*, edited by Robin Eagles (2014)

50. *A Free-Spirited Woman: The London Diaries of Gladys Langford, 1936–1940*, edited by Patricia and Robert Malcolmson (2014)

Previously published titles in the series are available from Boydell and Brewer; please contact them for further details, or see their website, www.boydellandbrewer.com